From Ramshackle to Resale:

Fixing Up Old Houses for Resale

Carol Boyle

TAB **TAB BOOKS Inc.**
Blue Ridge Summit, PA

FIRST EDITION
FIRST PRINTING

Copyright © 1990 by TAB BOOKS Inc.
Printed in the United States of America

Reproduction or publication of the content in any manner, without express
permission of the publisher, is prohibited. The publisher takes no responsibility for
the use of any of the materials or methods described in this book, or for the
products thereof.

Library of Congress Cataloging-in-Publication Data

Boyle, Carol, 1934-
    From ramshackle to resale : fixing up old houses for profit / by
Carol Boyle.
      p.   cm.
    Includes index.
    ISBN 0-8306-1362-5   ISBN 0-8306-3162-2 (pbk.)
    1. Dwellings—Remodeling.   2. Dwellings—Remodeling—Economic
aspects.   3. Profit.   4. Real estate investment.   I. Title.
TH4816.B663   1989
643′.7—dc20   89-35339
                                                                  CIP

TAB BOOKS Inc. offers software for sale. For information and a catalog, please
contact TAB Software Department, Blue Ridge Summit, PA 17294-0850.

Questions regarding the content of this book
should be addressed to:

    Reader Inquiry Branch
    TAB BOOKS Inc.
    Blue Ridge Summit, PA 17294-0214

Acquisitions Editor: Kim Tabor
Book Editor: Joanne M. Slike
Production: Katherine Brown

Paperbound cover photograph by Garth Francis, Fort Myers News-Press.

Contents

Preface

You've heard it often. The quickest way to make money—lots of money—is in real estate. Of course, everyone knows that it takes money to make money. But who says it has to be a lot of money—or *your* money? Let me give you a good first-hand example.

When my husband and I were both nineteen years old, newly married, and without a penny to our names, we went down to the local credit union and applied for a $2,000 loan. When the loan (cosigned by my father) was granted, we used the money as a down payment for our first home—an older, two-story building that was already converted into an apartment house.

While the upstairs apartment paid back the credit union, we struggled with the mortgage payments, my husband's college tuition, and raising two small children. The cost of our monthly mortgage payment, however, was still lower than the local rentals in this university town.

After my husband graduated, we sold the property and collected a decent profit, moved to the big city, and purchased a tract home across the street from his new teaching job. Two years later, although the market was flooded with mirror-image tract houses, we sold our home the very first day we put up the "For Sale" sign. Onward we trekked to Florida, to a new teaching position, a new home on the ocean, and a new life with two more children.

But that wasn't the end of our buying and selling. We had become hooked on recycling older buildings. Our addiction led us savaging through garage-, rummage-, yard-, and estate sales (which we called "family outings"). And the kids visited more than their fair share of flea markets, helping us gather up precious collectibles for our next venture. Eventually, we found a small mom-and-pop motel (a misnomer, as the children will loudly point out) at a bargain price. And then we found out why it was a bargain! The motel business was terrible: the work was excruciatingly hard and the hours were too long. It definitely was not our idea of a family-oriented business.

So we sold it the next year, cashing out (again) with a 50-percent equity profit. Besides the generous return on our money, there were other rewards. We learned a lot about human nature (at its worst and best). Sure, there were worrisome times, but a lot of laughs, too—enough to fill another book. And, as an additional bonus for all of our hard work, we came away with a pair of solid bronze vault gates (from the first bank in town) that were holding up the front porch of the motel. Former owners probably thought they were black wrought iron. But one day while sitting on the front porch, I became curious about the tiny authentic locks in each panel. I scraped the metal with a pin, and lo, gorgeous golden material was bared from underneath years and years of tarnish and encrustation. The solid-bronze gate doors are worth several thousand dollars and weigh as many pounds. They are certainly worthy of their humble place of honor flanking each side of our back-bar at home, reminding us of the good times, along with the difficult times. Most importantly, the doors stand as a constant reminder that perseverance pays off—if you can keep your sense of humor.

By the time we sold our motel, all four children were in school, and it was time to decide what I wanted to do with my free time and the rest of my life. My husband was still teaching industrial arts—something that became second nature to him by that time. I, too, decided to benefit from past experiences and do what I enjoyed most, so I opened my own interior design studio.

We purchased three lots with dilapidated buildings in an older downtown section of the city. One building we restored and transformed into the reception room of the interior design shop, the other two buildings were moved. It was charming: this little building with its Spanish-flavored, open-arch porch; wrought iron; high-ceilinged interiors; fireplace; and handsome tall, narrow windows (which were perfect for displaying opulent drapery designs). The new adjoining building was built by my carpenter-husband and housed the studio and workrooms. Today, with all but one son through college, and some of them with children of their own, this triplex rental unit belongs to a new owner. It was designed this way so it could be quickly converted and sold when it was time to let go of the business.

The moral of this story? You don't really have to have a lot of money to make money. What you do need is a little courage and confidence in yourself—and the knowledge that once you acquire and fine-tune your carpentry and decorating skills, your own abilities will make you a profit in real estate. Throw in a bit of imagination, elbow grease, and, of course, luck. When the dust settles—who knows—you just might be a successful real-estate tycoon. At the very least, you'll live comfortably in lovely houses, enjoy life, and have something to show for all those years of hard work: a paid-up mortgage on a retirement home of your choice, *before* your children even leave home!

Acknowledgments

In today's do-it-yourself world, we can find books on everything from curing our own ills to building an entire house. But the written word and instructions are useless if the needed components are not readily available to the reader. Fortunately for the readers of this book, in almost every community today there is a new phenomenon: the home center, a single building that stocks practically everything needed for your building or remodeling project—no matter how big or how small. Without the accessibility of such home centers and the companies who stock them with state-of-the-art products and services, it would have made no sense for me to write this book—and less sense for anyone to read it. My indebtedness, therefore, goes to the following companies and associations who have made this book possible: for their willingness and generosity in providing me with inspiring photos and concise and thorough information to pass along to you.

Georgia Pacific, Inc.
National Decorating Products Association
National Building Products Association
Color Tile, Inc.
Hoyne Mirror, Inc.

Introduction

If you think you can't make your fortune in today's economy, you're wrong! If you think that you can't have the house of your dreams, you're wrong again!

This country has produced many "sweat-equity" millionaires; people like you who started with next to nothing and who eventually evolved as principals in huge multimillion-dollar corporations. Consider these facts. Isaac Merrit Singer started with $40 in borrowed money and produced the Singer Company (1850); William Proctor and James Gamble started with equity capital of $7,192 in 1837; William Hewlett and David Packard invested their personal savings of $538 (1978) in their dream. What was their secret? Desire and a belief in themselves and what could be accomplished with sweat equity. They put equity profit from each project or product sold back into the next even bigger project until success was theirs.

It can be that way for you, too. Empty your pockets. Check your savings passbook . . . now your check book. Nothing? Then look around you. Your home, the house that you're in right now, could be your ticket to the top. It's a likely beginning point for you. You are most familiar with it's assets and drawbacks. Fix it up, sell it, and move on to your next venture. If your home is one that you can't bear to leave, that's fine. Find out how you can use its equity to purchase another candidate. You can pay off the second mortgage when the project is sold.

From Ramshackle to Resale was written to help you achieve these goals with the least amount of frustration and the largest margin of profit. Whether you intend to make old-house recycling a business or a hobby, this book will provide you with a wealth of information each step of the way, from buying to selling. Another book, *Do-It-Yourself Designer Windows* (TAB #1922) will provide the finishing touches for your "model" home. With this mini library, you will prove your worth as a carpenter, designer, and realtor and save—indeed, perhaps make—thousands of dollars.

The Candidate

What's the secret of successful old-house recycling? It's getting in, refurbishing, and getting out fast—*with* the profit you anticipated. The profit, of course, will depend on how much you pay for the property, what you put into it, how much you can ask for it under present market conditions, and how fast you can turn it around on the market once it's finished. This takes a little bit of homework.

First, you must have a pretty good idea of the minuses and pluses of the property. Then, you must have firm knowledge of existing home values in the neighborhood. In order to make the property saleable and still keep your profit line stable, you must be able to figure, quite accurately, the cost of your intended improvements. And last but not least, you must make the property appealing—more appealing than any other on the market. This takes getting involved with the decorating end of it. (You'll find that you usually are selling the house to a woman. If you can appeal to her instincts and her desire for style and fashion, you'll clinch the sale every time over what the run-of-the-mill carpenters/remodelers are offering.) Your successes will rely heavily on the blending of carpenter/handyperson/decorator skills, but you can achieve this with the help of this book. I've known couples, where one had ten thumbs, the other, two left feet, and they still made a lot of money in the old-house recycling market. You can, too.

This book will tell you how to buy intelligently, what bonuses to look for in old houses that will translate into extra profit dollars for you, what to stay away from so there will be no surprises to fracture your budget, how to make low-cost electrical and plumbing repairs yourself, how to insulate, how to choose the right refurbishing projects and figure the costs, when you should call in a subcontractor, and where you will most likely find old-house gems.

The book also offers decorating tips and home improvement ideas, with detailed instructions and illustrations to help you entice buyers: starting with relatively inexpensive options like covering up unsightly walls, floors, and ceilings with attractive fabrics, wallpapers, or paneling, and progressing to the more expensive option of rebuilding walls from scratch. Included also are extra-equity ideas to increase profits and the home's marketability. Before you're finished with your first renovation, you will be a handyperson with an eye for style. Your newly developed carpenter/designer talents will make each venture more successful. Just remember that your tools will include not only a hammer, saw, and ruler; but scissors, glue, and a sewing machine. And you will be able to master all of these while learning the secrets of how to recycle old houses successfully.

SIZING THEM UP

In your search for a likely house-recycling candidate, you'll find that most offerings fall into one of three categories: those that simply need face-lifts, those requiring more extensive cosmetic surgery, and those destined for major surgery or the wrecking ball. The ones requiring facials or minor reconstructions are the quick-turnaround investments: profitable prospects for first-time recyclers since all they need is a good scrubbing, scraping, and sprucing up before they can be put back on the market. These are usually the newer homes, victims of house abuse (usually rental property), or vintage estate homes that were well maintained but lack the modern conveniences that appeal to today's buyers.

On the other hand, we have the derelicts of the neighborhood, ramshackled houses that need complete gutting and extensive renovations before they can be made habitable. This may mean new plumbing, heating, and electrical systems, and often new roofs and siding. Although they are the most challenging and rewarding of the undertakings, it's best to wait on these until you have learned to master old-house appraisals, properly diagnose their symptoms, and know how to cure the ills of years and years of neglect. In addition, you'll probably have more difficulty receiving financial assistance for such properties, and your only alternative might be to finance them yourself with "sweat equity" money accumulated from previous recycling projects.

Both long- and short-term renovations can bring you a good return on your investment dollar, if you're mindful of a few basics.

Quick Turnaround Houses

Houses that need only superficial restorations or refurbishings are probably priced very close to their resale value already. Unless you add a generous dash of creativity that takes the house out of the ordinary class, and puts it into the showhouse category, you won't make a lot of money on the venture and it might not be worth your time. However, if you can rely on the magic of paint (the decorator's least expensive and most effective tool) and lean toward custom decorating, which costs a lot less than structural improvements, the profit is there. Just be absolutely sure you're getting the house for a rock-bottom price, and that you know what the top-dollar potential is for resale in that neighborhood.

Most old houses are valued for their gracious interiors and distinctive architectural details—but not for their antiquated heating, plumbing, and electrical systems; or poorly laid-out kitchens. But there is a strong market today for older, updated homes that are rich in artistic craftsmanship, and imbued with the personality and warmth found lacking in today's modern homes. If you can find an older house that's dark, dingy, and down-at-the-heels but has a good foundation and sturdy frame, you are also likely to find a bigger profit margin. Usually, sellers underprice these jewels because they're unable to detect the real charm and value hidden under layers of dust and grime. Yet, buried somewhere under tons of paint, peeling wallpaper, and yellowed varnish are the moneymakers: gems that can be honed and polished into highly desirable, livable dwellings.

Use ingenuity and elbow grease instead of cash. For instance, don't cross a house off your list because it has a fireplace that doesn't work when you can't afford to have it rebuilt. Use the chimney, hearth, and salvageable brick backwall for a new Franklin stove or freestanding fireplace (which, by the way, are far less expensive, just as appealing, and more energy efficient). If the traffic pattern or lighting is impossible, remove a wall, use a partial wall or partition to reroute the traffic, or open up the area of natural daylight. If there's something you can camouflage with inexpensive fabric, don't cover it with expensive paneling. If you find a floor worth refinishing under old carpeting, don't recarpet; strip and resurface the floors yourself.

With a conservative amount of money and a lot of creativity, use wallpaper, mirrors, carpeting, flea-market finds, fabric on the wall; with, perhaps, paneling on one accent wall installed in a herringbone pattern (instead of all over), painted walls with artfully arranged stock molding, and stripped and resurfaced floors stenciled to match the walls.

Rely on your decorating know-how inside and out. Instead of re-siding, repair the existing damage and repaint with an exterior paint color that makes the house look twice as attractive as its neighbors. Add some shutters and a few window boxes blossoming with brilliant geraniums or petunias. How could anybody not want to see what's inside after a welcoming like that?

Just don't get carried away with fuchsia kitchens or purple living rooms or eyebrow-raising exterior colors. Stick to attractive (but not wimpy) hues and schemes that are currently popular in home and garden magazines. Such cosmetic touches will cost you a few hundred dollars, but they'll add thousands to your resale price.

Also, don't take on costly customizing. Remember, you're not remodeling for yourself or for a friend—you're remodeling for resale to a stranger. So don't overdo it and price the house right out of the neighborhood, or your prospect's needs. Resist the temptation to bump out, add on, or build stylized work or study centers and greenhouses—no matter how trendy they are. Stay away, too, from stamping a room as a "nursery," "sewing room," or "child's room," no matter how well acclimated the room may seem for the purpose. And remember, the more you can do yourself, the better off you'll be.

Give yourself bonus points if you find a house with some of these blessings in disguise: stained, etched, or oddly shaped windows; high ceilings; tall, narrow windows; fieldstone cellars; dormer windows; plank or parquet floors; exposed (or the potential for exposing) beams; turrets; wraparound roofed porches with railings; usable attics; old-time woodwork in mint condition; open-rail central staircases, and lofts (FIG. 1-1).

For quick turnaround recycling, avoid houses with damaged roofs, water in the basement, termite damage, off-level foundations, sagging floors that can't easily be straightened, and paint-peeled shingles caused by something other than natural weathering over time—no matter what the bargain price is. If you don't have the time, money, or inclination to renovate properly, your profits will erode as the house stays on the market. Take on the more extensive renovating properties only when you're ready. The old saying "time is money" waxes true when you're making monthly payments on a home-improvement loan for property that you can't finish on time or sell.

Long-Term Renovations

Remember that initial drawbacks you detected on your first visit to the property will be visible to your prospective buyer, as well. There's no effective way to cover up a sagging or leaking roof, camouflage inadequate electric service to the house, or glibly pass off a failing furnace system. These repairs and replacements will have to be made at the outset, which means that the project will be longer termed. But if you have the time and can foresee a nice profit in the restoration or rehabilitation of the house, by all means, buy it.

RESTORE OR REMODEL?

You've seen them all. Every style, size, and scale imaginable. The row (after row, after row) house; the skinny tenement; your basic box tract home; the Victorian with its numerous little anterooms; the plain-Jane farmhouse; the two-story colonial; the one-and-a-half-story bungalow; the contemporary split-level; the saltbox; and the "born again" barn, loft, church, and stablehouse.

Architectural preferences in building styles are as individual as clothing styles. There is a growing class of Americans who consider it a privilege to live in a home that has been cherished and preserved down through the ages. It's their link to the past and a reminder of their heritage—days when housebuilders were craftsmen and built for posterity, as well as to provide shelters for their families.

Fig. 1–1. Ornate window detailing in Burrough's home, Fort Myers, Florida. Unusual-shaped, leaded, or diamond-paned windows are treasures unto themselves.

Others prefer straight-lined, no-nonsense contemporary houses like those built in the 50s and 60s. Many of which are now ripe for remodeling. And there is a huge market for eclectic homes designed with the elements of both past and present.

In tackling any house recycling project, the best rule of thumb is to restore where possible and remodel when necessary—without damaging the character that age has bestowed upon the dwelling. This not only keeps you on the safe side of both the preservationist and contemporary house-buyer, it also gives you an excuse to keep your recycling budget reasonable.

Whether your project is a refurbishing, restoration, or remodeling job, keep in mind your main goals: 1. to make the value sound, 2. to price it reasonably for the neighborhood, and 3. to make it absolutely irresistible to the buyer.

The Three R's

Three terms that we've been using to describe old-house recycling are "refurbishing," "restoration," and "remodeling." Although these terms sound interchangeable, they actually represent three different alternatives to recycling. *Refurbish* means to polish or spruce up, *restore* means to make new again, while *remodel* signifies change—to make over, or rebuild.

If you come upon a house that is architecturally pleasing, as well as very old, you have found a treasure, indeed. This project calls for a restoration. In dealing with a restoration, the basic plan should be to salvage as much of it as possible and reconstruct the lost or mutilated parts, using old-time materials, designs, and finishes in an attempt to restore the home to the way it looked at some specific point in time. These houses do not have to conform exactly to that period, but the house should retain the spirit, presenting a picture that reflects tender loving care, use, and growth. Stop short, however, of trading comfort for historical validity. Interpretive restoration is what you're after.

Many houses, while very old, have undergone transitional changes over the years that have entirely altered the original character of the house. Unsympathetic tampering destroys antiquity. Thus, these old houses, with modern picture windows, siding, and stripped or flattened exterior protrusions, will probably dictate a straightforward refurbishing or remodeling job to make them saleable again.

Many buyers prefer a combination of solutions: a preserved or restored facade, with a renovated (all or part) interior. For many recyclers, this is the more practical alternative, especially where time is a major consideration.

If a house is to be restored, or even adapted for modern living, no change should be made without proper consideration—backed by sound knowledge—or architectural styles.

A BRIEF HISTORY OF AMERICAN
HOME ARCHITECTURE

It's not surprising to learn that there was no one "typical" American home, in any period of our history. In this vast country, with its diverse and changing climates, each region developed its own style of architecture to cope with weather and environmental problems. All early homes were built strictly for function and economics. The designs reflected not only local climate conditions, but available building materials, along with the European heritage of the builder. Down through the centuries, as times got better and materials more available, and as new technologies brought us concrete, steel, and glass, home styles changed even more. We broke away from building for function and began to build for aesthetics and whimsy. American styles of architecture melded into an eclectic blend of past, present, and future. Traces of the colonial mansion with its shaded portico windows popped up in the cold Midwest and the North. The saltbox, designed mainly to buffer cold northern winds with its steeply sloped back, began to appear in the balmy South and West. On every street, in every city, flavorings of past and present styles found their way into today's modern homes. But the best and purest architectural designs of our heritage homes will never go wanting for buyers.

Knowing a bit about American architecture will enable you to spot an antique on your own and assess its proper value. Most sellers aren't knowledgeable about house antiquity or historical values—they're more interested in promoting its modern features. Even if it's not an antique, you'll want some background information on the history of the house, in order to establish its approximate age, and the age of the plumbing, heating, and electrical systems.

It's unlikely that you'll come across an authentic, old pioneer home (although, you might!). Most of these homes have already been restored and placed on historical preservation lists as museum pieces. What is available, though, are replicas of the originals, built 50 to 100 years or more ago. These houses have intrinsic, as well as real estate, value. Also, if you can recognize a house style and know its traditional floor plan before you make the initial inspection, you'll have important inside information on the remodeling problems you're likely to encounter: for instance lighting dark, dreary rooms, lowering too-high ceilings, and changing traffic patterns. You'll know also what you should poke around for: pine or oak flooring under linoleums and other layers, carved moldings, and fine stone fireplaces behind wall "modernization" attempts by previous owners.

Here are some obvious keys to antiquity that you should be on the lookout for:

- ▶ **Dates.** Look for dates on masonry or lintels.
- ▶ **Nails used.** The oldest nails are the hand-forged ones: long, square, and sharply pointed, with a roughly flattened head. These are eighteenth-century specimens.

► **Hinges and hardware.** Check cellars, attics, and closets where previous owners might not have bothered to replace them with modern ones. The earliest hinges were leather straps (seventeenth century). Others were hand-forged, distinguishable by burrs in the metal, and beautiful, unique designs such as the English cock's head, or those of German (Moravian), Dutch, or French origin.

► **Windows and glass.** The older the house, the smaller the panes. Eighteenth century glass looks old and wavy and has an opalescent tinge.

► **Bricks.** Early seventeenth-century, sun-dried clay bricks are larger than today's kiln-dried bricks.

OUR HERITAGE HOMES

At first, American settlers had to make do with simple huts or cruck-style dwellings made of bent trees, rush, and bark, but our ancestors didn't reside in primitive houses long. Fashion quickly followed function, and by 1650 when the settlers were acclimated to the land and firmly established, houses were being built by carpenters and masons schooled in the Old World traditions of their various homelands: Germany, the Netherlands, and England. Many of these houses, built over 300 years ago, are still standing today throughout the thirteen original colonies and Ohio's Western Reserve—testimony to their superior building skills and fine craftsmanship.

The first truss-roof, post-and-rail house was the half-timber cottage built in the colony of Virginia (FIG. 1-2). Its predecessor was the English Elizabethan Tudor countryside home, whose stalwart architectural features and earthy charm have been incorporated in contemporary homes down through the ages. Originally, the wall space between the post and rails was filled in with willow twigs and clay. Later, bricks were used. The walls were sealed over with plaster to keep out the weather, then whitewashed.

Still later, the half-timber home was covered over with clapboard, or siding. This simplified the whole building process, as the entire house could now be framed with huge vertical and horizontal timbers and encased with materials that were easier to handle and more accessible. Early clapboard (called "weatherboard" by our English ancestors) was of native oak, cedar, or pine. It was split from a log and tapered from ½ inch at the butt to 3/16 of an inch at the top. The boards were 5½ to 8 inches wide, and from 4 to 6 feet long, depending on the stud space used by the builder (usually 24 inches on center, or o.c.). Other homesteaders chose wide (12- to 18-inch) boards for their siding, fastening them horizontally to the studs. White pine shingles, originating with the Dutch on Long Island as far back as 1700, were also used as house siding. Original white pine shingles can be detected by their size: 3 feet long and approximately 10 inches wide.

Around 1640, the earliest clapboard house normally rose two and a half stories and had a medieval look (reminiscent of Tudor England),

Fig. 1–2. Mid-seventeenth-century Elizabethan half-timber cottage. Reminiscent of their ancestorial Elizabethan Tudor countryside manors, early English settlers along the Hudson River Valley built the first post-and-rail cottages of native timber wadded with willow twig and clay mortar.

steeply gabled roofs, and diamond-paned leaded windows. The two-foot overhangs on the upper floor were usually garnished with ornamental drops. The Garrison, as it was called, was the forerunner of later saltbox designs (FIG. 1-3).

In both the North and South, the simplest house consisted of a single, large room with a sleeping loft and an 8- to 12-foot-wide central fireplace for cooking and heating. The house was constructed with a steeply sloping lean-to roof—longer in the back than the front—and was known as the "saltbox," (more picturesquely termed the "catslide" in the South). The design was extremely useful for the colonists, providing them with much needed storage space and additional protection from harsh weather on the sleeping levels (FIG. 1-4). Long, narrow kitchens were located behind the chimney on the lower floor in the lean-to section. Directly off the kitchen, was the borning room, obviously located near a supply of hot water.

The central chimneys of these Early American homes rose well above the roofline. They were massive masonry structures of quarrystone or fieldstone, which supported numerous fireplaces, one for each room, positioned around the sides and back of the central flue. Usually, the stones were held together by clay and cow hair mortar.

Fig. 1–3. The Garrison (1640 to 1820). *One of the earliest settler houses, the garrison resembled a medieval English Tudor cottage with its diamond pane, leaded windows and steeply gabled roof. The two-and-a-half story clapboard dwelling has a large overhang on the upper floor and was usually garnished with ornamental drops.*

Fig. 1–4. The Saltbox (1620–1750). *The seventeenth-century saltbox, with its steeply sloping back roof provides for a lean-to kitchen and welcomed storage space. A massive central flue supports the many fireplaces needed for the living and sleeping quarters.*

The kitchen fireplace was always the largest; in some instances, spacious enough to contain built-in seats or benches in its opening for the convenience and comfort of the candle- or soap maker. Bake ovens were usually set inside the openings, too. These were large brick beehive-like recesses with sheet iron doors. To use the ovens, the door was opened, or removed, and wood curls were set afire on the oven floor. Sticks and then logs were gradually added. As they burned briskly, creating the proper draft, they were pushed further and further back into the oven. After an hour or so, the engulfing flames blackened the oven's interior. As the soot burned off and became clean again, the oven was deemed hot enough, and in went the whole meal—Indian pudding, brown bread, pots of beans, and eventually, the pies. With the sheet iron door in place, the entire meal could be forgotten for several hours.

Sometimes an arched opening constructed in the fireplace face held the fuel: logs and bake-oven wood chips. Some of the recesses, depending on where they were positioned, were used as ash pits. In the earlier Pennsylvanian fireplaces, many of the bake ovens are located in the back or side of the large kitchen fireplace.

Later in the seventeenth century, and into the early eighteenth century, the two-room, central chimney, single-story Cape Cod was developed in the Massachusetts Bay area. The basic Cape Cod was a four-square design with a fairly high-pitched roof that descended to the first-floor ceiling height. The single-story house had stairs leading to limited sleeping accommodations near the roof. The only upstairs windows were in the gable ends of the structure. Eventually, the Cape Cod acquired wings, or ell extensions, and dormer windows. The Cape Cod is characterized by its symmetrical facade; a central entrance flanked by a pair of windows (FIG. 1-5).

Most of the Dutch homes along the Hudson Valley in New Amsterdam were built of Bergen red sandstone, or a combination of stone and wood. The houses had a massive look, influenced by the deep window and door wells created by 2-foot-thick walls. In areas populated by the Dutch, English, Flemish, and Swedish houses sprouted attractive gambrel roofs, which were outfitted with dormer windows—mostly because it afforded extra upstairs room for little additional cost, but also because it was a tradition.

Of course, most gambrel roof shapes evolved from the different proportions of roof spans and the required head room clearance inside. But it's interesting to note that, more often than not, we can decode the builder's nationality by observing the shape and style of the roof he put on his house. For instance, there are two basic English gambrels: the high-peaked version is a derivative of the English Tudor-style home, the flatter shape is a carryover from a style that was introduced to England by Dutch engineers who lived there while designing the English dikes.

The Dutch Colonial is distinguished by a more prominently peaked

Fig. 1–5. Cape Cod. A four-square design, the Cape Cod has a fairly high-pitched, shallow-eave roof that descends to first floor ceiling height. Steep stairs lead to limited sleeping space under the eves, with windows at the gable ends only. Later, dormers were built into the roof.

roof with chimneys at the gable ends. The Swedish gambrel is almost flat where the two spans come together at the top.

But perhaps the most attractive gambrel of all, one usually—and incorrectly—referred to as the Dutch Colonial, is the Flemish gambrel with its gracefully curved eaves swooping outward from the side walls a foot or two (FIG. 1-6).

Between 1611 and 1629, brickyards were established in New England, and a few all-brick homes and mansions began to pop up in the more prosperous areas of Boston and New Haven. Still, most of the brick was used only for chimneys and bake ovens. It wasn't until the Georgian era, around 1740, that the use of brick for homes became widespread throughout all the states. The early two-room deep Georgian house, with its imposing central hall, and many rooms, began the elegant and formal trend toward home building that was to continue for the next century. Two huge central fireplaces could accommodate eight fireplaces downstairs, and more upstairs. Soft colors were used on walls in place of rustic pine paneling; sometimes carved dado was used on the bottom half, while the tops were detailed with fine moldings and cornices. Ceiling fixtures hung from splendidly cast medallions. Ornamental corner cupboards were built-in, and richly carved paneling embraced walls and fireplace surrounds.

Fig. 1–6. Dutch Colonial/Flemish Gambrel Roof (1700–1783). Most Dutch homes were built of Bergen red sandstone; the second floors were of wood. The 2-foot, deep-set window and door wells gave the house a massive look. An appealing characteristic was the Flemish gambrel roof with its flaring eaves.

The early Georgian façade was generally flat. Larger windows with bigger panes balanced the symmetrical front in units of nine or more, each decorated with a sculptured architrave. Simple doorways gave way to spectacular entrances, dressed up with pediments and pilasters, side lights at the doors, and fan-shaped windows above the doors. Clapboard exteriors were painted cheerful colors of blue, green, salmon, and yellow.

Later, the Corinthian-pillared portico rose to the second and third floor, and was often crowned with the rounded-top Palladian window (FIG. 1-7). Dormer windows were added to the top floor roofline; and sometimes the roofline, itself, was a huge, stately pediment, symbolizing classical Greek and Roman design elements. High-ridged roofs were replaced with lower ones, across which stretched the "widow's walk" complete with carved balustrades.

The Georgian era was truly one of the most elegant moments in American architecture, and the most-copied one today.

Over the next century, Georgian houses embodied two basic style characteristics. The first period after the Revolution (1785 to 1820), is known as the Federal Period. The second, from 1820 to 1860, is characterized as the Greek Revival. During the Federal period, the façades of the houses became somewhat severe. The fronts were flattened; bays, porticos, balconies, and other protrusions disappeared. Windows were still symmetrically arranged, but straight-lined pediments or simple, carved, stone lintels over the doors and windows replaced the beautiful, intricate carv-

Fig. 1–7. Georgian (1735–1790). The elegant Georgian mansion has gigantic flanking fireplaces on gable and walls and a symmetrical façade with precisely placed windows. Very often the high, hipped roof was spanned by a "widow's walk," complete with balustrade and deck. The shallow eaves are often decorated with moldings and modillions. Columned and pedimented entryways welcome guests.

ings of earlier periods. Instead of the two- and three-story fluted columns, simple, delicate pilasters flanked the entrance door, which may or may not have been softened by a fanlight window or a glazed panel on each side (FIG. 1-8).

The Greek Revival home, with its temple-like classic stylings, gained momentum after the Revolution. Instead of columns, they had refined corner pilasters, conspicuous with sculptured Greek symbols of anthemions, acanthus leaves and paterae. Even smaller houses were adorned with to-scale pedimented gables and portico entrances (FIG. 1-9).

After the Revolution, the population began to move to the cities where space was at a premium. Late Georgian/Early Federal brick row houses began to spring up in such cities as Philadelphia, Washington, and Boston. The three- or four-story rowhouse (or townhouse) was a narrow building, 15 to 25 feet wide, which shared double-thick walls with neighbors on both sides (FIG. 1-10). Each unit had its own front entrance and a garden entrance out back. The rowhouses were called "brownstones," a reference to the chocolate-colored sandstone veneer that covered the brick front wall. (Although many of the buildings had limestone, granite, and frame facades, as well as brick and brownstone.) Some of the brownstones had

Fig. 1–8. The Georgian/Federal-style home is as popular today as it was in the 18th century, with its symmetrically arranged windows, straightlined pediment, and delicate pilasters flanking the entrance door.

Fig. 1–9. Greek revival (1800–1861). The Greek revival home comes closest to true Southern architecture, with its white pillars and columns supporting enormous porticoes and verandas. Modillion (block-like) moldings and beautiful Greek sculptures adorn huge, pedimented gables and entablatures spanning the entire structure.

Fig. 1–10. Federal Period (1775–1820). The hallmark of the Federal house is simple elegance: straight-lined lintels over doors and windows garnished with Roman urns, garlands, and festoons; shallow eaves with delicate moldings; and exteriors of brick or clapboard in pastel colors. The Federal/Georgian townhouse is characterized by its balance and symmetrical design: columns and pedimented entryways; delicate hardware in both brass and iron. Wrought-iron fence and rails are commonplace.

stoops, or a short flight of stairs that led up to the living room and the formal front parlor. Separate kitchen entrances were reached by descending a short flight of stairs under the front stoop, slightly below street level. The original house had no central heating or plumbing. Outhouses stood in the backyard, and the homes were heated with large coal-burning fireplaces on each floor.

For years, the decrepit old row houses were shunned by buyers, as people moved away from the cities. But today, because of runaway inflation and high home costs and the scarcity of land close to urban workplaces, they are being snapped up and renovated.

The Victorian Age, which began in 1837, brought us back from austerity—in a rebellious manner. For the next 65 years, houses were emblazoned with sometimes beautiful, sometimes ostentatious ornamentation. Rambling buildings with high peaks and low valleys, rounded corners, and unbelievable blends of exterior skins characterized homes that resembled a mix of grand cathedrals and medieval castles. Our ancestors were obviously more than ready to switch from the sparse and somber neoclassical architectural designs to the more lacy, frivolous, and romantic Victorian detailings. The contagious mood spread throughout the country and lasted until well after the Civil War, with both large and small houses adopting the design trend.

The first of the Victorian styles, Gothic Revival, began in England and spread to America around 1840. August Welby Northmore Pugin, a religious zealot who was also an architect, designer, and philosopher, saw an opportunity to assert his interpretation of Christianity in existing styles, and his designs found their way into architectural history. In England, Gothic buildings were usually churches and public academic structures rich in ornamental stonework. But by the time the trend reached America, the English design elements of church and castle were integrated with good old American fantasy, inspired, no doubt, by the Gothic novels popular at the time.

Gothic Revival soon developed into American Carpenter Gothic and spread from the Northeast to the Midwest, and eventually, to the Far West (FIG. 1-11). Only the Deep South clung to neoclassicism. As machinery

Fig. 1–11. Carpenter Gothic (1837–1840). The carpenter Gothic house looked more like a Hansel and Gretel cottage than a home. Its steeply pitched cross-gabled roof was decorated with medieval-looking tracery bargeboards. Window styles varied in shape and size; sometimes, narrow and sharply-pointed lancet windows were set in a wall with other square-hooded windows. Typical also were fish-scale shingles and board-and-batten exterior walls.

replaced hand carving, and industrial nails became available, wood filigree could be easily mass-produced: cusps and crockets, pointed arches, spindles and rails, carved brackets, and fretwork adorned spires, pinnacles, turrets, and gables in a massive array of ornamentation that we now call "gingerbread."

The Italianate home, popular during the 1850s and 1860s, was part of a more subdued Victorian movement. It had a more or less flat roof with a centered, or off-center picturesque tower. Cornices, set on elaborately carved wooden brackets, detailed the eaves and doorways; arched windows were crowned with more sophisticated cornices and pediments. This style followed on the heels of the Late Georgian/Early Federal townhouse period. As a result, you'll find that cities like New York have more than their share of the simple, Italian-inspired brownstones (FIG. 1-12).

Fig. 1–12. Italianate (1850–1860). The Italinate is essentially a box-like structure with a flat or almost-flat roof having a heavily bracketed cornice or pediment. Its sole identifying characteristic is the centered, or off-centered, tower or cupola. But typically, it might have 5-sided, slanted bays—to ground level—or an oriel bay with bracketed supports. Heavy block-like modillions and cornice moldings are commonplace. Sometimes bold quoins decorate the corners of the buildings, giving it a very massive, yet opulent, look. Almost always, it features double-leafed doors with heavy moldings and hardware, and rounded or square-glass panes. The house windows are usually tall, round-headed or with a shallow arch; paired, or in a group.

Different interpretations of the Victorian gingerbread designs emerged quickly as prosperity continued, and the newly opened trade zones to Japan and other Far Eastern countries (1853) blended cultures into eclectic architectural styles resembling Moorish arches and Oriental fretwork.

The Queen Anne style came after the Centennial (1876) and represented a heterogeneous mix of structural protrusions that somehow retained an overall symmetrical balance (FIG. 1-13). Stripped of some of the ticky-tacky gingerbread adornment, the Queen Anne style emerged as a more purified and picturesque Victorian country house that still retained the popular bays, tall windows, turrets, odd-shaped gables, wrap-around porches, and steep, wide eaves. As the trend traveled across country to San Francisco, it was transformed into a citified version of the New York row house, and was aptly dubbed the San Francisco Stick, with its slim ornamental boards on the outside giving the illusion of structural framing (FIG. 1-14).

Another revival in France, the 1880 Second Empire, came to mean—in America—any house with a flat-topped, steeply-sloped Mansard roof (FIG. 1-15).

As we approached the twentieth century, native and international architects took us through several revolutionary phases of America's "rebellion/revival" architectural cycle.

Fig. 1–13. Queen Anne (1880–1895). The classic Queen Anne had tall-pitched gables, a turret, a recessed porch, stained, or beveled glass windows, and combinations of different exterior sidings. Rails and porch decorations included spindles, lattice, and scroll-shaped, chamfered and carved wood.

Fig. 1–14. San Francisco Stick (1870). Truly an American style, the Stick is ornamented with thin horizontal, diagonal, and vertical boards that suggest structural framing. The houses are known for their flat, 3-sided bay windows.

Fig. 1–15. French Second Empire (1870–1880). The most notable characteristic of the Second Empire home is its Mansard roof. Usually of red slate tiles, the steeply-pitched roof rises to a flat, or shallow deck and very often has cast-iron cresting on the rooftop. The roof's sides can be convex, concave, or straight. A paradigm French Second Empire home has dormer windows with detailed brick or tile hood moldings in it, providing daylight and fresh air for a full story above the eaves.

During the early 1900s, the conservative bungalow appeared: a smallish, one-story house that featured an oversized gabled porch. About the same time, the Shingle and Craftsman made their debut—styles that resemble stripped-down versions of the Queen Anne—totally clad in brown shingles but devoid of ornamentation (FIG. 1-16). The use of natural wood increased. So did the practice of building large overhanging eaves. And houses now sported large picture windows.

Leaving behind the splendiferous ornamentation, we were propelled into an era of modernism, with buildings that looked like cubes, stacked boxes, and glass towers—stark and sterile in contrast to the Victorian movement. Houses spread and flowed with the terrain, climbed hillsides, and projected their massive torsos of steel and glass far into the heavens. Their simplicity sometimes connoted a delightful, slightly Japanese feeling —other times, the starkness reminded us of a cold, empty box. The smooth and shiny-skinned houses were, of course, a rebellious retaliation from the overdone gingerbread. But this style, too, would soon soften into a more acceptable one, producing the most popular house ever built in America, the post-war ranch house.

The ranch style allowed you to buy just the right amount of house for your family and pocketbook. Sprawling ranches were built with ballroom-sized bedrooms, kitchens, dens, family rooms, studies, and triple baths. Smaller versions, called tracts, were constructed with two or three miniscule bedrooms, closet kitchens and living rooms with dining ells. Because of their popularity, millions of ranch homes were built in every state throughout the land.

What will the twenty-first century bring in architectural styles? What will our future homes be like? Experts predict that tomorrow's home will be radically different. All homes will be factory-built from synthetic materials, with precisely square and accurate, computerized measurements. They will have electromechanical cores that will supply energy for every household need. Everything will be computer-controlled.

Fig. 1–16. The Bungalow (1900–1920). The low-profiled bungalow often features a broad-gabled front porch roof with deep overhanging eaves. The one story house is usually set upon a raised foundation.

What this will do toward dehumanizing interpersonal relationships is questionable. Communication and interaction with family, neighbors, and community (the deliveryperson, gardener, paper carrier) is a very important part of our emotional well-being and sense of security. It was nurtured and sustained for centuries in our legacy homes. Will we bid a fond farewell to the kitchen range and family-style gourmet cooking; or to daydreaming dormers, window-watching bays, and hideaway havens, created by the add-ons and afterthoughts of our ancestors and endowing us with tiny, but precious, personal spaces and emotional recharging stations? Will it mean goodbye to brick and wood — materials that the land has provided us with down through the ages?

I think not. There will always be a place in the homebuyer's heart for the style of comfort and security that only America's architectural history can bestow — a heritage home.

THE INSPECTION

You've found what looks like a perfect candidate, and you're ready to give it a going over. Gather up your investigative tools: a flashlight, pocketknife, ice pick, magnet, and notebook; and wear old clothes and sneakers. If it's at all possible, try to make the inspection after a rainstorm.

Roof. Starting outside at the top, look for curling shingles — a sure sign of old age. Are any of them damaged or missing? Can you determine how many layers the roof has? It might be possible to just add another layer; if not, it could mean tearing the whole roof off and replacing it, along with the sheathing and new (or additional) insulation. Roof replacement by a contractor, according to a National Association of Home Builders' survey would run around $4,000.

Exterior walls. Are the exterior walls peeling, cracking, or blistering? You may not be able to correct the problem short of scraping them down to the bare wood, priming, and repainting. Check for chalking. Such evidence means that the old paint will have to be scrubbed down before a new coat is applied. Re-siding by a subcontractor, if that's what's called for, can also be a major expense: around $3,230.

Foundation and Basement. Walk around the house and look for mud-colored tunnels (½ inch in diameter) running up the walls, and discarded pearly-white, opaque wings. This could mean that termites are in residence. Check the basement, including sills, thresholds, stairs, and scrap lumber lying around. Since termites don't always reveal outward signs of infestation (and there can be as many as several thousand termites residing in a cubic foot of lumber — hardwood or softwood), check for them by digging a pocketknife or ice pick into the wood. If the wood is easily penetrated, the property might be infested.

Floors that slant or sag, and windows and doors that don't open and close properly, may mean foundation problems caused by settling or weakened main beams. Such ills are often cured with jacks or lollies; but if you find more than a few of these supports holding up the basement—beware! A complete basement replacement could cost $9,000 or more.

If the basement is dark and dank and smells musty, suspect leaking or condensation. Condensation is easier to correct, but if water seepage is the culprit, your job could be frustrating, time-consuming, and expensive. Often a waterproof surfacing can correct a minor leakage problem, but a bad drainage problem can mean excavating around the entire house and installing drain tile to reduce the pressure on basement walls, and diverting or rechanneling groundwater flow around the foundation. If you supply the manpower and rent a backhoe, you could accomplish this for around $400.

Water Heater. Examine the water heater. Is it sitting in a pool of water? Are there mineral deposits around joints? This could mean a replacement will be required soon.

Electrical System. Electrical service to the house can be determined by reading the label on the service panel (on the main disconnect switch), which indicates the total amperage the house is receiving. (It should register at least 100 amps, but 125 is better.) You can check the adequacy of the service further by turning on all the lights and other electrical devices at the same time. If the lights dim and flicker, or the circuit breaker trips, the system is indeed inadequate. If it takes the old-fashioned round screw-in fuses, the house has only two wires feeding into the box, or the wall receptacles accept only two-pronged plugs (newer ones take three), the system is antiquated and hasn't been updated in at least 15 years. This means that the electrical work should receive first priority on your remodeling list.

Before 1950, electrical service installed to a house provided only 60 amp/120 volt power, with two wires entering the service panel. Today, newer service providing 240 volts can be identified by three wires running into the house. With our voracious appetite for more and more electrical conveniences, anything less than 125 amperes/240 volts should be considered inadequate.

We measure electrical usage by watts (electric meters count these in kilowatt hours in units of 1,000 watts per hour). You can estimate what the electrical capacity should be for the house by multiplying the square footage of the house by 5 watts. This will give you a general wattage requirement figure. To this, add the wattage of all large appliances you use, such as central air conditioners, electric ranges, space heaters, water heaters, or clothes dryer. The wattage is usually listed on the metal nameplate attached to the appliance (amp × volt = wattage).

The total number of watts available in an existing system can also be calculated by multiplying the total amperage figure by the voltage figure on the service panel; for instance, a 200-watt, 240-volt service will provide a maximum of 48,000 watts. Now compare the two figures—your estimated required wattage for the remodeled house and what the house is actually capable of delivering. If the house is very old and the service is pitifully inadequate, you should probably replace the entire system, including the main electrical service to the house and the wiring. And you would be wise to call in an electrician to do the job. If you only need to add extra circuits to the existing system to update it (check to see if the service box has space for additional circuits), or add an additional subpanel, or replace or add extra electrical outlets, you can probably do these jobs yourself, assuming you understand the basics of an electrical system. But find out first whether or not your local building code will permit you to do your own wiring. Some codes allow you to install new circuits up to the service panel, but require a licensed electrician to complete the final hookup.

Flickering lights and faltering power doesn't necessarily mean that you have to replace the entire service panel and completely rewire the home. You may just need to update the wiring by adding extra branch circuits, so that each major appliance has its own separate circuit to the circuit breaker and the load is more evenly distributed.

The cost of upgrading the service will depend on the capacity you want installed, and the amount of rewiring needed. If you are subbing out the work, keep in mind that electricians charge around $8 to $10 per amp, and the bill may go as high as $2,000. But you may have no alternative, considering the risk. Faulty wiring is a major cause of house fires. Electrical fires often start inside the wall, smolder, then break out at night or when nobody is at home. So don't take a chance on an unsafe system. And before you undertake any electrical work on your own, make sure that you are properly covered by insurance. Some insurance companies will not pay on a policy if the work was done by an unlicensed electrician.

Plumbing. While you're in the basement, check the plumbing. Old galvanized pipes will rust and build up mineral deposits and eventually leak, or even burst. To determine if a pipe is galvanized, touch a magnet to it. It should stick if the pipe is cast iron or steel.

If you have to replumb with new copper, or even extensive plastic pipes, it could be expensive. Simple plumbing and the repair of leaking faucets and toilets can be done by almost anyone, but replacing outdated fixtures is another matter. A completely remodeled bathroom could cost around $1,850.

What about sewage? Is the house on a septic tank or city sewage system? Are there any noticeable problems?

Furnace. Turn on the furnace when you first arrive and let it run while you do your inspection. If it needs to be replaced, figure on spending upwards of $2,000.

Windows and Doors. Open and close all windows and doors. Do they operate correctly? Are they warped or damaged beyond repair? Is there evidence of dry rot around sills, thresholds, and jambs? Check by pressing a knife blade into the wood. It will penetrate easily if the wood is rotten. Exterior doors and window units can be expensive.

Floors. Since wall-to-wall carpeting has been around since colonial times, don't assume that you will uncover hardwood floors in all old houses. They, too, learned how to cut corners by using inferior grades of lumber where it wouldn't show. If the floor underneath happens to be hardwood, don't assume that it's in tip-top condition. Thoroughly check the whole floor before making a recovering or refinishing decision. Otherwise, figure recovering costs at around $15 per square yard (vinyl or carpeting, including pad and labor).

Interior walls. Check plaster walls by pressing on them with your thumb. If the paster moves or crumbles, a replastering or recovering job lies ahead.

Attic. Check the attic for rotting roofs, joists, and rafters. Are there signs of leaks or termites? Will the attic require insulation? Selling a home is almost impossible today without a guarantee of adequate roof insulation.

If you are lucky, your thorough house inspection might reveal a basically sound house—available to you at a bargain price—without too many expensive repairs. By replacing the most costly expense with your own labor, you can build up quite a "sweat equity" in the property. That's if you have appraised the house accurately, budgeted realistically, and follow your plan religiously. Be sure to set aside a substantial "unexpected expense" fund (at least 4 months worth of mortgage payments), in case you run into a few agonizing delays, more dirt and grime than you expected, or surprises like carpentry not conforming to contemporary standards. On any renovation or refurbishing project, such things go with the territory.

You'll get better at preempting trouble on your next house. For instance, you might uncover a wall built with 2-by-3-inch studs and spaced 26 inches o.c. Or bump into dry rot or a wall that has been destroyed by termites, which means tearing it down and replacing it with a new one. But expect good surprises too, like the solid bronze vault doors I told you about, or priceless wood held together with square nails and hand-hewn joints.

[2]
Remodeling Materials, Supplies and Tools

Some remodeling projects are straightforward and just about anyone can tackle them; others are more complex and require professionals or very skilled do-it-yourselfers. Most serious house renovators, though, usually enjoy taking on the more complicated projects, considering them to be challenges as well as learning experiences. While it might take you longer the first time to put in a new set of stairs, or install a skylight, eventually, as you become more adept, greater amounts of equity money are accumulated, the job is finished on time, and most important, you will be pleased with the results. You know the old saying: "If you want the job done right. . . ."

There are also many simple plumbing and electrical jobs that a do-it-yourselfer can do. Some building codes, however, require that only licensed professionals do the work. So be sure you go by the book. Take on only the projects that you know you can do and feel comfortable with. If you must consult with architects, engineers, or contractors, make sure that you have a well-thought-out plan and scaled drawings in hand before your meeting. Planning ahead will allow you to spot potential problems, ask the right questions, and get your ideas across more quickly. Planning ahead will also result in more accurate estimates. Hiring professionals on a consultation-basis-only can also save you time and a lot of headaches; they may be able to come up with solutions and ideas that never occurred to you. Consider, for instance, that a residential architect might charge around $50 an hour for his or her services—a worthwhile fee if the project is extensive, involves complicated building procedures, or working around building codes and restrictions.

The remodeler's building code book is his bible (or should be). These books are usually available in local libraries. The codes spell out minimum standards for the installation of wiring and plumbing and specify such things as how close to a property line you may build, minimum room height, fireproofing requirements, and so on. Be sure that all work conforms to local building codes or you may find yourself in costly litigation, or having to redo expensive work.

HIRING PROFESSIONALS

If you decide that a contractor should do all or part of the work, get the names of reputable companies from friends and neighbors who had similar work done and were satisfied with the results. Real estate agents, local utility companies, and other professionals might be able to give you recommendations, also. Check each contractor's background with the local Better Business Bureau.

Next, choose two or three contractors and call them in for estimates. Get everything in writing: approximate starting and completion dates, payment schedules, and who's responsible for what. Have them clearly detail the work they will do, specifying materials by brand name, style, model number, color, and size. This way each contractor is bidding on the same work and identical materials. Request separate labor and material costs in the bid. Bids should not vary more than 10 percent; be wary of very low bids, which may mean poor quality workmanship by inexperienced laborers or inferior materials. After receiving the bids, double-check the prices at the building supply store to determine if the contractor's price is fair.

The Contract

Contracts should include a *Waiver of Mechanics Lien Rights,* or an *Unconditional Lien Release* to prevent subcontractors from collecting from you if your contractor doesn't pay his bills. You'll also want an automatic arbitration clause inserted in the contract in case the contractor exceeds costs. A clause making the contractor responsible for damage caused by his workers' neglect, and a cleanup clause should also be included. You would be wise, also, to insist on a performance bond to guarantee the job will be completed satisfactorily in case the contractor goes bankrupt. Make sure the contractor knows about all restrictions and rules and carries them out in accordance with local regulations.

Be aware of a *Lien Sale Contract,* which makes your home collateral for payment to the contractor and gives him the right to foreclose on your home in order to obtain payment — even if his work was unsatisfactory! In fact, never sign any contract that involves a lot of money before your attorney has had a chance to look it over.

Payment. Usually, if the job is small, payment is made in full after the work is satisfactorily finished. On more costly projects, payment is made in several installments: the first when the contract is signed, the second when the job is half finished, and the final payment after the job is completed and you've had time to check it over.

Scheduling. If you decide to do the remodeling yourself, schedule your projects carefully and in sequence. Remember that it may take up to six or eight weeks for delivery of such items as kitchen cabinets or appliances, which could upset the whole project.

TOOLING UP

You probably already have most of the basic tools you need to get started—tools used around the house for general maintenance. Specific tools required for special chores can very often be rented from the people who sold you the materials. Ask before you buy. If you have to purchase new tools, remember to get the best quality you can afford.

Your toolbox should include:

☑ Hammer. A good curved-claw, 16-ounce hammer for pulling nails or driving them home.

☑ Nail set. A ¹⁄₁₆-inch nail set for sinking finish nails below a materials' surface.

☑ Saws. A 10-pt, 26-inch crosscut handsaw; a hacksaw for cutting through wire and metal; a keyhole saw for making cuts in tight places; a coping saw for intricate curves; and a miterbox and backsaw for making accurate angle cuts.

☑ Measuring Devices. A 25-foot steel tape with locking mechanism; and a wood folding extension rule.

☑ Screwdrivers. At least one blade about ³⁄₁₆-inch wide (which fits most standard screw heads); and a medium-sized Phillips (x-slot) screwdriver.

☑ Pliers. Regular mechanic's pliers with double-jointed jaws; and a pair of long-nosed pliers with wire cutters.

☑ Wrenches. A pair of 10-inch adjustable, open-ended wrenches; Allen set; and a combination wrench set.

☑ Framing Square. For checking and marking right angles and making stair and rafter cuts; a combination square to measure 45-degree (miter) cuts.

☑ Carpenter's Level. A 24-inch aluminum model with 3 spirit vials.

☑ Chisels. A ½-inch wood chisel; and a ½-inch cold chisel.

☑ Awl. For starting holes.

☑ Utility Knife. An all-purpose, light-duty cutter with retractable blades.

☑ Chalk Line. For snapping long, accurate guidelines.

☑ Planes. A 6-inch block plane for smoothing across grain; a 6-inch jack plane for smoothing with the grain; and a rasp plane that takes off a lot of wood–fast.

☑ File. A coarse, half-round, double-cut wood file.

☑ Clamps. Several pairs of 4-inch C-clamps.

☑ Pry Bar. For dismanteling or demolition.

☑ Sharpening Stone and Oil. For sharpening various tool blades.

☑ Electric Drill. A ⅜-inch variable-speed, reversible drill with a set of high speed drill bits, countersink, and masonry bits.

- ☑ Staple Gun and Staples.
- ☑ Electric portable circular saw. Blade diameter of 7 or 7-½ inches; depth adjustment for shallow cuts; angle mechanism for miter cuts; ripping fence to guide the saw on long cuts; and automatic spring-action blade guard for safety.
- ☑ Blades. Combination, carbide-tipped.
- ☑ Orbital/straight-line sander.
- ☑ Saber saw.
- ☑ Miscellaneous: Scissors; soldering gun; propane torch; glass cutter; tin snips; putty knives; masking tape; white glue; silicone rubber cement; plastic wood filler; synthetic lubricants; electrician's tape; pencils; an assortment of sandpaper; screws, nails; hooks; and wall anchors.

TIPS ON USING TOOLS

If you have never hammered a nail in wood before, the following tips may be helpful. Some of the information is very basic and rudimentary, but even the most experienced carpenter might find some merit in changing his or her style, sometimes.

Hammering

Hold the hammer as close to the base of the handle as possible. If you hold it too close to the head, it will reduce the force with which you can strike; it can also cause the nail to go askew or bend. The usual method for starting a nail is to grasp it between your thumb and index finger and tap the nailhead lightly once or twice. Once the nail is seated, remove the holding hand and direct a slow, easy swing so that the face of the hammer head meets the nailhead dead center. Never apply muscle power at the expense of accuracy. To start a short brad in wood, grip it between the first two fingers, palm side up, so that the knuckles are out of the way.

Wood will split if you use a nail that's too heavy, or nail too close to the edge of a piece of wood. To prevent splitting, blunt the nail head by turning it upside down and tapping the point gently with the hammer. When you nail in hardwoods, drill a pilot hole slightly thinner than the nail shaft before you hammer it in.

Cutting with a Handsaw

Keep the wood at least 3 inches in front of the surface on which you're working, in order to avoid sawing into it. Steady the lumber with your free hand, using the thumb knuckle to guide the first few strokes (FIG. 2-1).

Start with the butt portion of the blade near the handle and pull toward yourself with several short strokes to make the starting groove. When you cut, stay on the waste side of the line, never cut directly on the line. Because the crosscut saw cuts on both the forward and back strokes under its own weight, you need to apply only light pressure when using it.

Fig. 2-1. Guiding the handsaw.

As you saw, make an effort to cut with as much of the blade as possible, sawing back and forth in long, slow, even motions. Steady the lumber with your free hand so that the motion of the arm working the saw won't move the board out of position. If the saw wanders off the line, bring it back to the spot where it veered off and start again; don't bend the saw blade to get back on the line. At the end of the cut, always support the waste piece while you are making the final cutoff stroke; never break the piece off by twisting the saw blade.

Measuring

Never move a rule when measuring in increments, project off the extended rule. A fold-out ruler is printed in black, but every 16 inches it's printed in red. When you lay out studs in 16-inch intervals, this is a valuable time-saver.

Planing

Clamp or brace your work whenever possible. Turn the adjusting nut on the plane until the blade protrudes to the depth of cut you want.

Place the plane on the wood and start by applying most of the pressure to the knob at the front, rather than the handle in back. Glide it evenly over the wood, keeping it parallel to the surface. When you get to the end of the stroke, relax the knob pressure and finish in a smooth motion directed from the handle. Do not start or stop in the middle of the board. Always plane with the grain of the wood; it will gouge if you go against the grain.

Cutting with a Circular Saw

Adjust the saw blade so that one full tooth extends below the board you're cutting. If the blade is set deeper, you'll have less control over the machine (FIG. 2-2). The blade can be raised so that it makes groove cuts; or tilted to make 45 degree angle cuts.

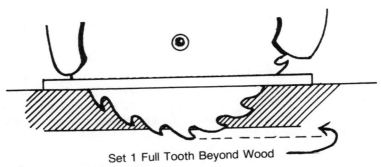

Set 1 Full Tooth Beyond Wood

Fig. 2-2. Adjust the saw blade.

To make straight, long, fast cuts with a circular saw, clamp a straight-edge or another board to the piece you're sawing to guide the edge of the circular saw.

Operating a Saber Saw

Insert the blade (teeth pointing out) by loosening, then tightening, a screw at the front. Notice that the teeth point up, meaning that it does it's cutting on an "up" stroke. Thus, always face the finished side of the material down.

The flat plate that extends in front and behind the blade is called the *shoe.* Turn the saw on to a fast rpm and lower the shoe flat onto the starting edge of the material. Inch the blade forward until it meets the penciled guideline, then push ahead slowly, watching the line—not the blade. Brace the material so it doesn't split at the end of the cut.

To start in the center of a piece of wood, you'll have to drill a large hole before you can insert the blade.

Using the Electric Drill

It's usually easier, and neater, to make a starting hole with an awl. Choose the proper bit (too small is better than too large). Insert the chuck key that's tied to the power cord into the chuck to open the jaws so that you can place the shank of the bit in. Now reverse the movement so that the jaws clamp the bit tightly. Remove the key.

Put the tip of the bit in the starter hole, hold the bit exactly perpendicular to the working surface, and start the drill at low speed by squeezing the trigger. Exert a little more pressure and switch to a faster speed. Don't tilt the bit. When the bit no longer meets resistance, withdraw it while the power is still on. Don't release the trigger and try to pull it out.

If you come up against something that slows the bit to a halt, withdraw the bit and change to a special drill bit for masonry, and so forth.

Power drills can be fitted with buffer, sander, and wire brush attachments and grinder wheels.

Electric Sanders

Start by selecting the correct type and grade of sandpaper. The two most common kinds are flint and garnet. Flint is less expensive than garnet and gums up more quickly. Garnet is tougher and longer lasting and works better for sanding all types of hardwoods. The closest thing to an all-purpose abrasive is aluminum oxide paper. It can be used on wood, metal, plastics and fiberglass. Silicon carbide is the hardest abrasive available for consumer use—nearly as hard as diamond. So it's ideal for sanding non-ferrous metals (metals that don't contain iron), composition boards, and plastics. It can also be used with water or mineral oil as a lubricant for rubbing down varnish, polyurethane, and lacquer finishes. The grade of an individual sheet of sandpaper is identified by the number on its back, ranging from a very coarse no. 12 to a superfine no. 600, with 22 increments in between.

For your sander, buy a supply of garnet or aluminum oxide sandpaper in each of three grades: coarse, medium, and fine. For especially rough jobs you may need extra-coarse paper. Don't use the cheaper flint paper on your electric sander.

Cut the sheet with scissors so that it fits neatly over the bottom of the sander pad. Leave about a ½-inch overlap at both ends so that you can secure the paper to the machine with either the clamp or lever.

To begin, hold the sander over the work and switch the power on. Gently lower the sander to make contact with the surface of the wood. Move the sander back and forth, working with the grain. You can start by cross-grain sanding to remove the first layer, but move quickly back to working with the grain. Replace the paper as necessary.

MATERIALS

Although there are many types of nails and brads, you'll probably find that four types will handle just about all of your nailing chores: common nail, casing nail, finishing nail, and brad (FIG. 2-3).

Nails

The common nail is the one used most often, mostly in applications where the head of the nail is not objectionable as in rough construction. It's length is identified by its pennyweight, notated by a "d." Years ago, nails

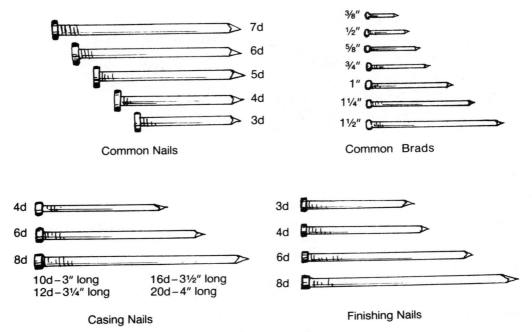

Common Nails

Common Brads

4d
6d
8d

10d – 3" long   16d – 3½" long
12d – 3¼" long   20d – 4" long

Casing Nails

3d
4d
6d
8d

Finishing Nails

Fig. 2–3. Nail types.

were sold by this term to designate the weight per hundred. Today, we use it just to designate length and size, thus there are 2d, 3d, 4d nails, and so on. "Spikes" are common nails larger than 4 inches. They're not identified by "d" but by length in inches.

The finishing nail has a rounded head. When the nail is driven flush, the round head is not as noticeable as a flat head.

Casing nails are used primarily on cabinet work or interior trim. They are similar to finishing nails but slightly heavier. The heads of casing nails are generally countersunk and covered with putty or wood filler.

Common brads are not identified by pennyweight. They are designated by length only. Used for light assembly work (attaching moldings, for example) where the head should be concealed, they are shorter and smaller than finish nails.

A good rule of thumb for choosing the proper size nail is that the nail should be three times as long as the wood it will be put through. This means that two-thirds of the nail will provide the holding power in the bottom piece.

We use a special-type nail for drywall, usually called sheetrock, or blue nail. This ring-shanked nail is designed to eliminate nail popping. Rings around the body of the nail give it extra-strong holding power. The dish-shaped head can be driven flush with the surface of the wallboard.

Another ringed-nail type provides a strong holding power for securing plywood to permanent flooring when preparing a subfloor for tile.

Lumber and Building Materials

Lumber and building materials are readily available today. Huge cash-and-carry stores handle all kinds of do-it-yourself products: building materials, plumbing and electrical supplies, home furnishings and appliances, and garden supplies. Building products can also be found in hardware stores and in some chain store departments. Of course, there's always the old standby: your local lumberyard and building supply dealer. If you're a novice, don't be intimidated by the product array or construction jargon. Wherever you shop, you'll find the salesperson ready and willing to assist you in any way possible. No matter how rough your sketch is, he or she will know the quantities and grades of materials you should be using. The salesperson can also give you technical advice and assistance and make other helpful suggestions. Most stores will even cut your materials to the exact size, saving you extra work and the worry of cutting materials to the correct size at home. But if this is the type of help you need, it's better to do your shopping during the week days, when the salesperson has more time to spend with you.

If this is your first remodeling job, the accompanying charts can save you time and money. The first thing you should know is that there is a universal lumber language. Lumber comes in different sizes and grades. The familiar terms, 2 by 4s, 2 by 6s, 1 by 8 and so on, are not the actual sizes of lumber you'll be getting when you buy it. These are called *nominal sizes*. The actual size has been slimmed down through the drying-out, planing, and finishing processes (TABLE 2-1). Of course, if you have your plan in hand, don't worry, the dealer will know exactly what you need.

Table 2-1. Lumber Sizes

Nominal Size (in.)	Actual Dry Size (in.)
1×2	¾×1½
1×4	¾×3½
1×6	¾×5½
1×10	¾×9¼
1×12	¾×11¼
2×4	1½×3½
2×6	1½×5½
2×10	1½×9¼
2×12	1½×11¼
3×6	2½×5½
4×4	3½×3½
4×6	3½×5½

Your materials list should be as detailed as possible. If your project calls for 12 pieces of 2 by 4 exactly 8 feet long, list it that way. Don't add them up to make it 96 feet of 2 by 4s, because the supplier might include a few pieces only 6 feet long. When you order lumber, do it as shown.

Amt.	Size	Type
12	2 × 4, 8-ft long	No. 2 Common White Pine

Lumber Grades

The success of any home remodeling project depends greatly on using the right grade of lumber for the purpose. Remember the best way to save when purchasing lumber is to: 1 Buy the lowest grade of lumber that will do the job (your description of the project will enable your dealer to suggest the correct grade); and 2. Buy the smallest quantity possible.

For boards (commons), siding, paneling, shelving, sheathing, and form lumber, follow these guidelines.

No. 1 Common. The ultimate in small-knot material for appearance uses.

No. 2 and 3. These are most often used on, or in, houses for paneling, siding, and shelving. Boards are generally available at building material dealers in 1 by 2 through 1 by 12.

Light Framing. (construction standard utility) This category is for use where high-strength values are not required, such as studs, plates, sills, cripples, blocking, and so on.

Studs. A popular grade for load- and nonload-bearing walls. Limited to 10-foot lengths and shorter.

Structural Light Framing Joists and Planks. (Select from structural no. 1, 2, or 3.) These grades fit engineering applications where higher strength is needed. For uses such as trusses, joists, rafters, and general framing.

An additional category is *S-Dry* for seasoned lumber, and *S-Green* for unseasoned, or "green" lumber. Be sure to use S-Dry for all enclosed framing.

[3]

Electrical Wiring

Whether a major revamping of the existing electrical system is required, or just a few minor repairs—don't postpone it. Updating the electrical system in an old house shouldn't take a backseat to other renovations. Getting by with an outdated system while you wait for the electrician, or neglecting to do minor electrical repairs that you could easily master yourself, could lead to a tragedy. Restoring a sound electrical system to the house should be your first priority; then the rest of your renovating can be done safely and with peace of mind.

Your inspection prior to buying the house indicated whether or not the entire electrical system had to replaced, or additional circuitry added. Your first clue was the number of lines running into the service panel indicating the system's ability to take the loads required by today's modern appliances. The second clue was the type of wiring used throughout the house.

SERVICE PANEL

In the 50s and 60s, before the advent of modern electrical appliances, 60 to 100 ampere service entrances were installed in many houses. As mentioned in Chapter 1, anything below 125 amperes, today, is considered inadequate, and 125-amp entrances are recommended for all new installations. If you have an older house with only 60-amp/120-volt power (two wires entering the service panel) you should have it replaced with 125-amp/240-volt service (three wires leading from the utility feed into the service box). This will require the services of a licensed electrician because, in most communities, any electrical work that involves rewiring *inside* the fuse or breaker box must be performed by a professional and is subject to an inspection. If you find that the installation of a subpanel is necessary, it's best to have an electrician do this, too, to make sure it's installed and grounded properly.

If you have an updated main service panel and wiring, you could possibly do the rest of the electrical work yourself (providing there is room in the main service panel to add additional circuitry). The job of extending an existing circuit, not requiring any modifications to the fuse or breaker box circuitry, is exempt from licensing requirements in most communities, and homeowners are allowed to install new circuits to the service entrance panel. In most cases, however, a licensed electrician is required to complete the final hookup. Check the code book and talk with an electrical inspector to determine what, if any, ordinances regulate minor home wiring jobs.

CABLE

Faulty wiring is one of the major causes of house fires. The old knob-and-tube system is still in use today in too many old homes and, almost surely, with overloaded and frayed wires just waiting to overheat.

Some years after the knob-and-tube wiring, BX metallic armored cable came into general use, but BX also had its faults, which caused the cable to overheat and result in fires. Today, BX too, is outlawed in many areas. Neither of these types of wiring should be connected into or extended.

Today we use a nonmetallic cable of tough plastic sheathing that carries hot (black) and neutral (white) copper wires, and a bare ground wire, in its casing. Nonmetallic wire cable, often called Romex, is now the most widely used wiring for residential use. When connecting into existing systems containing a ground wire or on new work, you should always use Romex. A similar moisture-resistant, noncorrosive cable is available for outdoors, or for damp indoor areas.

The ground wire allows you to ground outlets and fixtures. A grounded outlet has two slots for the plug prongs, and a U-shaped hole for the ground prong on the plug. This system provides a continuous ground for any appliance and provides an extra measure of safety.

RESIDENTIAL ELECTRICAL SYSTEM

Are you in the dark about how a residential electrical system works? Most people would never dream of doing their own simple wiring, for fear of electrocution, fire, or the unknown. Most of us are out-and-out scared when it comes to working with electricity, but there's nothing complicated about basic wiring. Even if you plan to hire an electrician to do all of the electrical work in the house, you should know how the system works, in order to lay out the lines according to your remodeling plans. Here's an overview of how a modern system works.

1. The power comes from a pole (or feed line) via a three-wire cable.
2. The three-wire cable is mounted to the house with anchors and clips. The bottom of the cable is fed into the utility company's meter on the outside of the house.
3. From the meter, there's a connection through the wall of the house to the main service panel (usually in the garage or basement). This

large, steel box splits up the power to various branch circuits inside the house. It has a main circuit breaker that can turn off all the power in the house, and individual switch breakers that control current going into separate branch circuits. Circuit breakers are safety devices that sense when a circuit has malfunctioned, or is overloaded, and in danger of overheating.

Today, we have modern circuit breaker switches, instead of the screw fuses that were once standard in old main panels. Fuses are one-time devices that must be replaced when they blow (evidenced by a blackened face); breakers are permanent devices that trip when overloaded but can be reset after the problem has been corrected. Breakers are the obvious choice for a modern and efficient electrical wiring system.

All installations—up to, and through service panel work—must be handled by power companies and licensed electricians. Once the main service panel is in place, there are many electrical installations that you can do yourself. Most do-it-yourselfers can add branch circuits, extra outlets and wall switches, install ceiling fixtures and fans, and even hot water heaters and other appliances—if they take the proper safety precautions during installation.

Safety

Safety precautions are of the utmost importance when working with electricity. All electrical work carries a risk of shock and can be fatal. Before you attempt any electrical work: *Shut the power off at the main panel, then, double-check the outlet you're working on with a voltage tester to make sure there is no current going through.*

A voltage, or circuit tester, has a small neon bulb between two metal-pronged leads. Put the probe to every combination of wires, terminals, and parts of the box. If the bulb lights, there's voltage going through, and you should shut the current off immediately before going any further. Also follow these precautions:

▶ Always use a rubber-handled screwdriver
▶ Wear sneakers
▶ Never touch pipes while you work on electricity
▶ Make sure the floor you're standing on is not damp or wet. Stand on a board or piece of plywood.
▶ Tape a note to the service panel so no one will restore the power while you're working in some remote area of the house.

Making an Electrical Circuit Diagram

Before a service panel can be installed safely, an electrical diagram should be made for the house, indicating the number of circuit breakers required and what their capacity should be. In making the diagram, you'll also be able to tell how the wires will be best threaded through walls, floors, and ceilings.

The diagram should show the location of all circuits and how many appliances or outlets there are on each circuit. Because most of today's small appliances take separate circuits, modern houses usually require at least two dozen circuits.

Knowing how many watts an appliance takes will help you to distribute the load more equitably. For instance, a 20-amp circuit (amp numbers are shown on front of fuses or breakers) can take 2200 watts, while a 15-amp circuit shouldn't be loaded beyond 1650 watts. For instance, you wouldn't want to gang a toaster that takes 1100 watts, with a rotisserie that needs 1400 watts to operate.

Appliances that must work at all times, like refrigerators, freezers, sump pumps, furnaces and the like, should be on separate circuits. Other small appliances can be ganged according to their wattage requirements to save on wire and expense.

For lighting you should figure one 15-amp for every 370 square feet of floor space, with light circuits split to prevent the whole floor from plunging into darkness in case of circuit malfunction. Lighting should not be installed on any appliance circuit.

Of course, separate 240-volt lines must run to the range, hot water heater, air conditioner, and dryer. Although you can buy 120-volt model appliances, the 240-volt models are faster and more efficient.

Outlet Locations

Once circuit needs are determined, you can decide where to put the outlets. In the kitchen and bathroom, an outlet should be installed every 4 feet along the countertop. If the spaces are divided by appliances or fixtures, each space should have its own receptacle outlet. Kitchen and bathroom outlets must be protected with ground fault circuit interrupters.

In addition, there should be no point along a horizontal wall farther than 6 feet from an outlet (this translates to outlets every 12 feet apart). At least one outlet is required in the garage and in the laundry room, no further than 6 feet from an appliance. An outdoor receptacle should be provided for each single-family dwelling.

All boxes should be installed flush with the finished wall at the following heights:

- ▶ **Switches** — 48 inches from floor to center of box, or 8 inches from countertop
- ▶ **Receptacles** or telephone outlets — 14 inches from floor to center of box, or 8 inches from countertop
- ▶ **Thermostats** — 54 inches from floor or 6 inches from countertop.

Be sure to mark switch and outlet box locations.

Running the Cable Wire

The capacity of the fuses or breakers in the service panel box *must* be equal with respect to the type of wire used for each circuit. Fourteen-gauge (no. 14) wire is the smallest wire permitted for homes under most local codes; the largest (no. 6) is used for heavy-duty appliances. The wire gauge number is printed on the cable's sheathing.

As a rule, circuits servicing house lights and duplex outlets require only 15-amp breakers run with no. 14 wire. However, no. 12 wire should be used from the service panel to the first lighting fixture or outlet box if the distance from the panel to the box is over 30 feet, with no. 14 used for the rest of the run. If the distance is under 30 feet, no. 14 wire can be used for the entire run.

The wire used for appliance circuits is usually heavier than other house wiring; dishwashers, sump pumps, garage disposals and room air conditioners are run with no. 12 wire protected with 20-amp breakers. Electric dryers and hot water heaters require no. 10 wire and 30-amp breakers. Electric range circuits are run with no. 6 wire, controlled with a 50-amp breaker.

Once you have made your electrical diagram, decided on the wire runs, wire gauge, and box locations, you're ready to thread the cable through the house leading out of the main service panel. If you're dealing with new construction or open studs and attic joists, this will be an easy chore. Just drill up from the basement through the sole plate into a partition cavity to where the outlet will go, or down from the attic through the top plates. If you have to go horizontally through the wall, drill holes in the centers of studs or other framing members to thread cable through (FIG. 3-1). On open floors in attics, nail a 1-by-2 board to joists to support the cable across the span and staple or clamp the cable to it.

Fishing Cable through Walls

If you're dealing with existing walls, floors, and ceilings, you'll have to break through at some locations, thread the cable through, and patch afterward. Fishing cable from one floor to the other is easy if you have some knowledge of house framing.

First, remove baseboard and trim on the wall where the new outlet will go. Then, drill ¾-inch holes diagonally, up or down, or both, between the studs until you open up a passage for the cable to get to the floor above (or below). Thread a stiff wire or weighted string down through the hole and tie the cable to it so you can pull it up (FIG. 3-2).

Once you have brought up wire for one outlet, you can run wire from outlet to outlet, behind the baseboard. Draw a light line along the baseboard before you remove it, then gouge out a channel below the line from the plaster or wallboard to expose studs. Ideally, you should drill holes through the studs for the cable, but where you're working in limited space, as in this case, it's easier to notch the front of the studs to make a

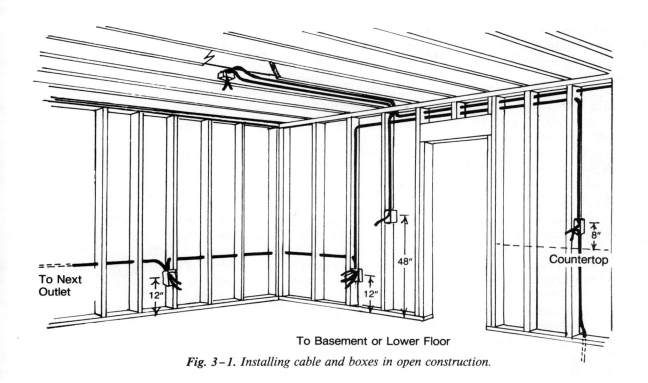

To Next
Outlet

12"

48"

12"

8"

Countertop

To Basement or Lower Floor

Fig. 3–1. Installing cable and boxes in open construction.

*Fig. 3–2. Fishing cable from one floor
to another.*

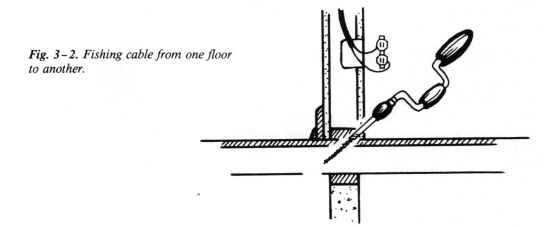

continuous channel. After the cable is threaded through the channel, cover the notches with metal plates (available at electric supply stores) to protect the wiring. Replace the baseboard, but be careful not to nail into the wiring.

To run cable around door frames and headers, start by removing the baseboard and door trim, notch spacers between wall and door jamb, the headers, and thread the cable around. Add protective metal plates and replace the trim.

Always leave plenty of slack in the cable and pull at least 8 inches out of the wall where the outlet or receptacle will go.

BOXES

Outlet, receptacle, or switch boxes come in many styles and sizes. Box depth depends on how much room you need to recess it. They are available as shallow as 1½ inches for a furred-out basement wall, or as deep as 2½ inches for regular construction. Box size is determined by the number of wires you must connect inside the box. Sectional steel switch boxes are needed when you must "gang" or attach more than one box in order to install several receptacle sets or switches.

When set in a finished wall, each new box is held in place by four pieces of metal: two tabs at the top and bottom to prevent the box from being pushed back into the wall cavity, and two drywall brackets that prevent it from being pulled forward.

All connections must be made in an approved box with the proper connectors—not by an open-line splice. If wires must be spliced, use wire-nuts, which are screw-on connectors that can be used with wire from no. 18 to no. 10.

Installing Boxes

The metal boxes have knockout plugs with built-in cable clamps for the type of cable used. Pry out the appropriate knockout plugs. Strip away about 8 inches of the plastic sheathing from the end of the cable and feed the end of the cable through the knockout hole, clamping it on the sheathing. Pull the stripped section out through the front of the box. Nail the box to a wall stud and prepare the wires for installation of switch, outlet, or fixture.

Installing Outlets and Switches

With a cable stripper or electrician's knife, taper the insulation back on each wire in the cable so that about ½ inch to an inch of bare wire is exposed. Take a pair of needlenose pliers and make a cup-hook loop at the end of each stripped wire to fit over the terminal screws (FIG. 3-3).

When the wire is hooked over the terminal screws, and screwed down, its open end will close up.

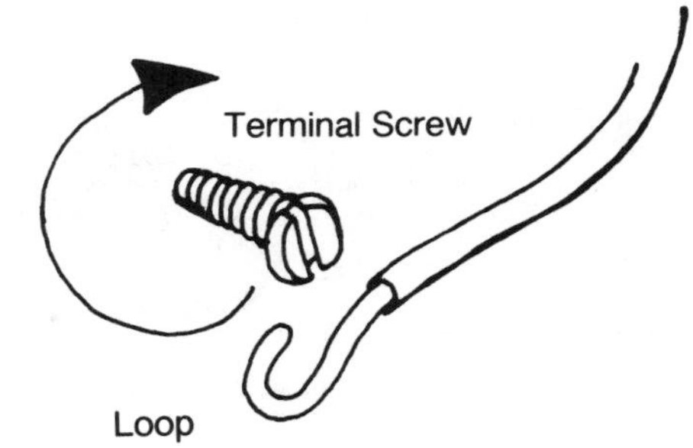

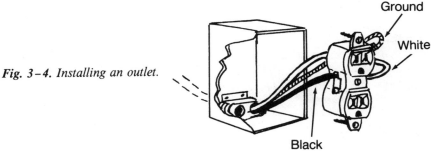

Fig. 3–3. Making proper loop for connecting wire to terminal screws.

Terminal Screw

Loop

Wires are color-coded to prevent wiring mistakes. Black wires connect to brass terminal screws or other black wire. White wire connects to silver (chrome) terminal screws or other white wire. Ground wires are connected to a green grounding, or hex-head screw, or to the box with a clip (check local codes).

Outlets. Connect the cable to an outlet by attaching the black wire to the brass terminal—the white wire to the silver terminal and the ground wire to the ground terminal (FIG. 3-4). Carefully fold the wires and tuck them into the box. Replace covers.

Fig. 3–4. Installing an outlet.

Ground

White

Black

Switches. Where you have a single-pole switch for a light fixture, connect black wire to black lead wire on fixture (FIG. 3-5A). Then, connect white wire on fixture lead to white wire on supply cable (FIG. 3-5B). Next, connect new cable's white wire to black lead at supply feed line (FIG. 3-5C). Then paint leads black at both switch and fixture.

Where you have a switch going to a receptacle, only the black (hot) wires are connected to the switch; the white wires are wire-nutted together, as are the ground wires (FIG. 3-6).

Connecting New Wire to the Last Outlet in the Run. To locate the last outlet in the wiring run, shut off the current and remove all the cover plates on the outlets. The last outlet in the run will have wires connected to only two of the four terminal screws.

The two unused terminal screws on the receptacle can serve as the starting point for wiring to the new outlet. *Be sure that you're using the*

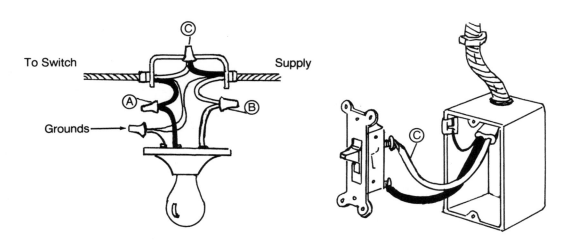

To Switch   Supply

Grounds

Fig. 3–5. *Installing a switch to ceiling fixture.*

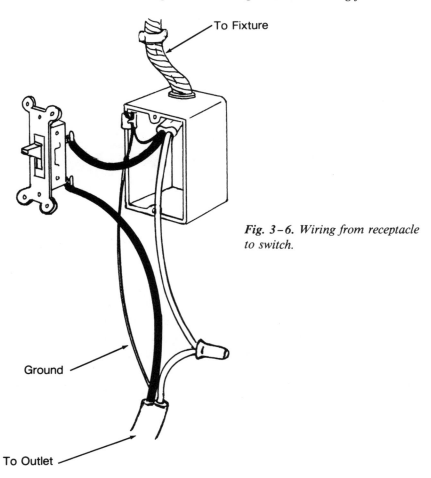

To Fixture

Fig. 3–6. *Wiring from receptacle to switch.*

Ground

To Outlet

exact gauge cable as was originally used. If no. 12 was used, use no. 12; if no. 14 was used, the new cable should be no. 14. To attach new wiring:

1. Loosen the screws holding the receptacle in the box and pull it out. Pull the new cable through knockout plugs in back of the outlet.
2. Attach new white wire to silver terminal—black wire to brass terminal and ground wire to green or hex-head terminal, or clip to back of the box (FIG. 3-7).
3. Set the receptacle back in the box and replace the cover.
4. Thread the new cable through the wall to the new outlet installation.

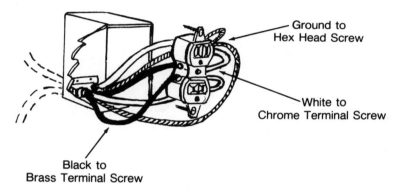

Fig. 3–7. Connecting new wire from last outlet in run.

Connecting New Wire to Junction Box. You can also tie new wiring in at a junction box, if there's room.

1. Shut off the current. Check the voltage of the cable in the box by tracing it back to the main panel. Be sure that you're not connecting a 120-volt outlet wiring to a run of wire provided for 220- to 240-volt appliances.
2. Locate the main supply cable coming into the junction box by tracing it to the main service panel. All white wires in the junction box will be attached to the white wire at the supply lines.
3. Knock out the unused plug on the junction box, and run the new line from the box as illustrated (FIG. 3-8).
4. Join black, white, and ground wires to their respective counterparts, using wire caps.
5. Fasten the new cable along joists in basement or attic with cable straps, until you can feed it inside a wall to the location of the new outlet box.

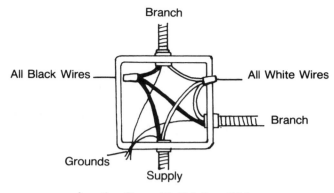

Junction Box with Existing Wiring

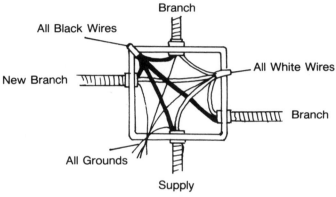

Junction Box with New Wiring Added

Fig. 3–8. Connecting new wire from junction box.

Connecting New Wiring to a Ceiling Fixture. If a light fixture is not switch-controlled, you can connect new wiring to it.

1. Shut off the current at the main panel.
2. Knock out a new opening in the outlet box and thread the new wire through.
3. Tie white wires to white wires; black wires to black wires as illustrated (FIG. 3-9).
4. Connect ground wires, then screw them to the back of the box. Replace covers.

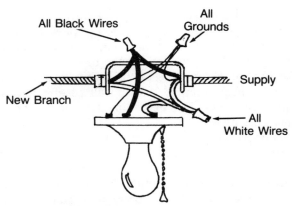

Fig. 3–9. Connecting new wire from ceiling fixture.

INSTALLING A CEILING FIXTURE

Mounting a new ceiling fixture is easy if you can make the initial electrical connections before finishing the ceiling, or if there's access to a finished ceiling from the attic above.

Most ceiling fixtures (other than recessed fixtures) are mounted to standard electrical boxes that are attached to a stud, strap, or hanger bar inside the ceiling cavity. In some cases, if your fixture allows, you can install a special shallow ceiling pan box directly to the bottom of a joist and mount the fixture to it (FIG. 3-10).

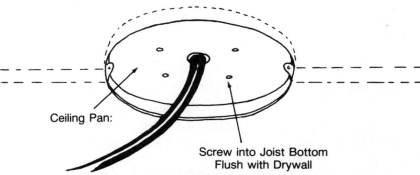

Fig. 3–10. Installing a shallow ceiling pan.

When additional mounting hardware is required, it's usually included in the fixture box. Read the manufacturer's instructions.

Installing an outlet box in a finished drywall ceiling is a little more time-consuming, but is not difficult.

1. Make sure that all power is off at the main panel. Mark the position on the ceiling where you want the fixture mounted. Probe until you

find ceiling joists on either side of the fixture's intended location. Then draw a rectangle on the ceiling one foot wide by the distance that spans the mid-points on the bottom of the two joists. (This will give you nailing space when you reattach the patch.)

2. Cut out the access hole in the ceiling according to the penciled rectangular lines; remove the drywall section and set it aside. Be careful when you cut into the ceiling that you don't make contact with hidden pipes or wires.

3. To support the electrical box, you can use a 2 by 4 nailed between joists, or a special metal hanging bar or strap (available at electrical stores). Some of the hanger bars rest on top of the joists; others are held in place with nails inserted through tabs and fit between joists (FIG. 3-11). Also available is a special adjustable bar that allows you to span irregular spaces.

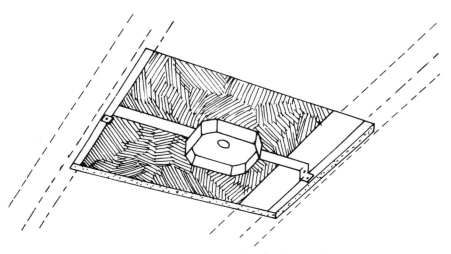

Fig. 3–11. Cutting access holes for hanger bar.

If your ceilings are of plaster, chisel out a narrow channel, the width of a piece of lath, and remove the lath. Install an offset hanger bar to support the box (FIG. 3-12).

4. Next, plan a route from the access hole in the ceiling to the wall switch location. If you can line up the spaces between ceiling joists and wall studs, do so. This way, you won't have to cut through too many studs or joists (FIG. 3-13).

Where this is impossible, you'll have to drill through or notch wood framing members to allow passage of the cable (FIG. 3-14).

5. After fixture, switch, and access holes are cut, start fishing the cable through the wall at the switch location. Run the cable from hole to hole, passing the cable behind drywall or plaster and in front of the exposed, notched framing members. If the wall contains insulation,

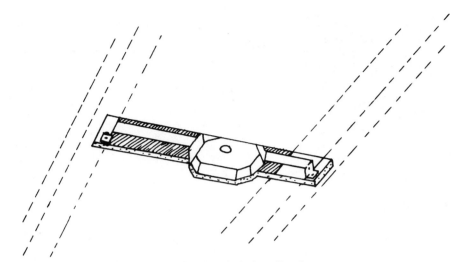

Fig. 3–12. Chiseling out a channel in lath for offset bar.

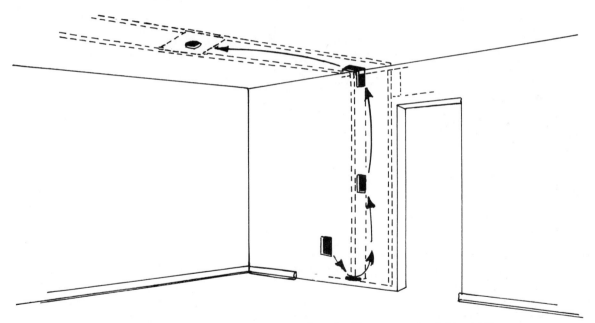

Fig. 3–13. Aligning wall and ceiling spaces for fishing cable.

keep the cable on the room side of the vapor barrier. You may find it easier to thread a stiff wire or weighted string from the ceiling access down to the wall switch access. Tie the end to a piece of cable and pull both back up through the ceiling access.

6. To connect the feed cable to the ceiling outlet box, strip away about 8 inches of the outer sheathing from the cable end and push it through

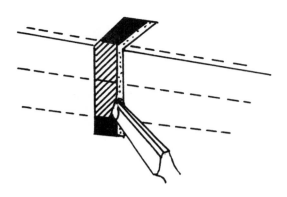

Fig. 3–14. Notching framing for cable.

one of the knockout holes equipped with a built-in clamp. Attach the box to your support.

7. Mark the exact dimensions and location of the box on the drywall patch and cut an opening for it. Nail the ceiling patch to the joists and finish with tape and drywall compound.

8. Support the fixture with a coat hanger as you connect black, white, and ground wires to their respective terminals. If the fixture does not have screw terminals, it will probably have short lengths of wire protruding from its back. Use wire-nuts to connect ends of like-colored wires together.

9. Finish installing the fixture according to the manufacturer's directions, using the enclosed hardware.

Plumbing

Plumbing, like electrical work, is often baffling to do-it-yourselfers. So baffling, in fact, that they eagerly turn the job over to professionals and pay a dear price. Actually, the only reason plumbing seems mysterious is because most of it's buried in floors, walls, and ceilings. The system itself is very simple. Let's get it out in the open and take a good look at it.

The typical home plumbing system has water entering the house, passing through a network of pipes to fixtures, then exiting back out again. The system is broken down in two parts: water supply and disposal. The disposal system (also called the drain/waste/vent system) is gravity-fed and requires larger pipes to enable waste to pass through without clogging and backing up. The water supply system operates under pressure, so the pipes are relatively small in diameter. The two systems never connect; this keeps the drinking water pure and uncontaminated.

A TYPICAL RESIDENTIAL WATER SUPPLY SYSTEM

Water enters the house from a municipal system (or well), and passes through a meter (A), which measures usage. A main shut off valve (B), located directly in front or back of the meter, controls the water supply to the entire house (FIG. 4-1).

After the main valve, the water splits into two parts: the hot water system and the cold water system. Shut-off valves at the beginning of each system (C) allow for isolation in case repairs are needed. Pipes after the main valve, or meter, should be of a ½-inch diameter for a 1- or 2-story house, or ¾-inch diameter for a three-story house.

The hot water system's pipe leads to the heater (D), which feeds cold water into the bottom of the tank; another pipe draws hot water from the top of the tank and leads it away to the rest of the house. Each time hot water is drawn from faucets or appliance feed lines, an equal amount of cold water is drawn into the heater and warmed. The pipe leading away from the hot water heater should have a shut off valve so the heater can be

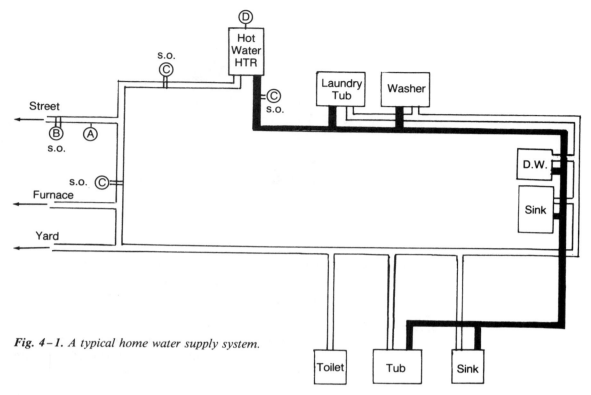

Fig. 4–1. A typical home water supply system.

isolated from the system for repairs or replacement. Also, "unions," or threaded fittings, should be attached to both entry and exit pipes so the heater can be disconnected easily with a wrench.

As the pipe leads away from the heater, it branches out to machines and appliances in bathrooms, kitchen, laundry, and so forth. Going back to the main shut off to trace the cold water pipe, we find the system bypassing the hot water heater and leading to all of the same areas, plus a few more, like the yard and garage.

A TYPICAL RESIDENTIAL DRAIN/WASTE/VENT SYSTEM

Drainage is very strictly controlled by legal code in most communities since it is the disposal of sewage. The drain/waste/vent (DWV) system starts at each fixture and appliance and ends at the city sewer or private disposal system. Drainage pipes and fittings are larger than those of the water supply, and where they cannot drop vertically, have gentle bends and slight downward slopes (FIG. 4-2) to aid gravity flow. (Water supply fittings of all kinds make abrupt 90- or 45-degree changes in direction). The pipe that's connected to the fixture or appliance is called the waste pipe. The

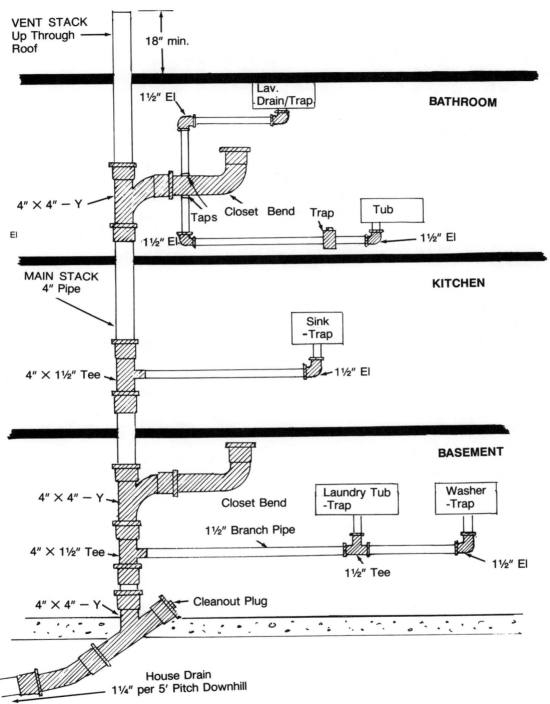

VENT STACK
Up Through Roof

18" min.

1½" El

Lav. Drain/Trap

BATHROOM

4" × 4" — Y

El

Taps   Closet Bend   Trap   Tub

1½" El   1½" El

MAIN STACK
4" Pipe

KITCHEN

Sink -Trap

4" × 1½" Tee

1½" El

BASEMENT

Closet Bend

Laundry Tub -Trap   Washer -Trap

4" × 4" — Y

1½" Branch Pipe

1½" Tee   1½" El

4" × 1½" Tee

Cleanout Plug

4" × 4" — Y

House Drain
1¼" per 5' Pitch Downhill

Fig. 4-2. A typical residential drain/waste/vent system.

toilet drain pipe is called the soil pipe. Waste and soil pipes enter a vertical pipe called a stack. The top end of the stack continues its run up through the roof and is left open; this is called the vent.

The lower end of the stack leads into the house's drain. The house's drain is a horizontal pipe, about 3 to 4 inches in diameter, that collects waste water from all the appliances and fixtures in the house, and carries it outside the house, into the city sewer in the street or into your private septic field.

Besides the pipes, there are other components of a drainage system with which you should become familiar: cleanouts to allow you to keep the system working and unclogged, a vent system to carry away the sewer gases, traps to seal the drain pipe and prevent gases from backing up into the room, and, where necessary, revents wherever there is danger of siphoning the water from a fixture trap, or, where specified by plumbing code.

Cleanouts

House drains have cleanouts at intervals to allow you to get at the heart of the matter when you have an overflow problem. Cleanouts are the Y-shaped sections of pipe with screw-off caps into which a snake can be inserted to unclog the line.

There's an outside cleanout plug at the curb in most city sewer systems to take care of that part of the sewer drain. Since it's in the city's system, it's their responsibility to correct the problem if it occurs at this point. But from about 5 feet of the curb to the house and inside your house, the responsibility is yours.

Traps

Traps are bent pipes (1¼ or 1½ inches) installed under sinks, showers, and tubs (FIG. 4-3). The bent portion holds enough water to seal against

Vent to Roof

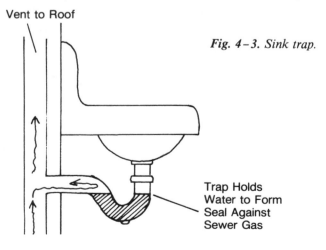

Fig. 4-3. Sink trap.

Trap Holds Water to Form Seal Against Sewer Gas

sewer gas, preventing it from entering the room. Every fixture except a toilet drains into a trap. (The toilet has its own built-in trap.) One end of the trap is connected to a tailpiece that extends below the fixture outlet; the other end is connected to the waste pipe that goes into the wall.

If a fixture drains into a wall connection, a P-trap is used. If a fixture drains into a floor connection, an S-trap is used. Some codes outlaw S-traps, claiming that they tend to siphon out the sealing water. (Refer to FIGS. 4-4, 4-5, 4-6, and 4-7.)

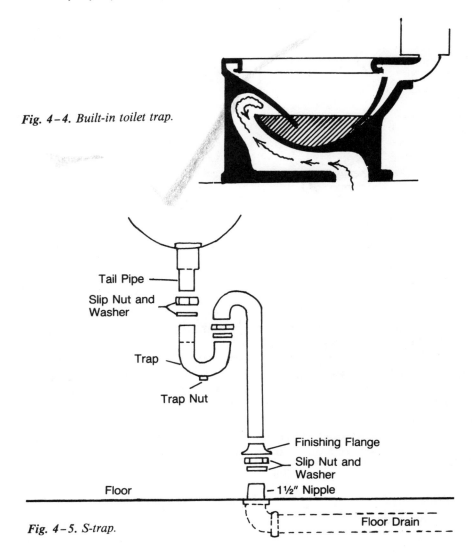

Fig. 4–4. Built-in toilet trap.

Fig. 4–5. S-trap.

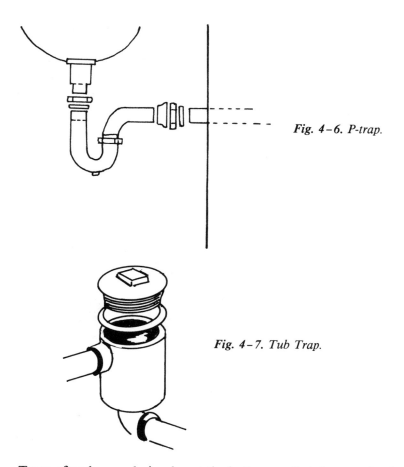

Fig. 4–6. P-trap.

Fig. 4–7. Tub Trap.

Traps often have a drain plug at the bottom so that they can be drained or probed without taking the trap off.

Fixture traps come in two general types: a swivel trap, which can be disassembled by loosening two slip nuts to let the trap drop free; and a fixed trap. A fixed trap requires a different disconnecting technique. You unscrew the top slip nut and loosen the lower one. Then let the straight section slide down into the trap and remove it.

Sink and tub traps are generally made of brass with chrome plating. Other traps that are hidden, like under shower stalls, are made of PVC or galvanized steel.

Vents

A venting system is the least understood of the DWV system. It is connected to the drain system, but doesn't carry water; it carries air. All drain pipes are connected to a stack hidden in the wall. Bad air goes up the stack through the roof and is dispersed into the atmosphere. The wastes go down into the sewage system.

The vent stack has another related function. Water going down a drain creates a suction action that causes all the water in the trap to be siphoned off, leaving you with no water in the trap to seal off gases. Venting prevents siphoning in your system (FIG. 4-8).

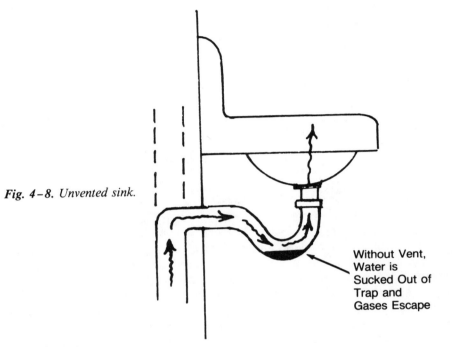

Fig. 4–8. Unvented sink.

Without Vent, Water is Sucked Out of Trap and Gases Escape

Another type of vent is installed close to the fixture. It's called a revent. A revent pipe is a short riser that leads upward from the fixture waste pipe. It bends as needed to connect with the vent stack above the highest fixture or another vent stack.

Air Chambers

An air chamber is the capped vertical riser that runs 8 to 12 inches up beyond the fixture fitting (FIG. 4-9). Air chambers prevent the "water hammering" noise, caused by the sudden damming when you shut off valves and faucets.

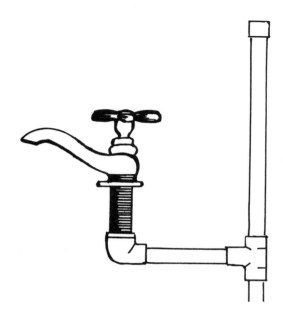

Fig. 4–9. Air chamber riser.

MAKING SMALL REPAIRS

Now that you understand how a basic plumbing system works, you can get a better picture of what the work will entail—how much is repair, how much is replacement, and how much of it you can tackle yourself. Since about 80 percent of a plumbing bill constitutes labor, you should be persuaded to do what you can in the plumbing department.

Generally speaking, on recycle houses, the rule is patch and piece before you rip everything out and replace. In many cases, a leak can be effectively patched with materials available from plumbing supply departments and stores. These "band-aids," designed for plumbing pipes and fixtures, will extend the useful life of the system well beyond the time it takes to sell and close on the house. Where a patch or filler won't suffice, remove just a short piece of deteriorated pipe or fitting, and replace it with a modern plastic part.

If the whole run is deteriorated so badly that it would cost you more to patch than replace, rip out the old pipes and install an all-new, modern plastic system.

Stopping Leaks

Pipe clamps can be purchased to stop small cracks from leaking on straight runs; fiberglass patching is available for sealing around joints and fittings.

To patch minor leaks in copper or plastic pipes, use a rubber-lined metal pipe sleeve that clamps around the damaged part of the pipe (FIG. 4-10). There are also heavier sleeve clamps for use on cast-iron drain pipes and steel pipes.

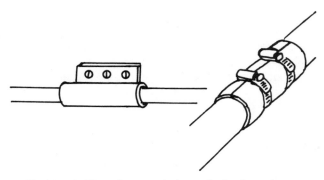

Fig. 4-10. Pipe sleeve and clamp for broken pipes.

Handy fiberglass patches can be used with an epoxy mastic to seal hard-to-get-at joints with fittings, and on lead pipes that are so soft that sleeves would crush them. Mix about ¼ cup epoxy mastic and butter it around the joint or fitting with a wood spatula; go 1 inch beyond the damaged areas (FIG. 4-11). Then wrap a strip of fiberglass cloth around the pipe, embedding it in the mastic. When the mastic hardens, apply another layer over the cloth.

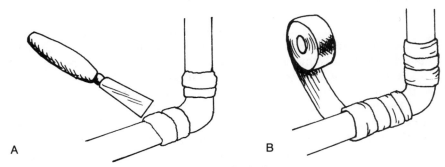

A   B

Fig. 4-11. Band-Aid for leaky pipes.

Old cast-iron drain piping is connected with bell-and-spigot joints. Each pipe section has a flared, larger-diameter opening at one end, and a regular-shaped opening at the other. The straight end is inserted into the bell-shaped end, then oakum, an oil-impregnated, rope-like fiber, is packed in to about 1 inch from the top of the rim. Molten lead is then poured over the oakum, completely covering it so that it forms a tight seal. You might get by fixing a small leak in these joints by just tamping down the soft lead with a hammer and chisel, or packing the joint with lead wool.

If these measures don't work you'll probably have to recaulk from scratch with molten lead. For this chore, you'll need a plumber's furnace, a cast-iron pot, an iron ladle, and a yarning and caulking iron—all of which can be rented. If the leak is in a horizontal joint, you'll also need an asbestos joint runner to direct the molten lead into the hub.

For safety's sake, wear long sleeves, gloves, and safety goggles when pouring hot lead, and make sure the joint is completely dry before you begin so scalding water won't spatter out. Make one continuous pour to the rim of the bell. When the lead has cooled about 30 seconds, use the caulking iron to hammer the lead and oakum firmly into the joint.

WORKING WITH PLASTIC PIPE

Today plastic pipe is used almost exclusively by do-it-yourselfers and master plumbers alike. It's less expensive and very simple to install. The development of this material has meant the elimination of hard work and special plumbing skills. Plastic pipe is self-insulating, noncorrosive, light-weight, and flexible. It can be connected with adhesive and cuts easily. This means that time-consuming soldering, threading, and aligning with elbows has been eliminated from most plumbing jobs. The only difficult thing about plumbing an old house today is trying to remove some of the antiquated piping materials that plumbers used to use.

When we talk about plumbing with plastic, we use the terms pipes and tubes. Pipes are thicker sewer pipes that carry household wastes below ground to public or private disposals, and the thinner drainage pipes that go above or below ground for non-septic runoffs. Tubes are flexible, smaller in diameter and are used for fixture drains, trap parts, and risers.

When you purchase plastic piping, choose from a list provided by a single manufacturer. Fitting tolerances for plastic pipes and fittings vary between brands. In addition, always use the solvent recommended by the manufacturer. Solvents actually dissolve a layer of plastic on the pipe. When resolidified, they make a permanent bond with the plastic next to it, so it's important that pipe and solvents are compatible.

The two kinds of plastic pipe that withstand hot water under pressure are CPVC (chlorinated polyvinyl chloride) and PB (polybutylene). CPVC is a tougher version of the older PVC and is almost universally accepted as a water-supply and DWV system material. CPVC is rigid and less expensive than PB. PB is used quite often in remodeling when you have to thread pipe through and between walls, and for riser installations, because it can turn corners without fittings.

PVC pressure pipe should be used only for cold water, outdoor installations like lawn sprinklers, irrigation systems and DWV sewer and drain pipes. Flexible PE is especially useful as deep-well pipe and for the unprotected outdoor uses.

Installing Plastic Pipe

1. Begin all plumbing jobs with careful measurements of pipe runs, allowing for the depth of the fitting sockets.
2. Check the ends of the pipe for cracks, gouges, dents, and abrasions. Replace with good material if damaged.
3. Test-fit pieces first. The pipe should slide easily into the fitting, but

meet with some resistance before it's all of the way in; in other words, it should not fall out when held upside down.

4. Use a hacksaw, crosscut handsaw, or knife to cut plastic pipes. (Use a miterbox to get square ends.) Remove any burrs from the cut end with a knife and chamfer the outer edge of the pipe slightly so it won't push cement from the joint (FIG. 4-12). Use a file or sandpaper to roughen up the plastic so the cement will adhere.

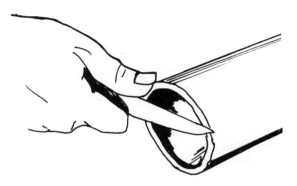

Fig. 4–12. Chamfer outer edge of pipe.

5. Wipe both pipe and fitting clean of oil, grease, and dirt with a soft cloth and the recommended cleaner/primer. Let dry.

6. The brush for the solvent is usually in the cap of the cement can. Choose the proper solvent and apply the cement liberally to the outside of the pipe's end and sparingly to the inside of the fitting socket (FIG. 4-13).

Fig. 4–13. Solvent weld joint.

Coat completely, leaving no bare spots. Then immediately join the pipe and fitting together to the full depth, twisting it slightly to bring it into alignment and forcing a small bead of cement out. Hold it tight for about 10 seconds (FIG. 4-14).

Fig. 4-14. Fit pipes and fittings together.

Note: You have about 2 seconds to turn it after cementing; after that, adjustment will be difficult and if a mistake is made, you'll have to cut the fitting off and start all over again.

Avoid prolonged breathing of solvents and cleaners. Work in ventilated areas and cap the cans after each use. Keep them away from open flames.

Couplings

Copper flex-connectors are the easiest to use when connecting existing copper pipe because they eliminate soldering (FIG. 4-15). Flexible PE pipe

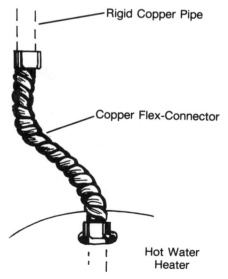

Rigid Copper Pipe

Copper Flex-Connector

Hot Water Heater

Fig. 4-15. Copper flex-connector from 18 to 24 inches allows you to bend the line in order to make the connection.

cannot be solvent-welded; you must use plastic or metal barbed fittings to join pipe and fittings. To make the connection, slide an accurately-sized worm-drive clamp over a pipe's end; push the other pipe all the way onto the barbed fitting and clamp about ¼ inch from the end of the pipe and tighten (FIG. 4-16). Flexible PB tubing is joined by patented o-ring seals.

Fig. 4–16. Worm-driven clamps are used to connect PE pipes.

PP tubular drainage pipes are joined by slip-jam-nut couplings. First, install the nut facing its threads. Then install the correct-sized slip washer with its flat face toward the nut. Adjust the length and direction of the tubular parts. Then start the nut's threads with its fitting and tighten with a pair of channel-locking pliers.

Each system has its own method of coupling, and most are not interchangeable. Follow manufacturer's instructions.

Joining Plastic to Metal

For adapting plastic water supply tubing to threaded metal parts, such as at water heaters and bathroom/shower valves, you'll need a fitting called a transition union. Transition fittings allow thermal movements between metals and plastics (FIG. 4-17).

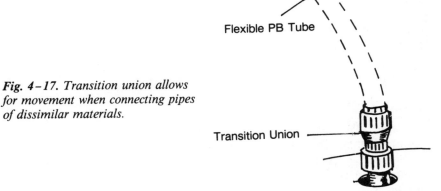

Flexible PB Tube

Fig. 4–17. Transition union allows for movement when connecting pipes of dissimilar materials.

Transition Union

Hot Water Heater

A male-thread adapter may be used for nonpressurized connections in spots like shower risers and water heater relief valve tappings.

Flexible DWV and sewer/drain pipe fittings are made of soft vinyl. They come with larger worm-drive band clamps and can be fastened securely to plastic or metal pipes. A flexible fitting can be forced into place over a pipe that's immovable.

Joining Plastic to Plastic

Use plastic slip couplings to join plastic pipes or add fittings. First, mark the portions of the old pipe to be cut away where the new pipe and fitting will be inserted, then saw out the length of pipe between the marks (FIG. 4-18). Slide a shoulderless slip coupling on each end of the severed pipe. (Push it back so that about 1½ inches are exposed for solvent welding.) Position the new fitting and stub pipes between the old pipe. Dope the pipe ends all around the joint with a heavy coating of solvent cement. Immediately slide the slip coupling into place over the joint, giving it a slight twist to seal the cement. Hold the alignment for 10 seconds before doing the other end.

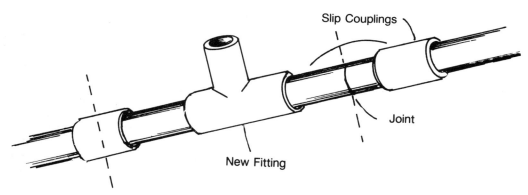

Fig. 4–18. Plastic slip couplings.

Burying Plastic Sewer Pipe

Lay the pipes in a trench of packed sand—not soft fill, which will settle and create low spots in the pipeline. Dig out depressions around couplings so they will lie flat. Backfill with sand.

Mounting Plastic Pipes

Large DWV pipes are hung by perforated metal strapping called "plumbers' tape" from joists. Space them a maximum of 4 feet apart.

Smaller water supply tubing is attached to framing by tubing hangers 32 inches apart. Don't bind the pipes. Leave about ¼-inch clearance between framing for expansion and contraction.

UNSTOPPING CLOGGED DRAINS, TOILETS, SEWER

The most common drain blockage problem occurs in the trap just below a fixture. If the drain is sluggish or backs up, and no other fixture is involved, you can be sure the problem is isolated in this spot.

If several fixtures back up the problem is further down the line. For instance, if you drain the bathroom sink and the tub backs up, this signals that the stoppage is in a portion of the DWV system that handles the flow from both fixtures. If the stoppage is in the main house drain, problems will show up most noticeably at the lowest point, like the first floor bathroom.

Backups that affect all areas simultaneously, for example, sinks, toilets, tubs, basement drains, mean that the problem is in the sewer system itself. Suspect your private or city sewage disposal system or the lines going to it. Often tree roots and clogs are the culprits.

Before you attempt to make any repairs, shut off incoming water. Fixture shut-off valves are usually under toilet tanks or sinks. A main shut-off valve will cut the supply to the entire house.

Sinks and Bathtubs

Pinpoint the problem area and start with the easy fixes. If you don't get any results, work your way up to the stronger and more complex methods of unclogging.

Sluggish Drains. If the drain is slow, but not completely stopped up, let the hot water run for 5 or 10 minutes to see if you can loosen coagulated grease and hair accumulations. If this doesn't work, try a good commercial drain cleaner, which will almost always do the job on a partially clogged drain. After using the chemical cleaner, flush the drain pipes with hot water.

Completely Clogged Drains. For stubborn blockages, try a plunger. In some cases, a simple suction action is all that it takes. Remove the pop-up stopper and fill the sink half full with water to increase the seal. If the sink or tub has an overflow opening, plug it with a wet washcloth to block incoming air from spoiling the suction. Cover the drain opening with the mouth of the plunger and push down hard on the handle. Pump the handle up and down several times to dislodge the material.

If none of these measures work, you'll have to probe the trap. Some bathtubs and showers have drum traps with access covers that have to be unscrewed. They're usually set flush with the bathroom floor, or in a basement or crawl space below. Sink traps can be worked on from above. Open a wire coat hanger and bend it to form a hook on one end. Then insert the hook in the drain and try to pull up whatever is clogging it. A probing by a coat hanger will tell you whether the problem is in the trap. If the wire meets with resistance, but you cannot dislodge the clogged material, you'll have to try to get at it through the trap.

Place an empty pail underneath the elbow, unscrew the plug on the bottom of the trap, and drain the line. Be careful in case water and debris whoosh out. If it's nothing more than a trickle, the problem is between the trap and the sink outlet. Use the coat hanger to dislodge the clog.

If the above fails, you'll have to remove the trap. Pad the jaws of an adjustable wrench, so you don't scratch the chrome pipe. Loosen, then slide back the two fittings on either side of the elbow that bind it in place; pull the trap free. Insert the coat hanger or snake and keep pushing until you break up the clog, so that it can be flushed away.

If the clog is beyond the elbow trap, you will need a snake or auger to dislodge it. A snake is a flexible steel cable that is inserted into the drain, and twisted and pushed until the drain is unclogged.

When reassembling the pipe, coat the threaded portions of the pipe with dope, or use Teflon tape or joint compound to make a tight seal.

House Drain

If the blockage isn't in the fixture, it could be in the house drain. Since all drains drop straight down from the trap to the basement or house drain, it isn't likely you'll find the clog in the vertical part. Proceed to the nearest cleanout in the basement or crawl space where the house drain goes horizontally, and attempt to unstop the pipe at this point. Remove the cleanout plug at the base of the plumbing stack. If it won't budge, try squirting penetrating oil around it and tap it lightly with a hammer first. Work your way to the outside wall, cleanout to cleanout, using the snake or auger.

If the drain is clogged by tree roots, you'll probably have to rent a motorized rotary drain cleaner, which has a sharp cutting head. As the drum turns, the cable spins and the head bores through the blockage, reaming it out. Wear gloves as you feed the cable slowly into the line, and use a garden hose to flush the blockage away as it's broken up by the cutting head.

Toilet

In most cases, a clogged toilet can be opened up with a force ball-type plunger, which exerts a lot more pressure for toilet cleaning than does the regular type. If this doesn't work, use a closet auger, which is a special tool with a sharply bent housing that feeds the snake up into the toilet trap (FIG. 4-19). Fill the bowl with water to just blow the rim to increase the pressure; this procedure will also let you know when the stoppage has been cleared. Start the auger into the bowl and continue to crank it until it becomes tight. This cranking and pulling action will usually bring up the object that's causing the problem.

Put about 6 feet of toilet tissue in the bowl, then flush it down with a pail of water. If this makes the toilet back up again, you'll know that some solid object is caught in the trap passage, letting the water through but not

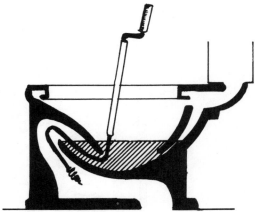

Fig. 4-19. *Unstopping a toilet with closet auger.*

the waste. If the stoppage continues, you'll have to remove the toilet bowl, turn it upside down and force the obstruction out from the bottom.

First, turn off the water supply valve and flush the toilet. As you do this, lift the tank lid up and hold the mechanism open that keeps the water in the tank. Sop up the rest of the water with a sponge, and proceed to remove the bowl from the floor.

If the toilet and tank are separate, as they are in many of the vintage fixtures, you need not remove the tank from the wall, but you'll have to disconnect it from the bowl. Place a bucket under the screw gasket on the curved pipe. If the gasket is corroded and can't be turned, sever the pipe with a hacksaw and replace it later.

If the tank and bowl are separate pieces but connected with bolts, unscrew the water supply pipe from the tank. Then reach inside the tank and loosen the gasket that connects the two. Next, remove the two hold-down nuts located under the tank at either side of the gasket; lift off the tank and store it in another room.

To remove the bowl, take off the ceramic appearance caps and unscrew the two hold-down bolts on the toilet bowl flange (FIG. 4-20). If they're corroded, cut them off with a hacksaw. Now lift the toilet bowl from the floor. As you do this, tilt it forward slightly, so that the bowl water doesn't drain out through the trap.

Pour the trap water into a pail and let the bowl dry. Invert the bowl on newspapers and work at the stoppage through the bowl's outlet. If you discover that the clog is not in the bowl but in the toilet soil pipe, ream it out with the drain auger. *Note:* After removing old toilet, or if you have to leave the waste pipe outlet open for any length of time, stuff it with old rags to prevent the escape of toxic sewer gases.

Before you reinstall the toilet, place a new wax toilet gasket around the outlet horn on the bottom of the toilet bowl. Also, position a pair of new toilet hold-down bolts in the slots of the floor-mounted toilet flange (FIG. 4-21). Place plumbers' putty around the bases to hold them upright. Invert

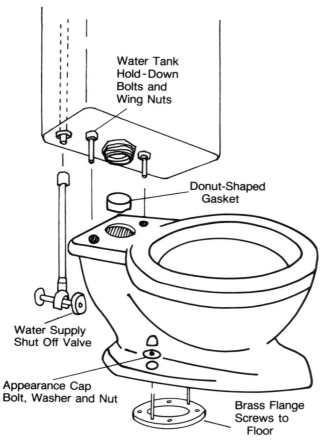

Fig. 4-20. *Dismantling a toilet.*

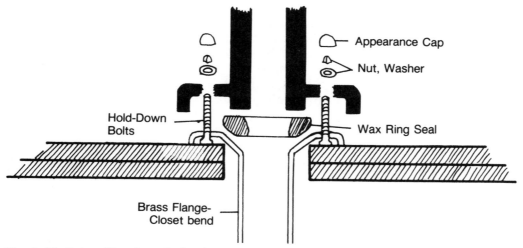

Fig. 4-21. *Reinstalling the toilet bowl.*

the toilet bowl right side up and lower its outlet horn with the wax gasket inside, directly onto the toilet flange. Press down and wiggle the bowl until it rests firmly. Then install the hold-down nuts and washers over the floor bolts and tighten them. Do not overtighten them; this may crack the bowl. Install the appearance caps.

Mate toilet tank to bowl with a new donut-shaped gasket, and snug down the tank bolts to slightly more than a hand-tightening.

Connect the water supply tube by joining it to the inlet valve at the upper end and tighten the take-up nut.

FIXING A MALFUNCTIONING TOILET

When you flush a toilet the handle raises the stopper ball valve off its seat and lets water rush out of the tank into the bowl. (See FIG. 4-22.) As the tank empties, the stopper ball falls back on its seat and closes the opening at the bottom. The float ball drops with the water level and the arm connected to it opens the ball cock valve to refill the tank. The float ball then rises with the level of the water as the tank is being filled; when the tank is full, it shuts off the flow of incoming water.

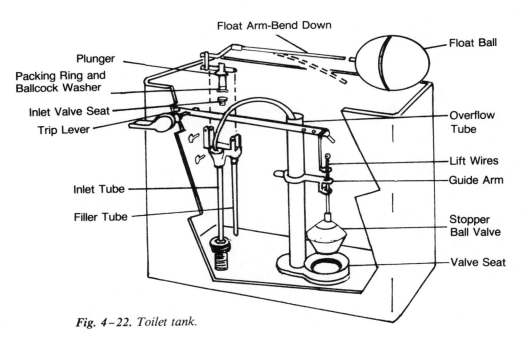

Fig. 4-22. Toilet tank.

The usual trouble is a "running toilet," caused by a malfunctioning float ball. The water comes in and then goes out the overflow drain continually. Usually the float itself just needs adjusting. Or the drain side is at fault. The ball-cock valve, which is supposed to close the bottom drain at the end of the flush, isn't seated right. Therefore, water continually runs out the bottom drain.

To correct the problem, take the cover off and look in the tank to see if it's full. If it isn't, the stopper ball valve is not seating properly due to improper alignment of the lift rods; or, the ball is worn out. Straighten the lift rods if they're bent and see if the stopper ball valve falls properly. Scour the stopper valve and seat to remove mineral deposits that may be preventing a watertight seal. Replace a worn stopper ball if it's defective. A full line of replacement parts are available and are inexpensive. Prepackaged kits include full instructions.

If the tank is filling properly, but the water is running out over the top of the overflow tube, lift up on the float arm to see if this stops the flow. If it does, bend the arm down slightly to shut the water off sooner. The water should stop within 1 inch of the top of the overflow pipe. If this doesn't solve the problem, you probably need a new float ball. Unscrew the float ball and shake it. If you hear water inside, this means that the ball was leaking and no longer floated properly, and the ball must be replaced.

If lifting up the float arm does not shut off the water, then the ball-cock float valve is defective and should be replaced. To do this, shut off the water supply under the tank, then flush the tank to empty it and disconnect the water line from underneath. On most models the float valve has two thumbscrews that must be removed. This frees the entire arm mechanism. Lift it out and install a new unit.

FIXING A LEAKY FAUCET

If the faucet leaks from the spigot, a worn washer is usually the cause. This is an easy job. Shut the water off under the fixture or at the main valve. Remove the handle (this may not be necessary on some older faucets) by unscrewing the phillips-head screw, which is usually under a decorative cap in the center of the handle. Remove the packing nut with a wrench and lift out the stem by rotating it in the ON direction. It will thread out. Keep the parts in order. The rubber seat washer is screwed onto the bottom of the stem. Find a washer in your assortment to replace it; install it rounded-side-down. If the screw on the bottom is corroded, replace it with a new brass one. Then reassemble the parts. (See FIG. 4-23.)

If the faucet continues to leak, chances are the valve seat is nicked or scratched and needs regrinding. The washer seat is located inside the faucet body. The seat should either be refaced with a seat-dressing tool, or be replaced with a new washer seat. Inexpensive seat-dressing tools are available in most hardware stores. Use the tool according to directions that come with it. With a new seat and washer, the faucet should be like new.

If the faucet leaks around the stem rather than the spigot, try tightening the packing nut with an adjustable wrench. Often a slight turn will stop the leak. Put tape or a rag around the nut to protect the finish.

If the leak doesn't stop, you must replace the packing. Remove the packing nut and wrap one turn of a nylon-covered or graphite-impregnated

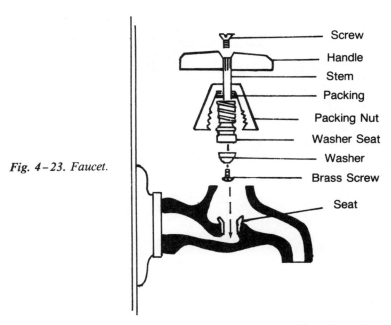

Fig. 4–23. Faucet.

Screw
Handle
Stem
Packing
Packing Nut
Washer Seat
Washer
Brass Screw
Seat

packing around the stem just beneath the packing nut. With the older string-type packing, inside the nut you will find a rubber washer and a dirty old piece of string. Don't use string. Instead, give the stem three complete wraps of the newer packing material. Some stems are O-rings rather than packing. If one of these leaks, replace the O-ring with a matching one and tighten the packing nut a half turn beyond hand-tight. Put a little silicone or pipe joint compound around the threads before reinstalling the faucet.

INSTALLING A WATER HEATER

If your water heater is more than 10 years old, rusted on the bottom, and sits in a pool of water, you can be sure that the tank has corroded through and it's ready to be replaced. Installing a water heater is a project that takes only a couple of hours, requires only a few plumbing tools, and a simple, methodical step-by-step approach.

Before you can connect the new heater, the old one must be emptied and removed.

1. Turn off the gas or electricity to the heater and shut off all water valves.
2. Drain the tank to the outside (or an inside drain) by attaching a garden hose to the drain valve at the bottom.
3. Disconnect wiring on top of the electric heater (use a voltage tester before you do this to make sure the electricity is off at the main panel.) On a gas heater (FIG. 4-24), disconnect the vent pipe on top by removing the sheet metal screw that secures it. After making sure the pilot light is out, disconnect the gas pipe at the union and cap it.

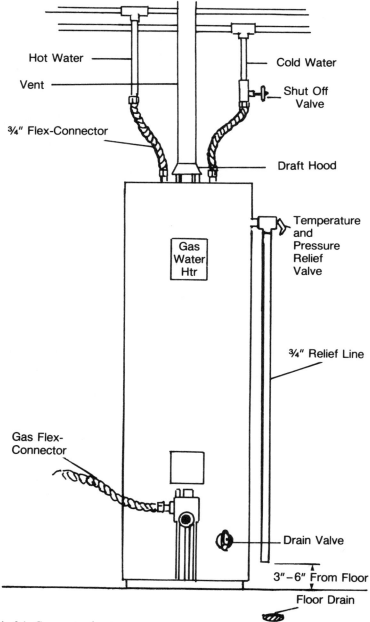

Hot Water

Vent

¾" Flex-Connector

Cold Water

Shut Off Valve

Draft Hood

Temperature and Pressure Relief Valve

Gas Water Htr

¾" Relief Line

Gas Flex-Connector

Drain Valve

3"-6" From Floor

Floor Drain

Fig. 4-24. Gas water heater.

4. Now remove the heater from its hot and cold water piping. If connected with unions take them apart with a pair of pipe wrenches. Pipes without unions will have to be hacksawed off. The old heater can now be hauled away for disposal.

5. Position the new heater to align with piping, particularly the gas vent pipe.

Replace the gas heater's new draft hood by inserting the draft hood legs in the holes on top of the heater jacket. Do not block the draft hood openings. Since every gas water heater must be properly vented, it's a good idea to replace vent pipe elbows with new, uncorroded ones. Most heater vents are sized the same. Vent up as far as possible, then begin a horizontal run to the outside that slopes up at least ¼ inch per foot.

6. Next, make the hot and cold water connections. Be sure the connections are made to the proper inlet and outlet—marked HOT and COLD on the heater. Install a cold water gate valve in the vertical section of the cold water supply. If the old connections were copper, use copper flex-connectors, available from the dealer. Flexconnectors are easily bent to reach where you wish to go.

With CPVC or PB plastic pipe, you'll need transition unions for connecting to the heater. Some manufacturers of plastic fittings also instruct you to use foot-long, threaded steel nipples between the water heater and the transition unions to isolate them from conducted burnout heat. If the rest of the house is not plumbed with plastic pipe, you'll need two more transition unions at the top where the plastic risers join to threaded metal water lines. (For the proper solvents and connectors, see "Working with Plastic Pipe," earlier in the chapter.)

7. An essential part of the water heater hookup is the temperature and pressure relief valve and relief line (FIG. 4-25). Install a new one in your water heater. The relief system is designed to let off excess heat and pressure automatically.

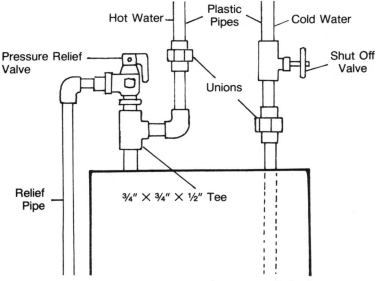

Fig. 4–25. Temperature and pressure relief valve.

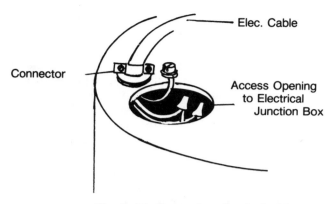

Fig. 4-26. *Connecting electrical wiring.*

After the plumbing is connected, close the heater's drain valve and open the cold water valve to fill the tank. Open a hot water faucet somewhere in the line to release trapped air in the top of the tank; close it as soon as water begins to flow from it. Check for leaks.

Finally, connect the gas or electric lines to your heater.

Gas Connections. Install a ½-inch male flare adapter into the inlet opening of the heater's gas valve. Connect the gas flex-connector collar to the flare adapter (no dope or tape) and tighten with an adjustable open-end wrench.

Electrical Connections. Be sure the wires serving the electric water heater are sized right to provide the proper voltage and amperage (FIG. 4-26). Hook up black, white, and ground wires to their proper counterparts. (See Chapter 3, "Electrical Wiring".)

[5]

Painting Everything in the House

Old-house remodelers use plenty of paint—gallons of it—because they know that it's the least expensive and easiest way to freshen up walls and protect surfaces. But many of them aren't aware of the decorating magic in a can of paint. In this chapter, you'll learn not only how to choose and use the right paint, but how to use it creatively and save a great deal of money in decorating costs.

What's so magic about paint? Well, to begin with, if you choose the right colors, you can visually alter space—and even change the mood of a room. By selecting the proper paint type, you can cover everything in sight with a coat that will last for years. With a simple twist in application, you can add exciting patterns and dramatic textures to your walls, not unlike expensive wallpaper. And best of all, this can usually be accomplished for under $50 per average-sized room. Now that's magic!

First, it's important to know a little about the properties and characteristics of paint so you can match the correct type to the job. Paying a lot of money for a good-quality paint and then putting it on an incompatible surface is an awful waste. Second, make sure that each can of paint that passes through your hands does several jobs: refurbishes the wall, adds decorative interest, and corrects many architectural mistakes as possible. This requires proper assessment and repair of wall damage, as well as knowing a little about what colors can do and the effect you're trying to achieve in a room.

WALLS

Take a good look at the walls you are about to paint. The problems you observe will determine the amount of time you'll have to put in before you can begin to apply the finish coat. About 80 percent of the total time it takes to achieve a newly painted wall is in the preparation. If the walls are in good condition, you'll be through in about an hour or two, otherwise, it may take days. But the amount of time invested in preparing a wall for paint directly correlates to the longevity of the wall itself. If you are keeping the property as a rental unit, you'll want to do a thorough job and eliminate frequent visits with the paintbrush and bucket. A good paint job requires only simple periodic washings. Even if you plan to put the house back on the market, proper wall preparation ensures an easier and better-looking job, allowing you to cover the wall faster, with fewer coats of paint.

Before you can accurately assess wall damage or paint failure, you'll have to remove the cobwebs, dust, grease, and dirt. Wash the walls down with a strong household detergent, like Spic and Span, or if they're really dirty, use a solution of trisodium phosphate (TSP) and water. TSP is available in hardware stores and home centers. Rinse with clear water and allow all surfaces to dry thoroughly. You may have to go over stubborn spots with a sponge or cloth dipped in turpentine or paint thinner. But be careful, these products are flammable.

Correcting Common Paint-Fail Problems

Here are some common causes of paint failure. Identify and correct the problems before you add a new coat of paint.

1. **Smoke, grease, and water stains.** Go to the source for the water stains, find the leaks, and fix them. Wash the stains and surrounding areas thoroughly with Spic and Span. When dry, block the stains with one or two coats of pigmented shellac sealer. Then prime the entire wall or ceiling before you paint.

2. **Rust.** Sometimes, when uncoated steel nails come in contact with excessive moisture, they produce rust spots, which eventually seep through the paint. Check for exterior leaks from the eaves, condensation on pipes, excessive humidity from kitchens and bathrooms, and the like. Correct the problem. Then sand the nails and the area around them, and dab on an undercoat or primer. Fill the nail holes with spackle. When dry, sand lightly and prime again.

3. **Mildew.** If not removed, this gray fungus will come right through a new paint job. Go over the walls with a stiff scrub brush dipped in a mixture of laundry bleach, powdered detergent, and water. Do not mix ammonia with bleach, this causes toxic fumes. A stronger solution of ⅔ cups TSP, ⅓ cup powdered detergent, and 1 quart chlorine bleach (Clorox) mixed in a bucket of hot water can also be used. Be sure to wear goggles and rubber gloves as any such solution is caustic. Rinse the wall thoroughly and let dry. Choose a paint with a mildewcide in it for the finish coat.

4. **Glue damage.** Occasionally, after removing heavy wall coverings or ceramic tile, you may find yourself with glue-damaged walls. Most adhesives can be dissolved with lacquer thinner or paint remover. (*Caution:* They're highly flammable so use with care!) Sand away any residual glue spots and scrub the wall with a TSP/water solution. Let dry, then prime with an alkyd primer-sealer before painting.

5. **Peeling.** Peeling paint usually indicates a serious moisture problem, but it can also be caused by paint that was applied over a glossy, greasy, or dirty surface. Check inside the walls for leaks and correct the problem if it's caused by moisture. Scrape peeling paint off the wall with a wire brush and sand the area smooth, feathering the edges. Wash the wall with a strong detergent and water mixture and let it dry. If the surface is glossy degloss it with sandpaper or a commercial deglosser. Follow with a primer and a coat or two of finish paint.

6. **Flaking.** Flaking paint is usually an exterior problem caused by moisture that gets behind wood siding. The constant swelling and shrinking of the wood caused by weather changes splits the paint film and allows it to pull away from the surface. Try to locate the source of the moisture and remedy the problem. Then scrape away all of the flaking paint plus a 12-inch area around the damage. Sand it down to the bare wood and apply one or two coats of primer before repainting.

7. **Checking and alligatoring.** Checking is a series of tiny cracks that appear on the top coat. Alligatoring is an exaggerated condition of checking with a crisscross pattern that resembles alligator skin. The problem can be caused by paint that was put on an unprepared surface or a surface that was incompatible, or by the use of an inferior paint with an inadequate binder. Checking is also caused by applying a second coat of paint before the first one has dried. All of the damaged paint must be removed. This will mean scraping and sanding with a power sander. Prime the wall after sanding. Spackle or caulk if needed, then apply an undercoat before repainting.

8. **Blistering.** Blistering is another common paint-fail condition caused by moisture. The sun's heat draws moisture to the wood's surface where it's trapped under the paint. The trapped moisture produces bubbles or blisters. Again, locate the source of excessive moisture and eliminate it. Then scrape away all the blistered paint. Sand thoroughly, dust, and seal any cracks with caulk. Prime the area before painting.

9. **Chalking.** Chalking is usually a symptom of a masonry wall that was not adequately prepared before paint was applied. If paint is applied directly to an unsealed porous surface, the binder in the paint will be quickly absorbed, leaving only the pigment, which appears white and chalky. Latex paints in dark colors have this tendency. If the problem is severe, apply a primer before you repaint. Otherwise, a coat or two of top paint should solve the problem.

10. **Wrinkled or wavy paint.** This is usually caused by applying the paint too heavily on a cold surface. The top film dries quickly, leaving the underpart soft, moist, and saggy. Remove the wrinkled paint and sand smooth. Repaint with a roller.

11. **Glossy paint.** Don't try to paint over a glossy surface; it won't stick. Sand the walls down, or use a commercial deglosser. Sometimes you can degloss walls as you degrease them with a heavy mixture of

TSP and water. Fill a bucket half full with water and pour in some TSP. Stir constantly. When the TSP is dissolved, add a little more until it no longer dissolves. TSP is caustic, so take care when using it. Use a sponge and wear rubber gloves. Keep it out of your eyes and off your skin. Use only in a well-ventilated room. Rinse with clear water and wipe dry. Use an enamel undercoat in bathrooms and kitchens, or where you'll be using a glossy or semiglossy paint.

In general, it's best to use paint with the same vehicle (the liquid part of the paint) that was used before: alkyd over alkyd, latex over latex, and so on. Compatible vehicles adhere best, but if you must switch, be sure that the present paint film is well aged, clean, and dulled. Then prepare the surface with a primer that is compatible with your new topcoat. To tell what topcoat is on now, wet a piece of paper toweling and tape it to the wall. Leave it on overnight and remove it the next day. If the paint has shriveled, it's probably latex. If not, it's probably alkyd or oil-base.

If you have to remove large portions of old paint, use a belt sander. Remember, there may be lead paint in some of the layers, which could cause health problems, so use a mask, goggles, and wear old clothes. Sanding is hard work. You may choose to recover the walls (with ¼-inch gypsum) instead of sanding them. This is a little more expensive, but faster and less messy in the long run. Always use a primer or sealer over patched walls or new drywall before painting.

Another alternative for covering badly distressed walls is to line them with canvas. Professional painters often canvas walls because it provides a permanent, smooth surface that covers disfigurements well and holds a crumbly wall together. Lining canvas, available in well-stocked paint stores, is a cloth coated with a mixture of vinyl and white acrylic paint. It's applied like ordinary wallcovering, with adhesive. A 16-foot roll will cover 36 square feet and costs around 50 cents a square foot.

Another alternative for badly cracked walls is to apply textured wall paint, mentioned later in this chapter.

12. **Painting over old wallpaper.** Strip away old wallpaper whenever possible and remove residual paste from the walls with TSP dissolved in hot water. (Strippable vinyl is easily removed.) Wallpaper that was glued to new drywall without a sealer applied first, is nearly impossible to peel off. In this case, lift up any loose edges and repaste, or peel away what you can, then sand the ridges and laps smooth. Spackle and feather the edges for a smooth transition from paper to wall. Fill nail holes and other defects in the wall at the same time. Sand again when dry, and apply a coat of latex sealer. The old paper is now a permanent part of the wall. When dry, apply the finish coat.

If the wallpaper has metallic ink, you'll have to use a pigmented shellac over it, which serves as a sealer and stain-killer. Over vinyl wallpaper that doesn't come off, use a oil-based primer or flat oil-base enamel undercoat. Unless you like the effect, avoid painting over flocked wallpaper.

13. **Painting over calcimine.** This water-thinned paint was used years ago on walls and ceilings. You can tell calcimine by the chalky residue it leaves when you rub it. You must remove all traces of calcimine before painting. Not even new calcimine will go over an old coat. Scrub it off with a stiff brush swished in a solution of TSP and hot water. Rinse, then use an oil-base primer to cover the surface. (Water soluble paints will act as removers.)

Choosing Colors

After the walls are prepared, it's time to think about color and finish styles. Color is the least expensive and most important tool with which we have to work. Selecting colors for a room — or a whole house for that matter — isn't difficult once you develop a general plan. First, decide on a main color. Then select a few pleasing color combinations that can be used with the main color. (If you're at a total loss for some good color combinations, browse through your dealer's wallpaper books.) Next, decide how each room will integrate into your scheme. Be sure to maintain a certain amount of color continuity throughout the house. Very often, the original floor color will dictate the scheme. If you use a monochromatic color scheme, you'll probably use the carpet color, or a lighter shade of it, for the walls, and various shades and tones of the same color for ceilings and woodwork. If you're going to keep a patterned floor or wallcovering, repeat the colors that are already in the pattern for the room, adjoining rooms, and halls. (*Tip:* Use the colors in the same proportions found in the pattern.)

You needn't paint all the rooms in the house one color. Just be sure that they all blend nicely and are well coordinated as you egress from the patterned room. It's considered safe to pick a neutral color found in the pattern's background for the shell of a room (walls, ceiling, floor), especially for living rooms, dining rooms, and halls. But venture out with the more vibrant shades of the pattern's colors for bathrooms, kitchens, and bedrooms.

Choosing a Paint Finish

Once you've decided on a color scheme, you'll have to decide on the paint finish. There's a wide variety of finishes available today with names that are more or less self-explanatory: flat, dull, matte, velvet, eggshell, satin, low-gloss, semigloss, and high-gloss.

The finish depends on its ingredients. There are four basic components in paint: pigment, vehicle, thinner, and drier. Pigment is a solid material that's ground into a fine, powder-like dust, which gives paint its color and hiding ability. The more pigment, the better the coverage.

The vehicle is the liquid part of the paint in which pigment is dispersed; it's composed of binder, thinner, and drier. Paints are usually designated by vehicle: oil, alkyd, or latex.

Thinners and driers are components of the vehicle. Thinners bring the mixture to a spreading consistency, and driers hasten the drying time. Additional ingredients, like colors and extenders, are added to produce different types of paints.

Flat paint contains more pigment than glossy varieties. Once flat paint dries, the pigments extend beyond the surface and create a nap-like finish that diffuses light. This gives it a soft, flat look, and great hiding power.

The amount and type of white hiding pigments in a paint, usually titanium dioxide, determines how well it covers. (Originally, we used white lead for the pigment until we discovered that it was toxic.) White pigments are used as a base in both white and colored paints. For colors other than white, a small amount of universal color tint is added. A white paint may cover better than a dark blue if the blue has less white hiding pigments in it. Likewise, a low-quality paint loaded with hiding pigments may also cover better than a superior quality paint with more vehicle and less hiding pigments, although the latter paint might wash and retain its gloss better. A well-balanced formula provides an all-around good performance in as many areas as possible.

Semigloss has a more evenly balanced pigment/vehicle ratio which, when leveled and dried, produces a soft sheen. Imperfections show up more readily, but it flows on easier. Hiding power is a little less than that of flat paint.

High-gloss paint contains more vehicle than either flat or semigloss paint, thus it dries to a harder finish. Since it also contains fewer pigments (which do not protrude beyond the surface), it produces a shinier, smoother surface. High-gloss paint has the least hiding ability and shows some brush marks, but it reflects light better and is easier to wash.

The shininess of a paint is usually indicative of the hardness of the finish when dry. High-gloss paints are best known for their durability and washability, hence, we use them in moisture-laden rooms, like kitchens and bathrooms, and rooms that are susceptible to grease and dirt. Semigloss paint is generally used on moldings and trim to highlight profiles and to facilitate wiping off fingerprints. Flat, or low-gloss paint is used on large surfaces that get light-duty wear.

To complicating matters we now have available today a latex flat enamel every bit as durable as many of the high-gloss varieties. So actually the choice of flat, sheen or shine, seems to boil down to personal preference.

An important consideration to remember about ultrashiny walls is that not only will they highlight architectural details, but they'll also call attention to every crack and lesion under the paint. Since deep, shiny walls are so undeniably sophisticated and cozy, however, you needn't deviate from your plan. Just make sure the walls are in good condition before you start painting.

High-gloss paints are sometimes known as "the poor man's lacquer." Lacquer is a finish involving many coats of a specially prepared varnish-based paint. Each coat must be sanded smooth after it dries. It results in a hard, durable surface, but it's labor- and material-intensive. For an easier, brilliant effect that resembles lacquer, apply two coats of semigloss paint on well-prepared walls.

TYPES OF PAINTS

Which type should you use? It all depends on the job, your available time, and what you want it to look like when you're finished. While some types are easy to work with and a snap to clean up, they tend to be less durable than others. Some types are more difficult to apply, and the cleaning up is a little more complicated, but the finish lasts longer, is easier to wash, and gives a certain look to the room. If you know a little about the different types—what they are, and what they do—you'll know what to expect of them, and it will be easier to zero in on the right paint and proper applicator for your job.

Latex Paints

Latex is the generic term for water-based paints, which happen to be the most popular type of paint used today. Latex is all but foolproof to apply. It won't leave brush marks, it's odorless and fumeless, it dries quickly (one hour), it's simple to clean up with soap and water, and it's quite durable. It has excellent coverage and is easy to touch up after the paint has dried. Its washability isn't all that great, but when applied to walls that require only light-duty wear, it'll last for years without color loss.

Latex is available in matte, semigloss, and gloss finishes. Latex enamel offers the best washability of the latex paints—a good choice for kitchens, bathrooms, and hallways.

Latex flat offers low light reflection and is a wise option for less-than-perfect surfaces and ceilings. The hideability of flat paint is the reason it's used so often on ceilings. Its napped texture helps diffuse light and makes ceilings look flat and smooth. Look for a latex labeled "ceiling flat white." It's a specially formulated, super-flat paint that covers soiled ceilings very well.

Remember that you can paint over latex with oil-based paint, or vice versa, if you sand or degloss the surface of the old oil-base paint first. Latex cannot be used successfully on porcelain, ceramic tile, or laminated plastic, but it covers just about every other surface quite well.

Don't pay too much attention to the designations of "acrylic" or "vinyl" latex. (Latex paint is made with plastic resins: acrylic or polyvinyl.) They're basically all the same.

So, if quick clean up and ease of application is your goal, latex is your paint. But if wearability and washability is a major requirement, use one of the alkyd or oil-based paints.

Oil-Based and Alkyd Paints

Oil-based paints provide first-rate, washable, abrasive-resistant finishes. They're also very beneficial in areas of high humidity, as they provide an excellent seal against moisture. But they have lost favor to modern latexes and alkyd paints because of their strong odor and extremely long drying-time. A strong-smelling solution (turpentine or mineral spirits) is also required for thinning and cleaning up.

Today, instead of interior oil-based paint, alkyd paint, made from a synthetic resin, is commonly used. The resin, a chemical blend, replaces the linseed oil in oil-based paints, which causes yellowing on the wall. Linseed oil is still used in exterior paints because the sun's ultraviolet rays prevent it from yellowing outdoors.

Alkyd is the most durable of all topcoats. It's relatively odor-free and stain-resistant. It gives a higher gloss and withstands a harder scrubbing. It applies easily with a brush or short-napped roller and requires about 4 to 6 hours of drying time. But it shouldn't be used on masonry or plaster, or over bare gypsum, unless an intermediate coat of latex paint is applied.

Perhaps the worst thing about alkyds and oil-based paints is the cleaning up. Flammable solvents have to be used. Be sure the room is well ventilated when working with these paints.

Glossier alkyds have good grease and stain resistance, and can be successfully scrubbed. High-gloss alkyd paints, however, should not be confused with high gloss enamel. Enamel is specially formulated for a specific job.

Enamel

Technically, enamel isn't a paint. It's a term that's applied to any topcoat that dries hard and smooth and has a washable, pigmented finish. This could range all the way from epoxy to alkyd and latex—in both flat and glossy finishes.

This scrubbable and stain-resistant finish is perfect for kitchens, bathrooms, and laundries, where it will also provide an excellent seal against dirt and moisture penetration.

In the past, we could always tell enamel by its glossiness or shine, but today, there's a new generation of enamels without shine. One of the most popular, latex flat enamel, has the scrubbability of high-gloss enamels and the easy cleanup of latex.

Use an enamel undercoater as a primer. Ordinary alkyd or latex paints do not have enough "tooth" to work well under enamel paint.

You can use a mohair roller to apply the enamel, but for a nicer finish, high-gloss enamels should be brushed or sprayed on. If you use a brush, load it up and "flow" the enamel on without brushing it too much. (*Caution:* enamel dries quickly.)

Primers, Undercoaters, Sealers

A primer, or undercoat, is the basecoat—a foundation for the finish coat(s). It's used when a topcoat of paint will not adhere well to an untreated surface. The primer must be compatible with both the surface to be painted and the top layer of paint. In other words, it must adhere well to the existing surface, and when dry, it must provide a rough surface so that the finish coat can adhere to it. We use primers to cover up discoloration or stains; to provide a bond, or "tooth," for a slick surface so the new paint will stick; or to seal unfinished surfaces so the finish coat won't be absorbed by it, causing an uneven-looking top coat.

If an existing painted surface has tooth and is in good condition, you can use it as the prime coat and paint right over it. Or, you can give an unfinished surface several coats of finish paint, the first one serving as the prime coat. This is considered an expensive primer, however, if you have use for the paint elsewhere.

There are three basic types of primer: latex, alkyd, and pigmented shellac-base primer. Other special-purpose primers are enamel undercoater, metal primer, and masonry primer-fillers. Pigmented-shellac, enamel undercoater, and metal primer are actually primer-sealers. Generally speaking, it's best to use latex primer with latex paint, alkyd primer with alkyd paint, and so on, but if in doubt—and for the best results— read the label on your topcoat paint for directions on which type to use.

Below are some instances where a primer or primer-sealer is absolutely necessary.

- ► Before painting new drywall, or any other previously unpainted surface, including drywall patches, use a latex primer. The slow-drying oil primers will raise the nap on the face paper of the drywall and leave the wall rough.
- ► Before painting mica, plastic, ceramic tile, glass, shiny metal, or any other nonporous, smooth surface, use a pigmented shellac primer to give the surface "tooth."
- ► Before putting a glossy enamel paint on a surface, use an enamel undercoater. Ordinary latex and alkyd primers do not work well under enamel.
- ► Before painting a light coat over a dark coat, use latex or alkyd primer, depending on first coat.
- ► Before painting over a badly stained surface, use a pigmented-shellac primer, which is also known as a "stain-killer."
- ► Before painting over brightly patterned surfaces, which might show through, use a pigmented-shellac primer to seal and prime.
- ► Before painting over cement-based products, use a latex prime coat that is resistant to alkali damage.
- ► Before putting paint over sanded, rusty metal, use a metal primer,

which will create a good bond and inhibit rust from seeping through new paint.

► Before painting over bare wood, use an alkyd primer to seal the wood.

► Before painting textured ceilings, use a latex or concrete block filler. Failure to do this will result in a splotchy finish and the waste of a huge amount of paint due to the absorption rate of the surface.

Apply primers the same as you would paint, with a brush, roller, or sprayer. Use soap and water to clean up latex, mineral spirits or turpentine for alkyd primers, and denatured alcohol for shellac-base primers.

Primers are almost always white, but you can have your dealer add a universal color to the top coat to get it closer to the desired color, or you can mix some of the top coat paint in with the primer yourself.

Two products are available that may be used in place of sanding: deglossers and bonding agents. Deglossers soften shiny, old paint and etch it so a new paint can take hold. A bonding agent is a clear adhesive coating that's applied to a glossy or glassy surface and forms a good bond for the top coat.

Special-Purpose Paints

Ceiling Paint. This is a special, extra-thick formulation that will not drip when you work overhead. It covers in a single coat and diffuses light with its napped surface.

Acoustical Tile Paint. This paint is designed so it won't clog holes that give acoustical tile its sound-deadening properties.

Deck and Floor Enamel. This floor paint will withstand heavy foot-traffic and all kinds of weather. It's chip-resistant and can take repeated scrubbings. It can be used on both concrete and wood porches and steps, and is available in low-luster or high-gloss finishes. These enamels are available in latex, alkyd, and polyurethane. A rubber-base paint, which is more expensive, is also an excellent choice for concrete floors.

Epoxy. True epoxy is not a paint. Like enamel, it's a type of finish that has a category all its own. It provides the hardest finish possible — one that resembles baked-on enamel. It comes in a two-part formula that must be mixed together before using. By a chemical process, it dries to a glass finish. (Latex and alkyd dry by evaporation and oxidation.) Although it cannot be used on all surfaces, it's the only finish for porcelain (tubs, sinks, toilets, and appliances) and it can be used under high-humidity conditions.

Epoxies are difficult to apply and are highly volatile and flammable. When applying, remember that they dry fast! Once the hardening starts, it doesn't stop. Epoxies won't go over other paints, but you can use them over old epoxy. For best results, spray or brush on, then throw away the applicator.

Epoxy Enamel. These are not considered true epoxies, but they are hard, abrasion-resistant paints for high-traffic areas where a tough wear-resistant coating is required. They can sometimes be used as both primer topcoat. Available in one-part formulas, they are used on floors and trin

Polyurethane Enamel. These enamels have much the same characteristics and uses as epoxy enamels.

Urethane Enamels. Urethane enamel is more abrasion-resistant than either polyurethane or epoxy enamels. It can be used as both primer and top coat. Since urethane enamels are cured by moisture in the air, they must be applied when the humidity is at a certain level. Once mixed, they must be used within a given time or they harden.

Glaze. Glaze is a clear, varnish-based coating used to achieve depth and effects not possible with opaque paint. It is slow drying and "tint-able" with oil color or paint.

Lacquer. Lacquer is tricky to apply and if you're a beginner, you should try to get the same effect from other paints and enamels, especially if you're planning on doing walls. First, the surfaces must be scrupulously clean and prepared. You cannot put lacquer over any kind of paint, enamel, or varnish, as it will dissolve the old finish. It is almost impossible to brush on a wall because of its tendency to weep and drip. It's highly flammable and volatile. If you spray it on, use some kind of nose and mouth protector so you won't inhale it. It's easier to work with on furniture where you can lay the piece horizontally in a well-ventilated area like a garage. But don't work outside in the sun, it sets up fast enough as it is.

When lacquering a surface, you should first apply a filler to cover pores and holes, then sand and dust thoroughly. Then apply a special sealer for lacquers. If a fresh coat is applied over a tacky coat it will "roll" or ripple, and the only solution is complete removal.

The above information is not meant to discourage you, but to alert you to the difficulty of applying lacquer to walls and large surfaces. You can get a very good lacquer-effect by using gloss enamels on your wall instead. But if you must lacquer, follow these directions:

1. Use a brush that's not too soft, or too coarse or stiff. The experts recommend a "fitch" brush.
2. After the surface has been prepared, use a clear, shellac-base undercoater specially designed for lacquers. The undercoater will also act as a sealer. Since the solvents in the lacquer will interact with the shellac, make sure you use a very thin coat.
3. "Flow" the lacquer on with the brush. Do not brush it out. Keep the bristles well supplied with lacquer and work as swiftly as possible. Brush marks should level off beautifully by themselves if the lacquer is applied correctly, but don't go back and try to touch it up. A second coat is generally not required. Allow the lacquer to dry for 48 hours.

Masonry Paint. Brick, concrete, and mortar are loaded with alkali, which causes alkyd or oil-base paints to deteriorate. Moisture leeches alkali to the surface and causes the paint to flake and peel off. Although you can use ordinary latex paint on brick in good condition, it won't work on all

...sonry paint is formulated to be alkali-resistant. The most ...masonry paint is a special latex that lets masonry breathe ...g. It comes in tough, glossy finishes, as well as flat finishes. ...latex paints are heavy-bodied for use on porous basement ...e labels on the cans for recommended uses.

...Apply latex masonry paints with a long-napped roller, but don't use this type of paint on cinder block or slag; these require a rubber-base paint.

Alkyd masonry paint is also alkali-resistant. This type of paint is mostly used for painting stucco. It is not recommended for new masonry or for surfaces that become damp. Before applying alkyd masonry paint on stucco, be sure the surface is completely dry.

Epoxy masonry paint is recommended for use on heavy wear-and-tear surfaces that are prone to moisture. Tile and glazed bricks are good examples. It comes in two containers that are mixed together before using. The paint, like all true epoxies, is difficult to apply because it dries so quickly. But if applied with care it'll wear like a coat of armor. Epoxies will not adhere to other paints, but will go over old epoxy or on unpainted masonry.

Cement Paint. You can buy a product called "Portland cement" for unpainted masonry in poor condition. It comes in powdered form and must be mixed with water before using. This heavy-bodied paint is about two-thirds cement when the right consistency is achieved.

Cement paint was once widely used, but with the emergence of the alkali-resistant latex masonry paints, their popularity has declined. You can use it on badly marred masonry or over small cracks, because it fills and covers at the same time, but don't use it on floors. Cement paint never quite hardens, even when dry. Apply cement paint to damp, unpainted masonry with a pliable fiber brush.

Rubber-base Masonry Paint. This is an expensive but excellent paint for basement floors, masonry stairs, and concrete walls. It provides a moisture-proof, alkali-resistant surface that takes a lot of wear and tear.

Textured Paints. Textured paint (also called sand paint or stucco paint) comes in both latex and alkyd, in premixed or powdered form. It's a great solution for walls that are in poor condition, because it covers cracks and small holes and produces an interesting three-dimensional effect. The ready-mix latex, textured paint is the easiest to use because it already has the right consistency. It can be brushed or rolled on.

Don't expect to get good coverage with textured paint — probably only one-fourth of the square footage you'd get from regular paint. But where it saves you repair or replacement of plaster or drywall, it's a good investment.

Apply the paint artistically with such items as shaggy rollers, sponges, brushes, crumpled newspapers, combs, whisk brooms, or trowels to create stippled, grooved, or stucco effects.

THE WISE PAINT BUYER

Once you've decided on your color scheme and paint type, gather up swatches of materials (carpet, wallpaper, and so forth) that you'll be using in the room and take them to the paint store with you.

If you're working with an existing carpet, and you can't find an extra piece lying around, snip off a smidgen from inside a closet where it won't be noticed; or pull, or cut tufts off the carpet, enough so you can "read" the color. Scotch tape the tufts to a white index card.

These swatches will aid you in color-card selection. Take several cards home with you. Color changes with light. The shade you see under the store's fluorescent lights will not necessarily be the same shade you'll see in daylight or under the incandescent lighting of your home.

Once home, lay the swatches out on a table in the center of the room. Mask off each color chip as you try different combinations. Then take your favorite, and walk around the room, holding it up with the other swatches of the chosen scheme. Study the layout under the different lighting conditions and exposures in the room. (Sometimes squinting helps; our eyes blend the colors together on a smaller scale, giving us a better idea of what we'll see when the room is finished.)

Mark your favorite choice, and jot down the color name, number, and brand of paint. Keep it in your wallet, just in case you have to order more, or want to use the color again, in another room or in another house.

How Much Should You Buy?

You can pretty accurately estimate your paint needs by measuring the room's perimeter and multiplying it by the height. This will give you square footage for the walls. Then divide by 400 square feet, which is the usual coverage for a gallon of paint. For the ceiling, width times length, divided by 400 will give you proper coverage. For trim, have the dealer mix you a quart of semigloss at the same time he's mixing the wall paint. This will cover the usual amount of trim in a room.

If you have not primed or properly prepared your walls, you'll use a good deal more paint. Having to go back for more creates the risk of not getting the same color, as mixed colors come from different batches and will probably be mixed by different people. Thus, you may end up with streaked or two-toned walls. This gets us back to the importance of going through all of the wall preparation motions—whether or not you're planning to sell the house immediately after refurbishing, short cuts could cost you a lot of money.

Buy the best paint you can afford. It's true that the better paints are the most costly, but considering all the work that goes into the finished product, you can hardly afford to skimp on the finish coat. Unfortunately, there is no way to tell an inferior paint by looking at a can. So buy a name brand that carries a money-back guarantee from a reputable dealer. Look for a paint that covers in one coat in most colors, resists stains, withstands repeated scrubbings, and retains its color. In addition, the label should tell you:

1. How to prepare the surface.
2. Whether or not a primer is needed.
3. What equipment should be used.
4. How many square feet it will cover.
5. How long it must dry.
6. How to thin and clean up.

Heed all warnings, and follow all directions.

After the clerk mixes the paint, have him open the lid. Take a bit of the paint on your fingertip and transfer it to a spot very near the selected color on the paint chip card. Blow it dry and check to see that it matches up before purchasing the paint. Remember that paint usually dries darker, not lighter.

TOOLS AND EQUIPMENT

Once you've purchased your paints and primers, the next step is to choose the appropriate applicators (FIG. 5-1). As previously stressed, if you have to buy new equipment, be sure to purchase the very best you can afford—especially if you plan to stay in the house-remodeling business.

Brushes

Don't be tempted to buy cheap brushes so that you can toss them out afterward. This won't save you time or money. Inexpensive brushes will slow you down and produce a second-rate job. Nothing is more nerve-racking than having to pick bristles out of fresh paint after every stroke, or brush marks that won't disappear because the paint can't flow from the brush properly. Poor-quality bristles pick up less paint, which means you'll be loading the brush more often. Since cheaper bristles aren't flagged to hold paint, you'll probably have it running down your arm in no time at all. The savings just aren't worth the frustration.

Superior-quality brushes are easy to spot, once you know which type to look for and what kind of paint you're using. Here are some guidelines for selecting a top-quality brush.

► Bristles are the most important factor in selecting a brush. Brushes are available with synthetic (nylon or polyester) bristles, or natural (hog, horse, or ox hair) bristles. Natural bristles excel where smooth surfaces are required, particularly when applying alkyd paints, varnishes, epoxies, and stains. Never use a natural-bristle brush with latex paint or a water-base product. The bristles will absorb too much water and go limp. Nylon or polyester bristle brushes cost less and can be used on most materials that require water for cleanup. They can also be used for alkyd and oil-based paints with

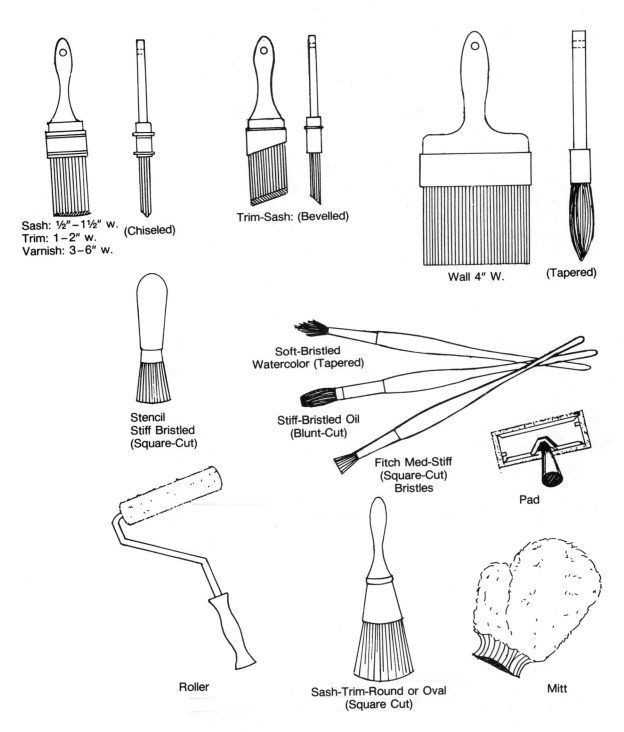

Sash: ½″–1½″ w.
Trim: 1–2″ w.
Varnish: 3–6″ w.

(Chiseled)

Trim-Sash: (Bevelled)

Wall 4″ W.

(Tapered)

Stencil
Stiff Bristled
(Square-Cut)

Soft-Bristled
Watercolor (Tapered)

Stiff-Bristled Oil
(Blunt-Cut)

Fitch Med-Stiff
(Square-Cut)
Bristles

Pad

Roller

Sash-Trim-Round or Oval
(Square Cut)

Mitt

Fig. 5–1. Paint applicators.

satisfactory results. Synthetic bristles wear longer than natural bristles.

▶ In either style, look for a brush with full, flexible, springy bristles. To test, press the bristles on the back of your hand, then release them. The brush tip should conform to the contour of your hand, then spring back into shape. If they don't, the bristles are too rigid or floppy. Good brushes have their greatest flexibility at the tips. Bristle length has a lot to do with flexibility: long bristles have a dragging effect and do a sloppy job; too-short bristles will result in a finish that looks like it was applied with a scrub brush. The rule of thumb is to purchase a brush with bristles that are half again as long as the brush is wide.

▶ Also, the bristles should be tapered from the base end to the tip, so the brush bottom is not bushy or blunt. Check this feature by viewing the brush sideways. Spaced plugs in the heel of the brush under the metal ferrule are designed to do this tapering, which allows the bristles to hold more paint. Be sure there is no hollow center. A brush that achieves its taper by the omission of fibers in the center of the clump will not release paint evenly. The fiber length should also be varied. You can check this by drawing the brush across your arm and watching to see if shorter bristles spring back before longer ones.

▶ Most important: the bristle tips should be *flagged,* or have split ends. Flagged bristles pick up more paint and spread it evenly without dripping.

▶ Don't be too concerned if a few stray bristles fall out when you tug at them. Even expensive brushes will shed a few. Once they are removed, the shedding should stop. Shake the brush and ruffle the bristles with your hand. If they continue to fall out, look for another brush.

▶ You'll need three brushes: a wall brush around 4 or 5 inches wide for large, flat surfaces; a trim brush 1 to 2 inches wide (the ones with chiseled edges are good for woodwork and cutting in); and an angled sash brush for muntins and moldings, and getting into tight corners. An oval sash brush is a handy addition for fluted surfaces on trim or rounded window muntins. Although wall brushes come up to 7 inches wide and obviously cover more territory, they may be too unwieldy and clumsy to use. Choose a brush that is well balanced and has a handle that feels comfortable in your hand.

wall brush
trim brush
angled sash brush
oval sash brush

Plastic Sponge Brushes

If you're bent on buying inexpensive brushes, purchase the plastic sponge types with chiseled edges. They leave very smooth surfaces, without brush marks or orphaned bristles. They're great for varnish, enamel, latex, or alkyd paints, but don't use them with shellac or lacquers. They were designed to be disposable, but if you clean them thoroughly, you can expect a lot of service from them before they deteriorate.

Rollers

When boxed cake mix first came out, it was considered a frivolous, "new-fangled" item. How could it be possible that this "dump" cake could be as delicious as grandmother's 10-step masterpiece? Yet, it was. Not only was it as good, but you could make it in three easy steps, and you were guaranteed the same quality every time. So it is with the paint roller and tray. Most of us will roll every surface we can before we'll pick up a paint brush, because we know it does a superb job in the shortest amount of time.

Just like brushes, roller covers must be selected according to paint types. Natural covers of lambs wool or mohair work best with oil and alkyd paints, epoxies, and polyurethanes, but don't use them with latex or they'll matt. Synthetic covers are best for latex and water-soluble products, and they can also be used for alkyd and oil-base paints; just don't use them with epoxies or polyurethanes.

The nap should suit the finish. For a texture-free or glossy finish, choose a short (⅛- to ⅜-inch) nap. Medium naps (⅜ to ½ inch) are good for all-purpose paints. Long naps (¾ inch) are used for textured paints and rougher surfaces. And deep-pile naps (1 to 1¼ inch) should be used over porous surfaces such as stucco and masonry. You can also buy specialty rollers: foam covers designed for acoustical tile, and small donut-shaped rollers, which help you to paint in corners where wall meets wall or ceiling.

Rollers come in widths from 2 to 14 inches. The larger the surface, the wider the roller should be — but you may find the 14-inch roller a bit too unwieldy to handle. A 7-inch to 9-inch roller is just about right for most wall and ceiling jobs. A 2-inch roller makes short work of door and window frames and sashes, as well as paneled wall or door sections. You can also buy 1- or 2-inch rollers for specialized work.

Look for covers with beveled ends that reduce lap marks. Get a roller with a grip end that's threaded for an extension pole or screw-in mop handle. Avoid rollers that are put on with wing-nuts. They create a terrible mess when you try to remove the cover. The newer ones simply slip on or off.

If you want to eliminate cleaning the tray, buy commercial tray liners, or make your own with aluminum foil.

Paint Pads

Pad painters are applicators made of flat-napped nylon or mohair attached to a little square frame with a handle on it. The paint is wiped on. Their best use is for cutting in at ceilings, around door and window frames, and other built-in obstructions where a roller can't reach. They're faster than a trim brush and leave clean edges and smooth surfaces. Look for a pad that has beveled edges or a device that allows you to get right up to the window and door frames without smearing paint on them.

Paint Mitts

Woolly paint mitts are great time-savers for painting pipes, radiators, balustrades, balusters, wrought-iron railings, or any other irregular, bent, or curved surface. Just slip it on your hand, dip it in the paint, and wipe the surface. To clean the mitt, wash out latex paint by holding it under a faucet, shampoo liquid soap into it, then rinse thoroughly. For alkyd or oil-base paints, use a paint thinner first, then shampoo and rinse.

Spray Guns

Spray guns are not really practical for indoor surface painting, as they require a lot of preliminary work. You have to mask and cover everything in sight that you don't want painted. Adequate ventilation is a must so you won't be overcome by paint fumes. Most do-it-yourselfers feel that paint sprayers for indoor work aren't worth the rental money, when you consider it takes so much time to prepare the room, set up the machine, then clean it before it's returned. But where you have shutters, louvered doors, and other projects too time-consuming to paint by hand, and where they can be moved outdoors or to the garage, it may be worth its weight in gold. Outdoors, they're fine for house exteriors, fences, screen dividers, porch furniture, and the like. Before you rent a paint sprayer, get complete instructions from the rental dealer, and make sure that there is additional printed instructions from the manufacturer. Heed all safety warnings. Some of the portable airless sprayers create very little fog, but they run at very high pressure. Never spray without proper ventilation or near open flames. Protect your hair with a scarf, wear gloves, and tie a handkerchief over your nose and mouth to prevent inhalation.

You should be able to spray a gallon of paint in 5 minutes with a portable airless sprayer. It will take you around 15 minutes with a power roller. Power rollers pump paint from the can directly to the roller. Control valves monitor the paint flow for no-drip application, and the pumps are powered by inexpensive CO_2 cartridges.

When you get the sprayer home, cover everything, including the garage floor, with drop cloths, fill the machine with water, and practice until you get the feel of it.

Remember that it's better to give a surface two or three thin coats than one thick, heavy coat. When you paint with a sprayer, always hold the nozzle completely parallel to the surface you are painting. Don't arc your swing or you'll end up with an uneven coating. Move the gun slowly across the surface at a uniform speed so that the paint doesn't pile up in one spot and weep. Keep the nozzle 8 to 10 inches away. If you move in too close it will run; if you hold the nozzle too far away, you won't get good coverage. Try to find the perfect distance from which to shoot.

Make a 3-foot horizontal pass. Start each pass slightly ahead of the target area. Squeeze the trigger just as you get to the target, release the trigger on the other side at the end of the target, and continue your pass slightly beyond. Now, move the gun back in a return pass, overlapping about 50 percent of your freshly painted area.

You can improvise a spray booth if you can locate a cardboard box large enough to fit around objects like shutters, doors and railings. Just remove one side and place the object in the center.

Aerosol Spray Cans

Techniques for spraying with an aerosol can are essentially the same as spraying with a gun. Shake the can well before you begin. Start your pass slightly before you get to the target area, then press the button all the way down and move the can evenly across the surface. Release pressure on the button just before you end each stroke in a follow-through motion. Slightly overlap each pass. Pause every few minutes and shake the can again. Spray paint containers require special handling. Keep them away from sparks and heat, and don't store them where heat can build up. If the spray hole becomes clogged, turn the can upside down and spray for a few seconds. Never stick pins, nails, or sharp objects in the spray opening. Before throwing the can away, turn it upside down, press the valve, and let the excess propellant escape. When nothing more comes out, the can is empty and can be thrown away.

Remember: all professional-looking paint projects begin with proper surface preparation. Clean dirt and grease off the surface before you paint. If the surface is extremely rough or glossy, sanding may be necessary.

Other Equipment

Besides basic paint applicators, other tools and equipment you'll need are: drop cloths and old newspapers to protect the floor and furniture; a supply of rags or paper toweling to wipe up smudges and spills; paint paddles or stirrers; masking tape; paint shields (long, thin sheets of metal or plastic for making neat lines at the edges of painted areas, or to keep paint from being smeared on adjoining baseboards as you cut in); and a stepladder. Even if you use a roller with an extension handle to reach high places, you'll need to cut in with a brush where the ceiling meets the wall. This requires a sturdy stepladder, tall enough so that when you stand on it, there are at least three steps left to the top, and one step on which to position yourself, which will leave approximately 3 inches of space between your head and the ceiling.

For deep stairwells, you may have to rent commercial scaffolding, but you can usually improvise your own for working on higher-than-normal ceilings by using two stepladders, sawhorses, or chairs of equal height, and a plank placed perfectly horizontal across them. This allows you to walk back and forth safely and does away with the tiresome job of climbing up and down, and repositioning the ladder.

SEQUENCE IN PAINTING A ROOM

The proper sequence when painting a room is: 1. ceiling; 2. trim (door and frame, window frame and sash, baseboards, and so on); 3. masonry (if any); and 4. walls. If you're going to paint the floors, do them last; however, if you're going to completely refinish the floors, sanding and all, do the floor first so you don't have to worry about the sanding dust ruining the freshly painted walls and ceiling. After the finished floor is thoroughly dried and cured, and before you start to paint, cover it completely with taped-down drop cloths.

This is a logical sequence. Painting the ceiling first prevents splatters and spills from dripping down freshly painted walls. Doing the woodwork and trim before walls ensures that a glossy trim paint, or one of a contrasting color, won't accidentally get smudged on freshly painted walls. Cleaning an enamel or contrasting paint off a flat wall surface and then retouching it with wall paint is much more time-consuming than wiping flat wall paint off of dried glossy woodwork.

Boxing Paint

If you've just purchased the paint, the dealer has probably mixed it for you on a machine, but give it a couple of quick stirs with a paint paddle anyway before you use it. Don't shake the can. Latex paints, polyurethanes, shellacs, and varnishes should never be shaken because this produces bubbles in the paint that are hard to brush out.

If the paint has been standing for any length of time, "box" it before you use it. Boxing is a method of mixing paint that ensures an even blend of vehicle and pigments, which guarantees good overall coverage.

First, pour off about two-thirds of the paint into a second, clean can or bucket. Then stir the remaining paint at the bottom of the original can until there's no sign of separation. Now, pour back the two-thirds paint and stir in a figure eight motion for a few seconds. Last, pour the paint back and forth between the two cans several times to mix it completely and get it to the proper consistency.

After the paint is thoroughly mixed, puncture a few holes around the rim of the can with a hammer and nail. This will allow excess paint to drip back inside the can instead of collecting in the groove and running down the label. If you've ever tried to tap the lid back on the can without doing this, you know the mess that can be caused by the splattering. This will also help to create a better seal for the paint.

Set the opened can of paint inside a topless shoebox, one that's large enough to include a can opener or screwdriver, rag, and other paint-daubed devices that could smear paint around or get lost under newspapers. If you don't have an old shoebox, take a couple of swipes across a paper plate with the paintbrush, then stick it to the bottom of the paint can. This, at least, will catch the drips and prevent paint from being tracked around.

Wear old clothes, cover your hair with a cap or scarf, and apply cold cream or Vaseline to exposed skin areas on back of hands, arms, and face to make it easier to remove paint specks from your skin. Don't grease up the palm side of your hand, though, or you won't be able to hang on to the paint brush!

After you've completely emptied the room and covered the floor with drop cloths, remove all switch plates and electrical-outlet coverings, drapery hardware, and brackets. Drop any ceiling or wall fixtures and slip plastic bags over them. Place related screws, nuts, and bolts inside the bag before securing it with a rubber band or masking tape.

Remove doorknobs, locks, and handles. If old paint-splattered hardware needs to be cleaned, place it in a container of paint remover while your work. This will soften the old paint and make it easier to remove later. If it's too much trouble to remove door hardware, put plastic bags around the handles and cover the rest with masking tape or a thin coating of Vaseline. After the neighboring paint is dry, you can wipe off paint spatters along with the Vaseline.

Use masking tape to separate areas not to be painted, or to be painted later. Always use masking tape across moldings. It's much easier to remove than misguided paint, and you'll get a nice, even line of demarcation between wall paint and molding.

Ceiling

If you're going to paint the entire room, it won't matter if you get a little white ceiling paint on the walls at the wall/ceiling joint. This will be covered later by new wall paint. If only the ceiling is to be repainted, however, you'll need to protect existing finishes on walls and woodwork from smears and splatters. Butt the top edge of 2-inch-wide masking tape to the ceiling line and press it to the wall. Insert (8-foot) sheets of 1-mil plastic under the loose bottom edge. Press them both to the wall all around the room, allowing the plastic sheets to drape to the floor covering walls, windows, and doors.

If you're painting over a sprayed-on texture, you should apply a coat of latex sealer underneath. The vinyl material used for spray texture is highly absorbent and takes paint unevenly. If you roll a sealer on first, you'll equalize the absorption and prevent a splotchy looking job. You'll also reduce the amount of finish paint required for good coverage.

Before you start painting anything, you should prime your applicators. If you're using a brush or roller with latex paint, wet them first with water, and blot the excess with paper toweling. The brush bristles or roller covers should be damp, not dripping. If you're using alkyd or oil-based paints, prime the applicators with paint thinner and blot dry, carefully disposing of the flammable rage or toweling.

If you're using a paint pad for the first time, you'll need to prime it also with water or paint thinner, depending on the paint you're using. Then, with the roller tray filled about two-thirds full, dip the pad in the paint. (Immerse the pad fibers only. Don't let the paint soak into the foam backing under the fibers.) Draw the pad up the slope of the tray, rock it back and forth, and lift it straight up to allow the excess paint to drip off. With gentle pressure, wipe the pad smoothly across the surface you want covered; never scrub it back and forth. When the pad begins to drag, reload it.

To load a new brush, dip it into the paint no more than halfway up to the ferrule, then lift it out and tap the bristles lightly against the inside rim of the can. Dip it in the paint again and gently stir the paint with the bristle tips so they open up and take on more paint. Tap the brush lightly against the inside rim of the can once more. You only need to do this initial priming/loading needs the first time you use the brush, not every time you take on paint. Later as you load the brush, dip, pause long enough for the drips to drop back, tap it gently against the inside rim of the container, and begin. Never drag the bristles across the rim of the can. This causes them to separate and clump up.

Begin painting the ceiling by cutting in a 2-inch strip around the edge where the ceiling meets the walls. Apply the paint with light strokes — neatly and cleanly — feathering your strokes so they'll blend in with the next application. Cut around ceiling fixtures if they have not been dropped.

Switch to a roller and start in a corner. To load the roller, move it back and forth in a tray of paint until the entire roller is covered. Let it saturate for several minutes, then draw the roller up the incline of the tray, pressing slightly to remove excess paint. As you lift the roller, tilt it from side to side and let the paint drip from the ends.

Now, roll out a rather large (3-foot-square) "M" with the first leg going away from you. Don't press too hard, or you'll release too much of the paint in one spot. Next, fill in the "M" by rolling vertically, then horizontally over it, feathering the edges as you go. The paint on the roller should be about depleted after each 3-foot section is finished. If you try to work sections larger than 3 square feet, you'll roll the paint on too thin. If your roller starts to drag before you've finished the 3-foot square area, the paint is being deposited too thickly. Go back and even out any strokes that are visible with light roller pressure.

Work section-by-section across the narrow dimension of the ceiling. When you reach the other side, go back in the opposite direction, overlapping and feathering the paint. You can make this job go faster if you attach a 4-foot extension handle, or screw-on mop handle to the roller. Then you can do the ceilings from the floor without using a ladder or scaffold. *Note:* Never stop painting in the middle of a large surface. Finish the ceiling or an entire wall before you take a break.

Latex paint will be dry enough in about an hour (at 70-degree temper-

atures) for a second coat. Don't remove the pla
you're sure another application isn't required. Wh
paint to dry, stick the paint-permeated brush insi
in the freezer. If you have to recoat, remove the
wait a few minutes, load it, and paint. (You can lea
for months without cleaning them. I know—I fo
while cleaning out my freezer!)

Woodwork

Follow the finishing instructions on pp. 164 to 169 in Chapter 7, "Moldings, Trim, and Woodwork," for doors, windows, bookcases, and cabinets.

Windows

Painting double-hung windows is not as difficult or as time-consuming as you may think, once you take a few preparatory steps and follow the recommended sequence.

1. Mask the windows around both sashes, leaving a hairline strip of exposed glass that can be painted along with the caulking. This will give you a better seal.
2. Raise the lower (inner) sash as high as it will go and lower the outer (upper) sash part way until you can get at the bottom rail. After the rail, paint the muntins (horizontal and vertical bars that divide the glass into sections), and then the stiles (vertical members of the sash). You may have to raise and lower both sashes to get at all the surfaces on the outer sash.
3. Lower the inner sash so that it is almost closed and paint the horizontal rails, the muntins, and stiles. Then paint the inner part of the frame, and the outer surfaces after that.

Doors

The sequence for painting paneled doors is as follows. Do the narrow moldings around the indented panels first, using a 1-inch trim brush. Don't overload the brush or excess paint will collect in the corners. Roll or brush the raised surfaces next. Last, paint the inner surfaces. A flush door can be painted with a roller, brush, or paint pad.

If two sides of a door are to be painted different colors, follow this plan. Open the door and paint the hinge edge the trim color of the room it faces. The latch edge and the top edge of the door should match the trim in the room they face when the door is open.

Paint all sections of the frame that are visible when the door is closed in the color of the room trim. If the door opens into the room, paint up to but not beyond the door stop. All the sections that are visible on the other side of the door when closed should match the trim color of that room.

or Built-in Cabinets

ove all handles, knobs, and hardware. Remove drawers and doors
er possible. Tackle the most difficult interior parts first with a pad or
brush in this order: interior back surface, undersides of top and
shelves, sides of walls, tops of shelves, and front edges. Then with a roller,
pad, or brush do all the exterior surfaces working from top to bottom.
Paint only the front surfaces, top and side edges of drawers; paint both
sides and all edges of doors.

Walls

Start each wall by cutting in the corners, along the ceiling and baseboard, and around any built-in cabinets, masonry, and door and window
frames with a 2-inch trim brush or paint applicator. Then, as you did with
the ceiling, switch to a roller. Start in a corner, at the top, and make an
exaggerated "M" with the first stroke going upward. Keep each "M"
section about 3 feet square. Brush across the "M" vertically, then horizontally, going from painted area to unpainted area and feathering the paint at
the boundaries by using gradually lighter roller pressure. Start the next
"M" below the first one. When you get to the bottom of the wall, start back
up at the top again. Work your way across the wall in this manner until the
entire surface is painted.

Stairs

Paint every other step with the appropriate paint (for concrete, wood,
metal). When the steps are dry enough to walk on, do the unpainted ones.
Paint the railing last, after all the steps are dry.

SPECIAL PAINT JOBS

Painting the remaining surfaces of a house would be so simple if we
could just go along rolling and brushing everything in sight with wall paint.
But we can't. Masonry, wood, metal, plastic, plaster, and porcelain all have
different characteristics and properties that call for special paints and
procedures. To make the paint stick, we have to abide by certain rules.
Here are some suggestions of what to use and where to use it that will give
you professional-looking results.

Painting Masonry

New brick, or masonry of any kind, should be completely set and dry
before a sealer or paint is put on. This may take anywhere from 6 weeks to
6 months. Always use alkali-resistant paint over new masonry that has
been primed with an appropriate sealer.

Brick Fireplace and Walls. If you've just uncovered a brick wall that
has never been sealed or painted before, but is very grimy, go over it
vigorously with a wire brush and vacuum cleaner to remove any loose dirt

or mortar. Then scrub the surface with a strong solution of TSP and hot water, and rinse. When dry, repair the mortar and wait about 2 weeks before you brush on at least two coats of a transparent masonry sealer. If the brick is in good shape, forego the wire brushing, and simply wash and seal it.

If the surface is dappled with a whitish, powdery substance, you have an alkali-related problem called *efflorescence*. Efflorescence is caused by excessive moisture in the air leaching out salts created by the alkali. It must be removed before any sealing or painting is attempted. Scrub the surface with a muriatic acid/water solution and good stiff brush, and let it stand for about 10 minutes. (*Caution:* Add 1 cup of muriatic acid to a gallon of water—never vice versa. Muriatic acid is caustic so protect skin and eyes!)

When efflorescence is dissolved, rinse the surface with clear water; then seal it with a transparent sealer within 4 hours before the efflorescence has a chance to reform. A second coat will protect it further against stains, and make it easier to clean in the future.

If you've repaired mortar around brick that has a good undercoat, you still should prime the area with a latex primer before you paint with an alkali-resistant masonry paint. If you're painting over an old coat (or coats) that is in substantially good condition, you can use either a latex or alkyd paint. The old coat of paint will act as the sealer.

If the old paint has "chalked," it must be cleaned with a TSP/water solution, then coated with a masonry conditioner or sealer before repainting. If the old paint is flaking or peeling, it must be removed. You may want to rent a power sander for this tough job. If this doesn't work, quite possibly you'll have to resort to hiring someone to sandblast the paint off. Vacuum the surface thoroughly before you apply a sealer and paint.

If you suspect old masonry has been coated with either calcimine or whitewash, don't try to paint over it. Remove the calcimine with a strong solution of TSP and hot water. Rent a sander to remove the whitewash. When you're down to bare brick again, wash the surface with TSP and water, prime it with a masonry sealer, and repaint. You could cover the old whitewash with another coat of whitewash, but it isn't recommended.

Ceramic Tile or Glazed Brick. You can give a face-lift to ugly-colored ceramic tile or glazed brick in your bathroom or kitchen. Wash the surface with a strong TSP/hot water solution, then spread a paste of powdered pumice and water over the surface. Rub it in vigorously with a cloth to roughen up the surface and remove any residual detergent or soap film. Then rinse and let dry. Paint over the old finish with a good epoxy following the instructions on the label very carefully. (See "Epoxy Paint," p. 84.)

If you want to change the color of tile or brick in an area that's not prone to water, a difficult epoxy finish isn't necessary. First clean and pumice the tiles or bricks, then coat them with a pigmented shellac-base primer. This primer will bond securely and will produce a surface over which you can apply any paint you want. Use denatured alcohol to thin and clean up shellac-base primers. The surface should be dry enough for a top coat within an hour.

Repairing Old Mortar. You can buy prepackaged mortar cement at paint or hardware stores. All you do is add water according to the directions on the box.

To prepare the surface, scrape out loose mortar with a small chisel. Use the corner of the blade to pick out small pieces to about a half inch in depth. Remove only what's necessary, being careful not to split adjoining bricks. Clean away dust and debris from the joint and dampen the area well with a brush dipped in water. Mix the mortar thoroughly. With the tip of a small triangular pointing trowel, pack the mix into the dampened crevice. As soon as the mortar begins to firm up, smooth it off so it blends with existing joints. Remove excess mortar with a trowel or a wet toothbrush before it dries too firmly. You can use the same mortar to repair cracks in the brick. Just be sure to keep mortar damp for at least 48 hours after application, then let it cure for at least 2 weeks before you apply a sealer or paint.

Concrete Steps, Floors, and Walls. Allow new concrete to cure for at least 6 months before coating it. Old, unpainted concrete should be washed down with a TSP/water solution and vacuumed when dry to get rid of dirt and dust. Remove any efflorescence with a muriatic solution. If any of the concrete surfaces are in poor condition, repair them before you apply any undercoat or paint. Hairline cracks will probably be covered by a heavy-bodied latex masonry paint, but larger cracks and small holes should be filled with a vinyl concrete-patching cement and a finely pointed trowel. Very rough or porous concrete can be filled and primed at the same time with a product called Primafil. While they cost a little more, such "block-fillers" save you time, do a good job of smoothing surfaces, and reduce the chances of paint failure.

Thoro-Seal is another product that you can apply as a coating to unpainted masonry that will seal and harden a surface. This same product can also be used to seal up chalky, previously painted surfaces before the application of new paint. Be sure to scrape off all of the loose paint with a wire brush and sand before you apply it.

If old paint on a concrete floor is in good condition (not flaking or peeling, but just soiled from heavy-duty car grease) wash it down with a TSP/water solution, or, if needed, buy a stronger commercial floor degreaser, available at automotive shops or garages.

You'll have a problem getting paint to stick to an existing surface if it's either too smooth or too rough. If it's too smooth, etch it with muriatic acid to give it "tooth." On the other hand, if the concrete is extremely porous, give it a coat of Primafil. If a waterproofing sealer is required, use a pigmented, rubber-base, epoxy-fortified product.

Latex floor enamels or rubber-base floor enamels are recommended for basement floors. Epoxies or urethane floor enamels are recommended for garage floors. The speediest way to apply the paint is with a roller and extension handle. Pour the paint in an exaggerated "Z" directly floor and roll it out, then blend it in. For best results, apply two co paint, abiding by the between-coat drying time recommended on product's label.

Apply cement paint with an inexpensive whitewash brush. Even quality brushes don't hold up well on rough concrete.

Cinder Block. Although cinder blocks aren't used much today, they're still found in basements and cellars of older homes. These slag-type blocks have iron deposits in them that tend to bleed through latex paint, so it's advisable to use a rubber-base masonry paint. You may have to roll on two or more coats.

Flagstone and Slate Floors. Flagstone and slate floors are seldom painted, but they're often treated with a clear masonry sealer to make them more stain-resistant and easier to clean. All dirt, wax, and grease must be removed from the floor before applying the sealer. Wash with a strong TSP/water solution and rinse thoroughly before applying the sealer.

Stone Fireplaces and Floors. Stone can also be coated with a clear masonry sealer to help keep it stain-free. To clean smoked areas around fireplace openings, rub off as much of the stain as you can with an artgum eraser. Then dip a sponge into a strong TSP/water solution and wash, soaking and scrubbing the surface with a vegetable brush. Rinse with clear water.

If this doesn't do the trick, dissolve 4 ounces of naptha in 1 quart of hot water. Cool, then stir in ½ lb. powdered pumice and 1 cup ammonia. Mix thoroughly. Apply the mixture with a paint brush. Allow the solution to remain on the surface for 1 hour, then scour it off with a brush and warm water. Rinse with a sponge saturated with clear water.

Stucco. A clear sealer can be applied to stucco to help keep it clean and easy to wash down. Stucco can also be painted. Use a latex masonry primer on new stucco. If it's been painted before, use either an alkyd masonry paint or latex masonry paint. Wash the stucco thoroughly before painting or priming, but be sure that water does not accumulate in the depressions. The surface has to be completely dry for the alkyd paint to adhere.

Painting Metals

Ferrous metals like iron and steel will quickly rust when exposed to air and moisture. Other metals will also pit and corrode with oxidation. The use of primers on metal is strongly recommended, not only for protection from deterioration, but also to improve the surface for the application of paint. Always read the label on your can of top-coat paint for the recommended primer. Different metals require different primers.

There are basically two metal primers. *Zinc chromate* is a white primer commonly used on metals that are not exposed to excessive moisture. *Red primers* are recommended for surfaces that are constantly exposed to harsh outdoor elements. White zinc chromates can be tinted with universal color (ask your paint dealer to do this for you) so the prime and

applied in one step. Several manufacturers make a ☆
that has a primer built into it, so you can prime and
ration. Other manufacturers put all the rust inhibitor
ll an alkyd enamel top coat to go with it. Be sure to
know what you're buying, you won't duplicate your

_____ paint type, all metal surfaces have to be cleaned and
prepared before you start. Remove oil, wax, grease, and dirt with a strong
solution of TSP and water. To remove rust and chipped paint, wipe the
surface with a rag dipped in mineral spirits (ventilate the area well and
don't work around open flames or pilot lights), then scrape and sand until
you get down to bare metal. Fill any dents with a special metal filler. Blend
and feather all edges so they will be invisible under a new coat of paint.
Next, spot prime, or fully prime, bare metal with a rust inhibiting metal
primer before you apply a compatible top coat. If you want to paint over
glossy paint that's not chipped or peeling, roughen up the surface with
sandpaper first to give it tooth for the new paint.

Metal surfaces that must endure hard wear and tear should have a
high-gloss alkyd paint applied to them. Alkyd is also an excellent choice for
anything that must withstand high heat, like radiators and heat pipes.
Enamel is the most frequently used type of paint for metals, but a flat latex
paint can also be used anywhere indoors. It just won't give you the soil-re-
sistant, durable finish that alkyd paint affords.

Aluminum. To clean and renew aluminum window and door frames,
alternately wipe surfaces with a metal conditioner that contains phosphoric
acid, and rub with steel wool until the surface appears bright and shiny
again. Then, preserve the shiny look with several coats of clear, nonyellow-
ing acrylic lacquer.

If you're going to paint new aluminum, roughen up the entire surface
with steel wool or coarse sandpaper, so the primer will adhere. Then use
any metal primer or a primer specifically designed for aluminum. Paint
with any latex or alkyd paint that's compatible with your primer.

To paint over old aluminum, wipe the surface down with mineral
spirits. Remove any rust, corrosion, and peeling paint with coarse sandpaper, steel wool, or a wire brush. Spot prime the exposed areas before
painting.

Note: Aluminum paint is very difficult to paint over. You may have to
remove it with paint remover before repainting. Old lacquer will also have
to be removed with lacquer thinner and steel wool before repainting.

Aluminum Railings: For intricately sculptured railings, sand with a
powered wire wheel or a cup brush attached to your electric drill. They
come with ¼- to 1½-inch shanks and in a variety of diameters ranging from
1½ inch to 4 inches. Use the coarsest grade for removing paint and rust.
This is one job where you might find a painter's mitt a little handier than a
brush. Dip the mitt in paint, wrap your hand around the irregular surface,

and draw the paint across the openings and down the side bars, coating both sides at once.

Heat/Air Registers: One or two coats of latex interior paint will cover registers nicely, so they blend in with walls. Paint them the same time you're cutting in ceiling, floor, and corners with a trim brush. Alkyds cannot be applied to aluminum anywhere, without a special metal primer.

Chrome. Chrome can be refinished if it's badly scratched or chipped. Clean it thoroughly with mineral spirits and scrape away loose particles. Use coarse sandpaper to remove rust and to roughen up the entire polished surface for the new coat of paint. Use a finer grade of sandpaper to blend in and smooth the old edges of the chipped finish. Prime the entire surface with metal primer before you apply a new chrome finish.

Heating and Hot Water Pipes. Clean the surface with mineral spirits. Scrape away loose and peeling paint with a wire brush. Sand, then prime the pipes with a moisture-proof red primer. Choose a high-gloss alkyd enamel that's formulated specifically for use on metal. *Note:* Never paint when the pipes are sweating. make sure they are thoroughly dry.

Radiators. Ideally, radiators should never be painted. It's better to encase them in a decorative radiator cover that will allow them to emit heat efficiently. A painted coating will restrict the flow of heat into the room. However, if you must paint them, a high-gloss alkyd enamel paint results in the least heat loss. Don't use a latex or an aluminum paint which has a very low emmittance rate.

Clean the entire surface with a special radiator cleaning brush dipped in a strong TSP and water solution. Scrape away rust and peeling paint with a wire brush and power sander. (If the radiator has been painted before with aluminum paint, it must be removed entirely before repainting.) Wipe down the radiator with mineral spirits and prime with a red primer. Then brush on the paint. Use a long-handled bottle brush, or a painter's mitt to paint hard-to-reach places.

Metal Furniture. Clean all surfaces with mineral spirits and remove rust with a wire brush and sandpaper. If the furniture was painted before and still has a gloss finish, degloss it, or roughen it up with sandpaper. Spot prime where necessary and repaint with a compatible top-coat paint.

Wrought-Iron Furniture or Railings. Remove rust and flaking paint with a powered wire wheel and coarse sandpaper. Then wipe down the surface with paint thinner and apply a metal primer that's compatible with your top coat. Use a painter's mitt for fast and easy coverage of the primer and paint.

Tin Ceilings and Cabinet Fronts. New or corroded tin must be wiped with mineral spirits and rubbed with sandpaper until the surface is rust-free and deglossed. Then apply an alkyd metal primer. For a top coat, choose a compatible alkyd enamel. If you're using tin in a bathroom or moisture-prone laundry or kitchen, apply an epoxy enamel as the finish coat.

Metal Tile. Scrub grout areas with a stain-bleaching cleanser and toothbrush, then clean the entire tiled surface with a strong TSP and water solution and rinse with clear water.

When the surface is dry, sand the tile with medium-fine sandpaper. Prime with an epoxy primer and finish with an epoxy enamel paint.

Metal Cabinets. If you have a deft hand with the spray gun and can remove the cabinets, take them to the garage for spraying. Otherwise, buy the best semigloss alkyd enamel brush that you can afford and paint by hand. Spraying indoors is too messy and dangerous, especially where open flames or pilot lights are involved.

Unscrew knobs, handles, and hinges and secure them in a plastic bag along with the screws for safekeeping. Cover anything else that you don't want painted with masking tape or petroleum jelly. Whenever possible, remove drawers, doors, and shelves.

Mix a super-strong solution of TSP and water and scrub the cabinet surfaces until they are free of wax, grease, and grime. The surface will also be deglossed by this strong solution. Sand away any rust that may have accumulated. Then rub sandpaper over the entire surface to additionally roughen it up so the new paint will adhere.

Spot prime with a metal primer, then paint. Do all the interior surfaces first before you paint the exteriors. Lay doors and drawers horizontally on a makeshift work table, so the paint will not drip or weep. Apply several thin coats rather than one thick one, letting the paint flow from the end of the brush without working it back and forth too much. Enamel dries quickly, so don't overbrush the surface. Let the brush marks smooth by themselves. Allow each coat to dry thoroughly, sanding lightly between coats.

Metal Shower Stalls. Rusty, grimy shower stalls can be rejuvenated quite satisfactorily with a little elbow grease and a can of paint. Rinse, then towel dry. Sand away any rust, undercoat the entire shower stall with a red primer, then apply a coat or two of a high-gloss enamel formulated especially for metal.

Appliances. You can effectively repair small chips in appliances with a special epoxy touch-up enamel by following the directions on the package; but for large scale restorations, it's best to enlist the help of an auto body shop. Many body shops specialize in this type of work, and will pick up and deliver the appliance for you as an added convenience. Get a complete cost statement in writing before you sign the contract.

If you attempt to refinish the appliances yourself, be aware that there isn't a brush-on finish available that will last long on range tops where extreme heat and abuse exists. However, for a temporary finish, wash the porcelain enamel top thoroughly with TSP/water solution, sand once over lightly, and apply an epoxy enamel. On the less-durable, baked-on enamel sides, prepare and finish with an enamel specified for use on metal.

Porcelain Bathtubs, Sinks and Fixtures. Stained porcelain enamel fixtures, or those with thinly worn spots, can be effectively resuscitated with a good-quality epoxy paint. First, wash the tub or basin out with a strong detergent/water mix, and rinse. Then, make a paste of powdered pumice stone (available at hardware stores) and water, and scrub the entire surface with a sponge or cloth. This will remove any trace of soap film and roughen up the surface so it will hold the new paint. Be sure to work the areas around soap dishes, built-in holders, and faucets assiduously. You may have to add some heavy-duty scouring powder to the pumice paste and rub with steel wool to remove rust or green copper pipe stains. Rinse completely and let the fixture dry thoroughly before painting.

[6]

Where There's a Wall, There's a Way!

Any dramatic change that you may effect in a house will surely involve a wall. Knocking down, raising up, and recovering or resurfacing existing walls with new materials can cause the metamorphosis of a dark-and-spooky Victorian into a light-and-airy contemporary home — or a ramshackled ranch, into an imposing house with traditional overtones. Just as the artist creates on canvas, you too, can breathe new life into every room with creative walls. In fact, the artist is somewhat limited, for you have the additional option of physical transformation. You can change the size and shape of your "canvas," and even perforate it with openings to achieve your remodeling goals.

* * *

Since most people prefer good traffic patterns and updated interiors to outdated ones (even if it means sacrificing the original floor plan) you must first consider which walls stay and which ones go. Then remove existing walls, or build new ones, to improve traffic flow, increase natural light, or free up more convenient space.

If you feel there is more potential for the resale of your house in the contemporary market, streamline its interiors by eliminating some of the tiny, dark anterooms that honeycomb most turn-of-the-century houses. A few possibilities: enlarge a small kitchen by incorporating the butler's pantry, create a more spacious bedroom by removing the partition between it and a sitting room annex, do away with the claustrophobic entrance hall and replace it with a wide-open passageway that presents a sweeping view of the adjoining living room.

On the other hand, if the grand old house has colossal but ill-planned rooms, divide and conquer with partitions. It's common to find four or five doorways that open into a single room, with a traffic pattern that crisscrosses occupants through the center of one room to get to others. Many bedrooms, resembling ballrooms in size, have disproportionately sized closets. (Wherever did they hang those hoop skirts and ballgowns?) Personal space is almost always at a premium, for bathing, exercising, dressing, wardrobes, and entertainment equipment. But by compartmentalizing some of the larger rooms with new walls, you can create hallways that bypass private rooms, and other personal amenities that sell houses — like an extra bath, a dressing room, and maybe even a luxurious spa and exercise room.

If the house you're remodeling happens to have been built within the past 30 years, you'll find the problems aren't so much with traffic flow and room layout as they are with cramped space and lack of natural light. Low ceilings and box-like rooms have a stifling effect. Also, more often than not, it's devoid of a personality of its own. So here's your chance to alleviate the visual (and physical) space problems and improve aesthetics at the same time with the creative use of walls. Some suggestions: Open up areas by enlarging doorways with wide arches, or span an even larger area with an exposed beam; change the shape of the wall — curve it, run it at a right angle, or puncture it with interesting openings; and, if you can, raise the roof to the rafters.

BUDGET AND DESIGN POSSIBILITIES

Since budget is always an issue when you remodel for resale, start out with a plan that does the most for the house with the least amount of money. In many cases, walls can be left intact with only minor patching and a coat of fresh paint to overcome aesthetic problems. Sometimes you can kill two birds with one stone and cover badly scarred walls with a decorative product, like textured wallpaper, which enhances the decor as it camouflages cracks and bumps. Or create sculptured "plastered" walls (achieved with new paint products) to conceal ugly cracks and blemishes while giving the room an Old World look. Then, there's paneling, unrivaled for its warmth and coziness. It's capable of covering a multitude of sins.

Consider, also, other ways to achieve the effect of drastic change without actually making it: mirrored walls that hide unsightly surfaces and reflect light around a dark room; elaborate, but inexpensive, moldings; arches and niches, embellished with vintage, mail-order millwork that gives the house character.

If you must deal with unwanted walls or inconvenient space that needs to be divided, read on! You'll find that putting up, or removing, a wall is considerably easier than you think.

REPAIRING DRYWALL AND PLASTER WALLS

Two of the most common gypsum walls found in houses today are plastered walls and walls of plaster board (also known as drywall, wallboard, gypsum board, and Sheetrock — a trade name). When gypsum — a natural rock that's mined throughout the world — is crushed and heated in kilns, all the moisture is removed and the rock is reduced to a fine powder called plaster of paris. After the powder is mixed with water and dries, it returns to its former rock state. All gypsum products produce walls with durable surfaces that resist the spread of fire.

We use plaster of paris extensively for patching small cracks and holes. It's also used as the base for wall plaster. Sand or perlite is added to the main coat, and lime is added to plaster of paris for the final, or finish coat on "wet" walls.

Wet plaster, with its lath framework and many coats, has almost virtually disappeared from houses since the advent of drywall, which is quicker and easier to install, and much less expensive. Although it doesn't produce a finished surface (as does plaster) it provides a smooth and durable base for paint, wallpaper, tile, and other decorative sheet converings. Since drywall does not require the skills of a master plasterer, it's the most logical do-it-yourself choice for interior wall sheathing.

Plaster walls can be brought back to mint condition quite easily, however, and you should pursue this option whenever possible. Plaster walls are more sound-resistant than drywall, and you'll save the time and aggravation of tearing them down, plus the cost of replacing them with new materials.

Major and Minor Plaster Repairs

A fresh coat of paint can do wonders for a somber room. But if you try to paint over plaster walls that aren't ready for it, you'll be wasting your time, as well as the paint, and the room will appear sloppy, making future buyers skeptical of the house's stability as a whole.

Cracks and Small Holes. Paint may or may not hide hairline cracks, but it's a little disconcerting to find out later that the cracks you thought would go away with a coat of paint are even more conspicuous after the paint has dried. Don't take shortcuts that could risk the sale of the house. Small fix-ups, like cracks, take only minutes to remedy.

If the plaster is still firmly attached to the wall, purchase a can of spackle and a 1½-inch putty knife. Then widen and deepen the crack with a beer can opener, so the filler has adequate adhering space. Brush out any loose material, then wet the crack down with a plant sprayer (atomizer), a wet sponge, or a brush, so the existing dry plaster doesn't absorb the moisture from the newly applied spackle and weaken it. Put a small amount of the filler into a dish, then take some up with the tip of your putty knife and force it into the crack or hole, letting some ooze over slightly. Next, draw the putty knife across the crack with one swift stroke, removing the excess and smoothing the surface in one motion. A single application should be enough, but if you find the surface has sunk after it's dry, you'll have to give it another coat. If you take care to smooth the wall with the putty knife as you apply the spackle, you can eliminate the light sanding afterward.

Another method of fixing cracks and crevices is to use a fiberglass bandage. You can purchase a roll of adhesive-backed fiberglass mesh tape at almost any home center. The mesh tape costs a little more than the regular paper drywall tape (a 300-foot roll will cost you around $5), but it's worth it. It's stronger, more flexible, and you don't have to embed it in a layer of drywall compound first. Simply cut off a strip, press it on the wall over the crack, then apply a layer of joint compound over it. The joint compound oozes through the mesh and bonds the tape firmly to the wall. You can maneuver the mesh tape over crooked cracks more easily, too. The stiffer paper tape has to be cut and the chore started over each time the crack veers off slightly in a different direction.

Large Holes. As plaster ages, it becomes dry and brittle, and cracks from structural movement. Eventually, it separates from the lath and falls away from the wall in chunks. Spackle doesn't work well on larger crevices or holes, because it shrinks too much as it dries. On holes 3 to 4 inches in size, use patching plaster or plaster of paris. Plaster does not come premixed; you'll have to add water to the powder according to the directions on the bag. If you use plaster of paris, which hardens within 10 minutes, add a dash of vinegar to the water before you add the plaster. This keeps it at the desired consistancy longer. To mix plaster of paris, put water in a coffee can, then add the plaster to the water and let it soak up without mixing. When you're ready to use it, scoop up a small amount and work it in the palm of your hand until it's the right consistency. The plaster should not be lumpy.

As with spackle, brush away all loose material from the edges of the hole, wet the opening, and apply an initial thick coat. After the initial coat has hardened, moisten it again and apply another coat, making the final coat as smooth and level as possible. Plaster is much more difficult to sand than spackle, so if you have trouble smoothing the plaster while you're working on it, go over it with a folded wet rag or sponge until you can get it near perfect before you let it dry.

Sometimes there will be lath or boards to support the new plaster. Other times you'll find nothing but a gaping hole and dead air space. If the hole isn't too large, stuff it with crumpled newspaper. Then insert a piece of cardboard (cut a few inches larger than the hole) through the opening to keep the newspaper from projecting into the hole while you're working on it. Mix some extra-thick plaster and pack it in, building up the sides as much as possible. When it's dry, build it up again until the hole is closed. This will give you a good base on which to apply your final coat of normal-consistency plaster.

If you think the new plaster is going to require more support over the hole than what the crumpled newspapers can offer, buy hardware cloth at the lumberyard and cut a patch several inches larger than the hole. Thread a piece of string through the cloth's center, then push the hardware cloth through the hole and overlap the opening on the back side of the wall so that it's even all around. Pull both ends of the string forward and tie them tightly around the center of a wood stick that overlaps the front of the hole. This will keep the hardware cloth in place as you work.

Now, fill the hole with a thick plaster mix. When the base coat is dry, cut the string, remove the stick, and proceed as above. On larger holes, use the back edge of a trowel to smooth the plaster, keeping the front edge slightly raised.

Extremely Large Holes. Technically, we repair surfaces with like materials: plaster with plaster, wood with wood, mortar with masonry. But if the damage is extensive in a plastered wall, it might take days, plus buckets of plaster, to fill a huge, gaping cavity, so it makes more sense to bridge the hole with a piece of drywall and finish the joints around the two dissimilar materials with drywall tape and joint compound. This may sound easy — cut out the damage, insert a patch of drywall, then tape over it. But there's a potential problem. Since plaster is rarely of uniform thickness, even when the lath base is level and even, you might have some difficulty blending the edges. A piece of ½-inch drywall might set flush on one side and rise above the surface on the opposite side. In most cases, you can insert shims (of cardboard or some other thin material) behind certain areas of the drywall to flush it with its surrounding surfaces, or trim away some of the backing to level it if it's too high.

To repair a plaster wall with a drywall patch:

1. Mark the section of damage off in a rectangular shape, using a chalkline or carpenter's square and a pencil. (Go a bit beyond the damaged area.) Score the plaster along these lines with a utility knife. If you don't end up on the center of a lath strip or stud, cut it back until you do. Then, with a hammer and chisel, chip away the plaster carefully. Work from the damaged center to the scored lines, removing small areas at a time and taking care not to damage the areas outside the chalklines.

2. Cut a piece of drywall to fit into the opening. An easy way to do this is to tape a piece of paper over the hole and trace the edges of the hole with the side of a soft lead pencil. This will give you a pattern for the exact size and shape of the hole. Using the pattern, cut out your patch and insert it into the opening. Check its thickness with that of the surrounding edges of plastered walls. If it's level, and you're working on a base of lath, drive flathead screws through the drywall into the lath, setting the heads slightly below the surface of the drywall.

3. If some areas need shimming, cut wood strips to fit inside, around the perimeter of the opening, and nail them partway into the lath or studs. (See FIG. 6-1). Drive shims under the strips as needed, in order to flush the piece of drywall level with the plaster. Then finish driving the nails all the way in.

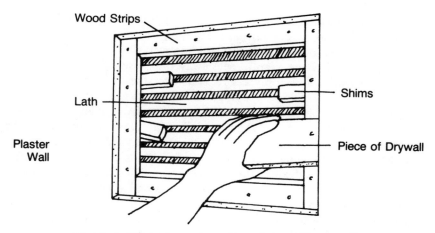

Wood Strips

Lath

Shims

Plaster Wall

Piece of Drywall

Fig. 6-1. Shimming a drywall patch in a plaster wall.

4. Refit the piece of drywall into the hole and nail its corners into the wood strips, through lath and wood framing members. Finish securing the drywall patch with drywall nails spaced 6 inches apart.

5. Tape the joints, using a 4-inch-wide drywall knife. First spread a ⅛-inch-thick layer of drywall compound over the entire joint and embed the tape into the compound. Apply enough compound layers (wait 24 hours between each one) over the tape to bring the drywall level with the plaster, all the way around the patch, extending each layer 2 inches further than the one underneath.

When you're working the corners—the day after the tape is put on and embedded in compound—sand lightly, then apply the second coat to one side of the joint only. Let it dry. The following day, sand lightly again, apply another coat over the entire joint and feather it out 2 inches on each side. On the day after that, apply a coat to the skipped side only. Repeat this process until you have applied the final and finishing coat over the entire patch. Give it a final sanding with fine-grit paper when dry, being careful not to sand the paper coating as it becomes fuzzy and hard to hide under paint.

Repairing Damaged Outside Corners. Nail a temporary straightedge (a scrap board that's longer than the damaged area) to one side, flush with the corner. Fill the other side with plaster. Remove the straightedge and tack it over the plastered hole. Repeat the procedure for filling the opposite side, shaping the corner against the straightedge. Finish with joint compound.

Major and Minor Drywall Repairs

Drywall doesn't crack and chip like plaster, but there are several common types of drywall damage—all of which can be easily repaired.

Hammer Dents. When drywall is installed, the nails are purposely set below the drywall surface and covered later with drywall compound.

Sometimes the installer misses some of these dents. To repair, fill the dent with spackle. Apply it carefully, eliminating any light sanding, as the drywall paper coating does not take sanding well.

Loose Drywall Tape. Gently peel away the loose tape, scrape off old drywall compound, and apply a new coat over the seam as if you were installing a new wall. See "Drywall Installation" in this chapter.

Nail Popping. This is a common, but easy-to-fix problem. It happens when an installer uses longer than needed nails (drywall nails should be only about ¾ inch longer than the thickness of the drywall you're using), or when the drywall is installed over wet ("green") studs. As the stud shrinks, it pushes the nail back through the joint compound. To repair, drive in two more nails, one above and one below the popped nail, about 2 inches apart, so the drywall is back tight against the studs. Sink the nails just below the surface of the drywall, without rupturing the paper coating. Reset the popped nail with a nail set, then cover all three nails with spackle. Sand lightly when dry.

Cracks Around Doors and Windows. These cracks are usually caused by the house settling. Repair as you would for a plaster wall. Use the paper drywall tape or adhesive-backed fiberglass tape.

Holes or Openings 3 Inches or Larger. Cut strips of joint tape several inches longer than the hole. Spread joint compound across the bottom of the hole and embed the first strip of tape. Apply more joint compound, then overlap with another strip of tape, and so on, until the hole is completely sealed. Cover the entire area with drywall compound and finish the wall as per instructions for drywall installation in the chapter. You can also use the adhesive-backed fiberglass tape on this type of damage: overlap the strips until the hole is sealed, then apply the finishing coats of drywall compound over the taped area.

Plug Method of Drywall Repair. Many people prefer the "plug" method of repair where you need — but don't have — backing support. Cut away the damage in a rectangular shape, tape a piece of paper over the hole, and trace the size and shape of the opening. Untape the paper and cut out the rectangular pattern. Place the pattern on the back of a scrap of drywall and trace the opening. Then draw another rectangle an inch larger, outside the first. Cut the piece of drywall to this outer rectangle. Score the inner rectangle (make sure you're working on the back of the piece of drywall) by cutting through the paper, but barely into the core. (See FIG. 6-2.) Cut from edge to edge on each line. Break the board on the scored lines and carefully separate the loose pieces from the front paper. You now have a 1-inch flange all the way around the plug.

Test-fit the patch; then coat the area around the opening with joint compound. (See FIG. 6-3.) Embed the flaps into the compound and proceed to finish the drywall repair by layering successive coats of the compound and sanding until the hole is completely disguised.

Very Large Holes. Cut a piece of drywall to fit an enlarged rectangular-shaped hole. (Cut the hole back until one half of the studs are exposed

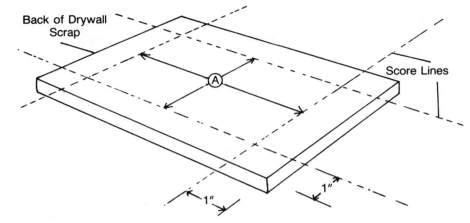

Fig. 6–2. Scoring a drywall patch.

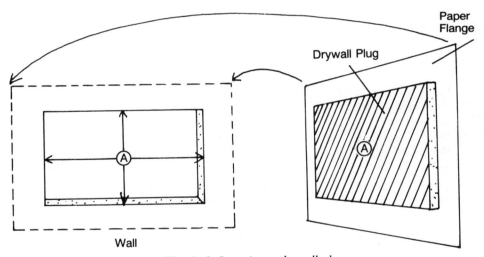

Fig. 6–3. Inserting a drywall plug.

on each side, giving you nailing space for the new patch.) Cover with joint compound and tape, and finish as you would a new wall.

BUILDING A NEW WALL

Most walls look alike—on the surface. But some are created to help support the weight of the structure overhead. These are called *bearing walls. Curtain walls* are nonbearing and simply divide up interior space for convenience and privacy. The flow of traffic throughout the house is governed by the placement of walls and doors. Furniture arrangement is often decided by walls and partitions. All of these functions should be considered carefully before you build an interior wall.

In residential construction, wood stud framing is commonly used because it's less expensive and readily available. A stud wall is also the easiest to build or remove.

Basic components of a frame wall are the horizontal top and bottom plates (the bottom plate is also called a sole plate), and vertical studs. The studs are nailed between the plates, and the skeletal frame is then fastened to the ceiling, floor, and end walls, providing the core and a nailing surface for eventual wall coverings. If door and window openings are located in the wall, the studs must be cut off at the openings and reinforced. The shorter, vertical studs that start at the top plate and go down are called *cripples*. *Jack studs* are the less-than-wall-height vertical members that go up to some other member like window sill or header. In most cases, the plates and studs are made of 2 by 4s, but headers may also be of 2 by 6s, 2 by 8s, and so on. The greater the width of the opening, the wider the lumber for the header must be.

Walls are usually laid out and built flat on the floor, then tilted into place. Extra studs may be required for nailing surfaces where the new wall meets an existing wall, or in a case where it turns a right angle, at the corner, for instance.

Nonbearing Partition Walls

Nonbearing partition walls carry no weight, so they can be less sturdy and easier to build. However, since local building codes dictate construction procedures, be sure you know what's required before you buy materials and lay out the wall. Some codes stringently require 16-inch on-center spacing for all studs; others allow 24-inch on-center spacing. Sometimes you can get by with 2 by 3s for the vertical members, other codes stipulate 2 by 4s. Door and window openings have to be reinforced with certain trimmers and headers if they exceed a particular measurement. Some builders can use single sole and top plates, others must double them up. You may also be required to use firestopping between studs to prevent the concealed spaces from acting as flues and spreading the flame during a fire.

The following partition wall is easy to construct and it's generally accepted by most building codes. But since no one wants to be told to rip it out, and do it over, be sure to check first. Make the necessary additions or revisions according to specific codes in your area.

Most wall-surfacing materials (plasterboard, gypsum, paneling) come in 4-by-8 sheets, so if you use 2-by-4 studs, 16 inches on-center, you'll always have the necessary nailing space to apply outer materials to.

Planning New Wall Location

The first step is to determine where you want the partition to go. But before you mark it off, consider the following: The top plate must be anchored to the ceiling securely. If the planned partition runs perpendicular to the ceiling joists, you have no special problem once the joists are located; just nail the top plate into them at the intersection points.

If the partition runs parallel to overhead joists, you may want to move the new wall a bit to the left or right, and center it directly under one of the joists where it can be nailed solidly. If this is not possible—and the partition falls somewhere in between—you must install nailing blocks between the joists in the ceiling. Sometimes, in order to do this, you have to rip the ceiling open. At the very least, you'll have to crawl up in the attic with more lumber and nail the blocks between the joists in the open attic. By checking stud location first, you might be able to sidestep this probelm and adjust the new partition to accommodate existing ceiling members.

Locating Joists

If the joists in the attic are exposed, mark the center of the joists on a board, carry the board downstairs, and transfer the joist locations to the ceiling (FIG. 6-4). (If a subfloor covers the joists in the attic, nail heads will indicate their locations.)

When an upper floor conceals joist framing, locate the joists in the room with a stiff wire probe, or nail (FIG. 6-5). Small holes can be made in the ceiling, which will reveal the direction of the joists. When the probe encounters a joist, mark it. Several of these marks will indicate the spacing pattern of the hidden ceiling joist .

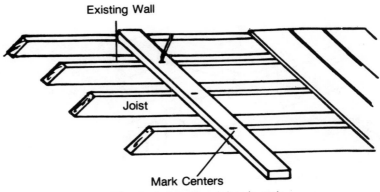

Existing Wall

Joist

Mark Centers

Fig. 6-4. Locating joists in attic.

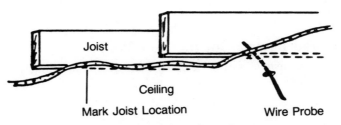

Joist

Ceiling

Mark Joist Location

Wire Probe

Fig. 6-5. Probing for ceiling joists.

Installing Nailing Blocks

Where a partition falls between ceiling joists—and if the joists are accessible from the attic—nail 2-by-4 blocks every few feet between the joists as illustrated in FIG. 6-6.

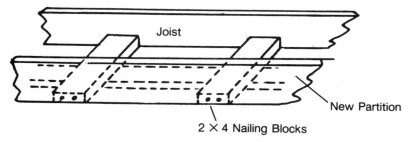

Fig. 6-6. Inserting nailing blocks from attic. Where joist are accessible from attic, existing ceilings below can be left intact. Nail 2-by-4 pieces between joists, flush with bottoms of joists. Then nail partition through ceiling material into nailing blocks.

If you can't get to the joists from above, you'll have to open up the ceiling to install the nailing blocks. If you go this route, nail an additional 1-by-6 board (down the center) over the 2-by-4 blocks, to allow ample nailing room for the ceiling covering as shown in FIG. 6-7.

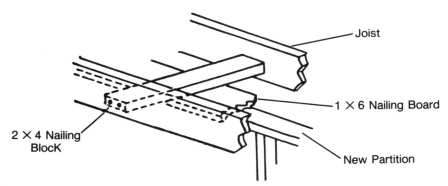

Fig. 6-7. Installing nailing blocks in open ceiling. Where nailing blocks must be installed by opening up ceiling, remove ceiling material between three joist spans. Nail 2-by-4 blocks between one section of joists. Nail a 1-by-6 board down the center of the blocks (flush with joist bottoms) to provide a nailing surface for the new ceiling drywall.

Measuring and Laying Out the New Wall

Remove or cut away existing baseboard and ceiling molding where the new partition will go. Toenail two full-length 2 by 4s into the (hidden) top and sole plates of the existing wall. Plumb the 2 by 4s with shims, if necessary.

Mark the location of the wall on the floor and ceiling by snapping a chalk line between the two edges of the 2 by 4s as shown (FIG. 6-8). Measure accurately between the 2 by 4s for partition length, and floor to ceiling for height.

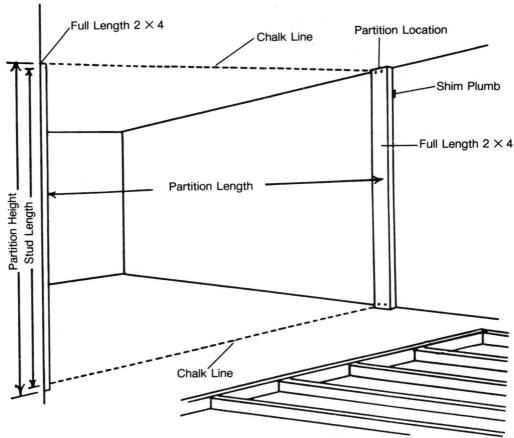

Fig. 6-8. Measuring and laying out a new wall.

Begin your layout. Cut the top and sole plates to identical length measurements. Then lay them side by side on the floor and mark stud locations simultaneously. Work from left to right. Place an "X" at the very end for the first stud, measure 15¼ inches from the end, and draw a straight, vertical line across both plates with a carpenter's square. Mark with X's (or C's for cripple and J's for jack studs), and then finish measuring the rest of the plates in 16-inch increments (See FIG. 6-9). Do not alter the spacing at the end if the studs do not come out even. Instead, simply set the last two studs closer together. By deducting ¾ inch from the first measurement, you're ensuring that, whether you apply drywall or paneling, the sheets will fall in line at the proper nailing space on the studs.

Cut the studs the height of the ceiling, minus the sole and top plates.

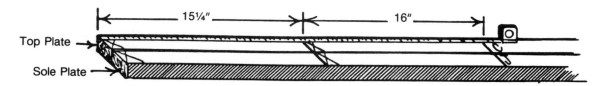

Fig. 6-9. *Marking stud location on plates.*

(On a wall 8 feet high, precut studs are 7 feet, 9 inches—minus ½ inch for clearance for raising the wall, or 7 feet, 8½ inches). Set the plates on their side edges on the floor, with the studs placed in position on their marks. Brace your work against a wall to make nailing easier, then butt-nail the plates and studs together on the layout marks with 16d common nails. Omit the studs where door or window openings fall. (See FIG. 6-10.)

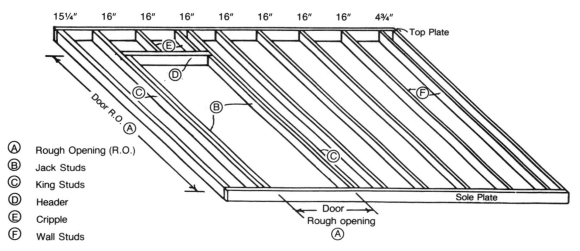

(A) Rough Opening (R.O.)
(B) Jack Studs
(C) King Studs
(D) Header
(E) Cripple
(F) Wall Studs

Fig. 6-10. *Constructing the wall.*

Framing Door and Window Openings

Rough opening sizes for doors (or windows) are furnished with the prehung units. Generally the rough opening for any door is about 2½ inches wider than the door at the side jambs, with a 3-inch margin at the top.

Cut two jack studs to the door's rough opening measurement and nail them to two wall-height (king) studs. Nail a 2-by-4 plate (header) across the jack studs and through the king studs. Then nail these double studs to the plates to frame the door opening. Reinforce with cripples at the marked 16-inch intervals. Leave the sole plate section in until after you raise the wall.

To frame a window, follow the same procedure as for the door, except nail a 2-by-4 sill across the bottom opening. *Note*: Toenail studs with 12d nails; butt-nail with 16d common nails.

Corner Construction

If your new wall is made to turn a corner, you'll have to provide nailing surfaces on both sides of the partitions for wall coverings. When you lay out the walls, reinforce one partition with a stud-block-stud corner post as shown (FIGS. 6-11 through 6-13). The blocks can be 2-by-4 scraps at least 12 inches long. When the two walls are raised and plumbed in place, use 10d nails driven through the studs and nailing blocks to secure the corners.

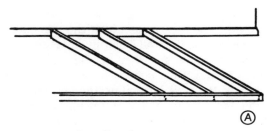

Fig. 6–11. Corner construction. Step 1.

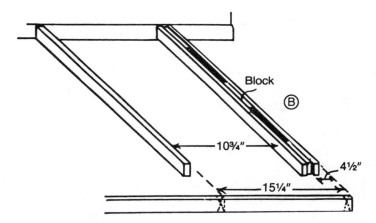

Fig. 6–12. Corner construction. Step 2.

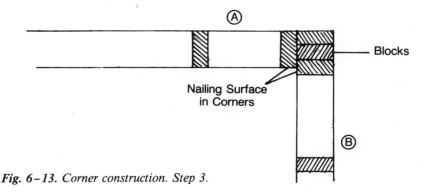

Fig. 6–13. Corner construction. Step 3.

Raising the Wall

The best time to square a wall is when it's still lying flat on the floor, before you tilt it up into position. Measure the wall diagonally from the top left corner to the bottom right corner, and from the top right corner to the bottom left corner. Assuming you measured correctly and cut both top and sole plates to identical lengths, and that the ends of the wall are equal to each other, your diagonal measurements will be the same, and the wall will be square. Nail temporary 1-by-4 braces diagonally across the partion to hold it in place as you tilt the wall up.

You'll need several helpers to get the wall up on the marks and plumb. Before you start to raise the wall, be sure that the sole plate, when raised, will "toe the line." Now raise the wall carefully, meeting up with the chalk lines. Shim between sole plate and floor so the wall is flush against the ceiling. Then, with a level, get the new partition plumb all the wall across the span. Next, secure the wall by nailing the end studs to the 2-by-4s anchored to the wall, the top plate to the ceiling joists or nailing blocks, and the sole plate to the floor or subfloor (use concrete nails or masonry anchors on a slab floor). Saw and remove the sole plate section at the door opening.

Install any new electrical outlets in the open framework before any wall covering is put on. (See Chapter 3, "Electrical Wiring").

REMOVING A WALL

If your remodeling project calls for opening up and expanding a room, eliminating a hall, or adding an extension to the house, the very first problem you're likely to encounter is dealing with a wall that's in the way. This could be a small undertaking, or a very large problem, as we shall see.

To the uninformed do-it-yourselfer, wall removal might seem like a simple enough task. Beware! The wall you tear down could be a structural wall that can cause the house to list to one side, or worse, collapse! Accidentally discovering electrical conduit and plumbing stacks inside a nonbearing wall is no minor irritation either. Removing load-bearing walls and rerouting electrical and plumbing lines can be very time-consuming and expensive. You may decide to alter your remodeling design to something more in tune with your skills and pocketbook if you're faced with removing a load-bearing wall.

Outside walls are usually structural, or load-bearing; but it takes more than guesswork to detect where they are inside. You literally have to become a "house" detective and look for clues to tell the difference.

It is possible to remove a load-bearing wall, providing you have a complete understanding of house construction and the wall's function. Reinforcements, usually in the form of beams or headers, must be installed. A word of caution: if the house has two or more levels, or if the span is unusually long (over 14 feet), call in a pro to do the work.

Determining if a Wall is Load-Bearing

Although there are exceptions, the following rules of thumb will help you to determine if a wall is load-bearing or not.

First, knock against the wall with your fist. If the resulting sound is a thick, dense thud, it's most likely a load-bearing wall of solid concrete, block, or brick. (*Caution*: Some inside walls were solid exterior walls before extensions were added and have been covered over with furring strips and drywall. This will result in a more hollow sound.) If the sound is resonantly hollow, you are probably knocking on a non-bearing wall, which is usually a vertical-stud-network sandwiched by layers of plaster, as well as lath, paneling, or plasterboard. But don't draw any conclusions just yet. Confirm your suspicions with a basement and attic inspection.

If a beam or a row of support posts are found in the basement, you can be fairly sure that a bearing wall will be running parallel, and directly above.

You might discover individual wood framing pieces in the shape of triangles holding up the roof in the attic—these are called *trusses*. A roof truss spans the narrowrest dimension of a house, distributing the roof weight to the two longest, outer supporting walls. Partitions beneath these trusses are not weight-bearing and can be removed without much difficulty. Also, the short end-walls of a one-story house that has a trussed roof can be removed for additions or extensions without disturbing the basic structure. However, if you want to expand by opening up part of a long outside bearing wall, you'll have to reinforce the span with a supporting beam.

If the roof is not trussed, but of the conventional joist-and-rafter construction, and the unwanted wall runs parallel to ceiling joists, you should have no problem—it's nonload-bearing. Bearing walls almost always run at right angles to ceiling joists or beams, and parallel to (and directly under) the roof ridge. The top plates of an interior bearing wall usually support lapped joists (see FIG. 6-14). This wall is there to carry the major part of the house's weight and to minimize the size of ceiling lumber needed. The longer the span, the longer the lumber, and long lumber is expensive. The longest distance that ceiling joists are able to span without support is 18 feet. But heavy loads above, such as bathrooms or kitchens with heavy fixtures and appliances, definitely call for professional advice. Your architect or engineer can also help you figure optimum beam dimension and type, for the distance you have to span on a load-bearing wall according to the weight the beam must carry. Span charts are also available at most lumberyards, indicating your needs as to size and type of beam, according to weight load. (See TABLE 6-1.)

Another note of caution: you might have to throw all "rules of thumb" to the wind, if you're remodeling a house that was built in the 1800s. Sometimes the joists run in three different directions because the original builder couldn't obtain the proper lengths of lumber; but in most large, old houses the "right-angle" rule will lead you to bearing walls. If

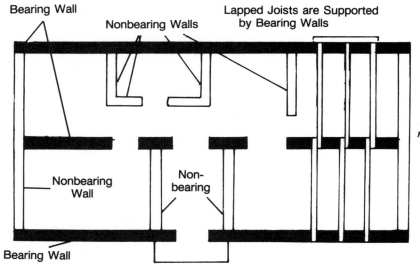

Bearing Wall

Nonbearing Walls

Lapped Joists are Supported by Bearing Walls

Nonbearing Wall

Non-bearing

Bearing Wall

Fig. 6–14. Bearing and nonbearing walls.

you're going to do large-scale remodeling anyway, open up a small portion of the ceiling and offending wall and take a look.

Table 6–1. Header or beam dimensions.

Maximum Span	Board Size
3′–6″	2×6
5′–0″	2×8
6′–6″	2×10
8′–0″	2×12

Over 8′, use steel I-beam.

Checking for Electrical Conduit and Pipes

The other issue that may change your remodeling plans is the existance of electrical conduit, or plumbing pipes and stacks inside the wall. Changing the location of plumbing stacks presents a major problem for the do-it-yourselfer. It's wise to call in a professional and "pay the piper" on this one.

A wall containing wiring is easier to take out — but still requires extra work. Existing outlets in the wall will suggest that there's wiring inside, of course, but electrical wiring may also be hidden, running from the room above down through the wall to the basement.

To determine what's inside without breaking through the wall, remove the floor molding and saw through the plaster or plasterboard behind. (Shut off the electricity, and take care not to cut so deep that you come in contact with any wiring or pipes that might be inside.) If there's too much involved, simply replace the floor molding.

Support Beams

Support beams (also called *headers* or *lintels*) can be of solid wood or laminated double or triple 2 by 4s, 2 by 6s, and so on (FIG. 6-15). Do-it-yourselfers usually choose the laminated beams over the solid wood because they are less expensive. Some beams are steel (*girders*); and another type (*flitch beam*) is a combination steel plate sandwiched by wood. Steel I-beams are called 8 by 17s (8 inches deep and 17 lbs, per ft.) and are available from steel suppliers. I-beams are used for spans greater than 8 feet.

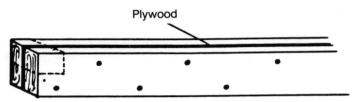

Plywood

Fig. 6-15. Laminated wood header beam. Headers are usually made of two pieces of 2-inch limber set on edge. A half-inch piece of plywood is sandwiched in between to build the header up to the 3½-inch thickness of a 2-by-4 wall. If the header is to be fitted into an adjoining wall, notch out the upper corner (3 inch deep by 3½ inches long) so it will accommodate the top plate of the adjoining wall. Nail together from one side using 16d common nails.

Beams can be installed below the ceiling (if there's enough headroom) and left exposed, or they can be stained or painted, or boxed in and drywalled. They can be installed on joist hangers so they're flush with the ceiling, or hidden above it, suspended by strap hangers. The latter two choices are very costly, since the beam's support system has to be built into the ceiling.

If headroom is not a problem, you can leave the top plate in and install the new beam beneath it. This may be easier than trying to separate the top plate from adjoining walls. But be sure to take this into consideration when you measure and cut the leg posts.

If you are installing an I-beam, you must leave the double top plate in (See FIGS. 6-16 and 6-17). The I-beam should be 6 inches longer than the distance it will span.

Each end of the beam is supported by a leg post (4-by-4 inch to 8-by-8 inch, as needed) that transmits the weight load below and distributes it evenly to receiving structural components (post and beams, foundations, and so forth). The leg posts, depending on size, can be set inside the wall, flush (make sure you add 3½ inches to your measurement for the end of the beam that goes into the wall), or outside the wall as exterior columns (FIG. 6-18). Leg posts can be of solid wood, or constructed of two or more pieces of 2-inch lumber.

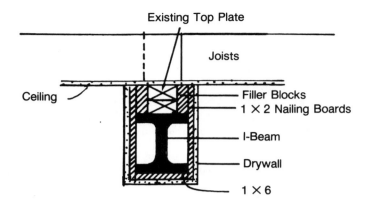

Fig. 6–16. Installing an I-beam.

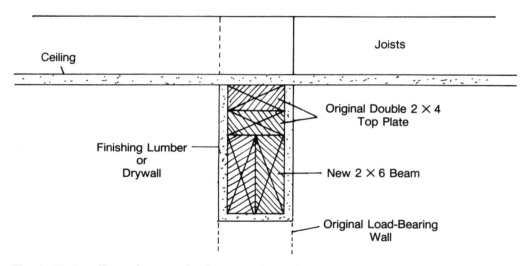

Fig. 6–17. Installing a beam under the original top plate.

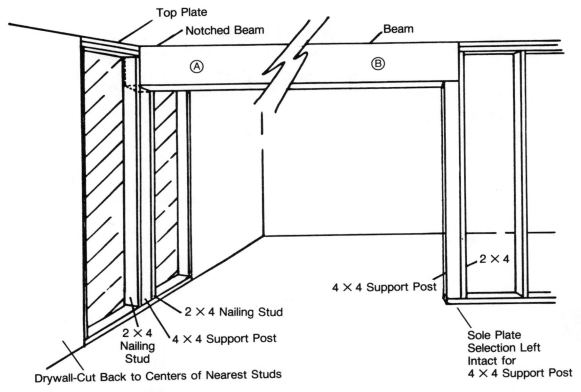

Fig. 6-18. *Two methods of installing ceiling beams. A notched beam can be installed inside a right-angle wall so the adjoining walls stay flush (A); or, it can be installed on exposed leg posts (B). In which case the top plates are cut flush with the stud and the bottom plate extends out to support the leg post. Beams can be unfinished, stained, painted, or covered with drywall.*

Temporary Support Systems

When you tear down a load-bearing wall, you have to devise a temporary support system to carry the weight of the doomed wall until the new beam is in place. There are two commonly accepted ways to do this: 1. use double sets of jack posts; or 2. construct temporary 2-by-4 frame support walls, one on each side of the wall that's to be removed. Jack posts can be rented in a range of sizes. A post that measures 8 feet, 4 inches when totally extended, can telescope down to 5 feet for transporting. But while they're quick and convenient to use, they're also very heavy to transport. A built-up beam of 2 by 4s is placed across the top of the jackposts to accept the load from the ceiling, and a 2 by 6 is placed on the floor under the posts to transmit the weight evenly to the floor joists below (FIG. 6-19).

If jack posts are unavailable, build temporary support walls of 2 by 4s, the same as you would for a partition wall, with a sole plate on the bottom and a top plate on top. The temporary frame support is shimmed against

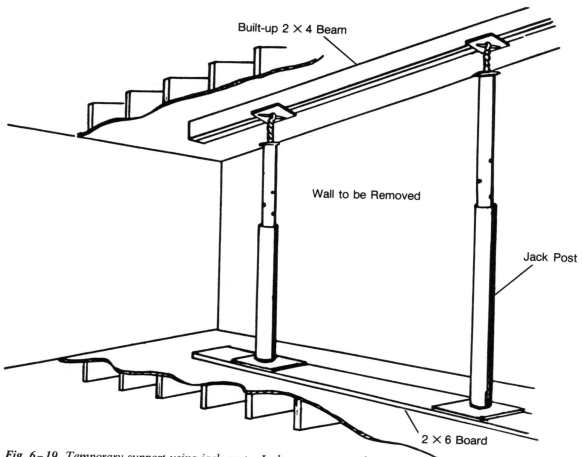

Built-up 2 × 4 Beam

Wall to be Removed

Jack Post

2 × 6 Board

Fig. 6-19. Temporary support using jack posts. Jack post temporarily support the weight of the doomed wall until it is demolished and the new beam is set in place. (not shown: On the other side of the wall, an identical set of jack posts equalizes the weight load. The new beam rests on the floor near the wall that's to be removed, ready to be raised into position.

the ceiling joists overhead with wedges of shingles or lumber. (The ceiling joists must be located beforehand, and their positions marked on the ceiling.) Expect a little ceiling damage as you pound the shims into position.

Before you put your temporary support walls or jack posts in place, set the new beam on the floor in front of the wall that's being removed, as it's nearly impossible to get it into this position after the support system is in place.

Install your temporary support systems 30 inches from each side of the wall that will be taken out. Remember that you cannot support the load carried by the bearing wall with a single set of jack posts or wood framing on one side of the wall. Both sides of the ceiling joists must be supported before any part of the bearing wall is removed.

To determine what length the leg posts will be, set a 2-by-4 block (sole plate allowance) on top of the beam as it rests on the floor, and measure from the top of the block to the ceiling (or top plate if you're leaving it in). In older houses, because of the shifting of weight over the years, this measurement could be different on either side. So, be sure to measure each leg post separately to ensure a good, tight fit. Cut the leg posts to the proper measurements.

Note: You might have to add additional support beneath the new leg posts. Reinforce with blocks, or, in a basement, install permanent jack posts.

Preparing for Demolition

If there are plumbing, electric, or gas lines in the wall, shut off the gas, water, and/or electricity and prepare for demolition. Severe conduit and pipes; reroute and reconnect them later. Wear goggles and a face mask to protect yourself from plaster dust and dirt. Cover everything in sight with plastic drop cloths. Close off adjacent rooms, and open all the windows in the rooms you're working in. Have a dumpster and wheelbarrow available for trash disposal. Grab your claw hammer and crowbar, and go at it.

Remove doors, moldings, baseboard, and trim, first. Save the trim by pulling nails as you go. Pound a starting hole through the wallboard (or plaster) with a hammer, or use a keyhole saw or drill—whatever is needed —on other wall compositions. Peel away wall surfaces from both sides. Remove studs intact by knocking them out with a sledgehammer, but don't knock out the last stud, which is usually nailed to a built-up stud running at a right angle in the adjacent wall. Saw it instead, and pry away the pieces. Pounding on this stud with a sledge will damage the existing wall. After the studs are removed, saw and pry away the portion of top plate that will be replaced by the new beam.

Saw, then pry away the sole plate segment from the floor. Now, while two helpers raise the beam and position it against the joists above, have two more helpers place the end posts in position under the beam, and drive the endposts in tightly between sole plate and beam. (Shim, if necessary.) Then, toenail the posts to the beam and plates.

Remove the temporary supports and refinish the walls. (For information on how to repair a hardwood floor after a wall is removed, see p. 176 in Chapter 8, "Floors.")

WORKING WITH DRYWALL

Drywall is a fire-resistant sheathing with a plaster core sandwiched by two layers of heavy-duty paper. The seamless, cream-colored side (the good side) faces the room. The darker face is installed against the wall studs.

The sheets come in standard 4-foot widths, up to 16 feet long, and in several thicknesses. For resurfacing existing walls, ¼-inch-thick drywall is usually used, ⅜-inch drywall is often used as backing board under plywood paneling; ½-inch drywall is most commonly used on walls and ceilings; and the ⅝-inch thickness (usually stipulated by code) is mainly used for its fire-resistance and sound-control qualities.

Special-purpose drywall includes foil-backed drywall for extra insulation, drywall that comes with one side prefinished with vinyl, and a water-resistant variety (blue or green), which is available for moisture-prone areas like kitchens and bathrooms and is usually used under tile.

Drywall is fairly durable, but it will break if it's bent too far, or dropped on one of its corners. You shouldn't have too much trouble working with drywall (it nails cleanly and saws quickly), if you can handle the bulkiness of the sheets. Since drywall is quite heavy (about 60 pounds per 4-by-8-by-½-inch sheet), you might find it easier to use double sheets of drywall where you need the extra thickness for soundproofing, fire resistancy, or building up a wall to match it's plaster counterpart, in order to use existing trim and molding.

Usually, drywall is nailed directly to the studs or joists, or over furring strips, but it can also be glued right over the old wall. The long edges of the sheets are beveled; the short (4-foot) sides are squared. The butt ends are usually positioned at inside corners when the panel is installed horizontally, or if you're using it vertically, at the floor and ceiling lines. When the beveled edges are butted, a slight trough is created for the joint compound. Thus, it's very difficult to hide a butt seam where the compound and tape sit on top of the seam and surface material; and it's almost impossible to hide a seam where one edge is beveled and the other squared. Keep this in mind when you're laying out the room for drywall.

Measuring and Estimating

If you measure the room and make a scaled drawing, you'll know exactly how many drywall sheets the job will require. This simple exercise will also help you decide what direction to run them in—parallel or perpendicular to the studs. As you measure, keep in mind that no matter which way they're installed, each sheet must begin and end at the center of a stud. If the walls are constructed with 16-inch o.c. studs, you shouldn't have any trouble landing on nailing space. The main idea is to end up with the fewest cuts and the least number of eye-level joints. Most professional drywallers prefer to run drywall horizontally for these reasons. For instance, if they use 12-foot-long sheets, they reduce the taping on an 8-by-12-foot wall to one horizontal seam across the middle; and it's a lot easier to tape and finish a horizontal joint at shoulder height than it is to tape from ceiling to floor many times across the span. This method should also be used on high-ceilinged walls and in halls where vertical joints would be especially noticeable. The problem is, unless you have a helper, you may not be able to carry or lift the sheets into place, and the alternative would be to use the more manageable 4-by-8 sheets in a vertical position.

Plan to use only full sheets around windows and doors, and to butt only beveled edges. This automatically implies that you will have waste. But since ½-inch drywall, nails, joint-sealing compound, and tape cost a mere 15 cents a square foot, the waste will be worth it. If you use scraps, you'll end up with countless seams to finish and hide, on a job that will seem like forever to finish. Of course, sometimes it will be impossible not to butt some 4-foot-square edges, and you'll have no other choice but to spend the extra time taping and finishing them. Try to avoid butt joints or at least keep them at a minimum.

Materials and Tools

Besides the drywall, you'll need:

Nails. Use only the annular ring-shanked nails made especially for installing drywall. They have the best holding power. Make sure that the nails are long enough to penetrate the drywall, plus about ¾ inch of the stud.

Buy 1⅛-inch annular ring-shanked nails for ¼-inch backer board; 1¼-inch drywall nails for ⅜-inch drywall, 1⅜-inch nails for ½-inch drywall, and 1½-inch nails for ⅝-inch drywall. It will take about 1 lb. of nails for every 200 square feet of surface.

If you're installing ¼- or ⅜-inch drywall over an existing plaster surface, use the longer 1⅞-inch cement-coated nails (1¼ lbs. per 200 square feet). For ½- or ⅝-inch drywall over existing plaster or new backer board, use 2¼-inch cement-coated nails. If you're installing double layers of drywall, you'll also need gypsum adhesive.

Joint Tape and Compound. You'll need about 100 feet of tape and a gallon of ready-mixed joint compound for every 200 square feet of wall surface.

You can buy the perforated tape, which allows the compound to seep through, but most do-it-yourselfers find that the plain tape is easier to finish because you don't have to contend with the compound oozing up through the holes, or the holes, themselves, showing through if too thin a coating is applied.

Get the ready-mixed joint compound that comes in a plastic bucket. The consistancy is just right, it's free of lumps, and it will keep for over a year if resealed properly.

There are certain precautions to take with the joint compound. Don't apply the compound to cold and damp walls. Warm the room to at least 55 degrees before drywalling, and keep it around this temperature for four days afterward. Don't allow the compound to freeze, but don't overheat the room either. High temperatures will cause the compound to shrink. It will also cause excessively high humidity in the room (make sure you provide adequate ventilation). Allow 24 hours drying time after each application.

Metal Corner Beads for Outside Corners. These are long metal strips, folded to form a right angle, that slip over corners to protect them and keep them straight and square. They are perforated, so they can be embedded in a layer of joint compound. You'll need one strip for each outside corner.

Furring Strips. Furring strips are available at lumberyards so that you can flush out a crooked wall before applying the new drywall.

Hammer. The best hammer for drywall is the crown-head, which has a rounded top. This style will dimple the drywall without breaking through the paper coating, as flat-headed hammers have a tendency to do.

Plasterer's Hawk. A square, flat plate or board with a handle underneath that holds a convenient amount of drywall compound while you work. Use the edges of the hawk to scrape the compound off the drywall knife.

Drywall Knives or Scrapers. These are similar to putty knives with flexible blades. You'll need at least 2 sizes (three is better). Purchase a 4-, 6-, and 10-inch scraper. You can also use a 12-inch trowel for some of the finishing work.

Inside Corner Tool. This is a very helpful tool for installing drywall tape at inside corners. It makes a neat right angle and feathers the compound on both sides simultaneously as it's drawn down an inside corner.

Utility Knife. A sharp pocketknife or utility knife for scoring and cutting the drywall.

Straight Edge. A 4-foot T-square or steel straightedge to ensure a clean, straight cut.

Keyhold or Sabre Saw. For making cutouts in drywall.

Steel Tape and Pencil. For measuring and marking.

Crowbar. For demolishing old walls. You can also use it as part of a foot lever needed for raising drywall off the floor.

Sandpaper and Sanding Block. You can use an orbital sander, but do-it-yourself beginners are advised to hand-sand. Buy several grades of sandpaper to wrap around the wood block.

Stepladder. For installing the drywall.

Goggles and Dust Mask. For safety precautions.

Preparing the Walls

Stack the sheets flat on the floor in a dry place. Always take the necessary safety precautions to prevent harmful dust from getting into your lungs, eyes, and hair—wear a dust mask, goggles, and a hat.

Carefully pry off old door and window casings, trim, and moldings, and save. Strip away old plaster or drywall, and hammer in any protruding nails. If you're drywalling over an existing wall, smooth its surface first, or install furring strips over incorrigible walls.

Move electrical boxes forward ¼ or ⅜ inches (depending on the thickness of the drywall), so they will be flush with the new wall surface.

Then locate the studs, and make light pencil marks on the ceiling and floor, indicating their centers to facilitate nailing the drywall.

Installing Drywall Over Masonry Walls. When installing drywall on masonry walls, either above or below grade, waterproof the walls with a waterproofing compound before applying the furring strips. The strips should be installed with concrete stub nails 24 inches apart (both vertically and horizontally) with spaces left between the horizontal strips for air circulation. If you're going to insulate the wall first, see the chapter on Basements.

Installing the Drywall

Butt the first sheet of drywall tight to a corner and snuggly to the ceiling. Make sure it's plumb and straight, then work your way all around the room with successive sheets, keeping the nailing edges on the centers of the studs. If necessary, cut panels narrower to fit studs. Make your cutouts for outlets, fixtures, or doors and windows as you go around the room. After all the drywall is nailed on, you are ready to begin taping.

Techniques to Make the Job Easier

Even the experienced carpenter can benefit from a few common-sense tips.

Cutting. Never cut a panel even slightly larger than the space allotted to it. Edges and corners will crumble if you force the piece in place. Instead, cut the panel slightly smaller than the opening, and rely on tape and compound to fill any small gaps or joint cracks.

When you cut drywall, draw guidelines on the finished side of the sheet, then score along the lines with a utility knife and straightedge. If you're cutting on curved or irregular lines, take your time. It isn't necessary to cut all the way through, because the sheet will snap neatly on the scored line. If you're cutting out a right-angled piece, such as one leg of a door opening, cut right through the short line; score and break the drywall on the long line. Breaking and snapping drywall is easy if you place a 2-by-4 under the scored line and press downward on one side. Don't let the weight of the cut rip the paper away from the back, however. Then, position the scored drywall sheet so it's bent at a right angle, and separate the pieces by slicing the paper on the underside, drawing the utility knife upward.

Use full sheets for door and window openings. Measure down from the ceiling to the top and bottom of the jamb, and from the edge of the last installed sheet of drywall to the first edge of the opening. If the sheet surrounds a door or window, you must also measure across to the furthest jamb. Transfer these measurements to the face of the sheet, connect the lines, and cut the openings.

If you have help, there's a more accurate and faster way to mark outlets. Hold the drywall sheet in place and have a friend mark the outlet from the next room in back of the open studs. Make sure that the panel is aligned so that it's plumbed tight to the ceiling and the side edges center on studs.

Drill holes through the panel inside the four corners, then cut from hole to hole on the face side with a keyhole or sabre saw. The hole can be slightly larger than the opening itself. The rough edges will be covered by trim or switch plates later.

Nailing. For a better-quality installation that cuts down on nailhole finishing afterwards, use the adhesive/nail-on method. Apply a ⅜-inch bead of adhesive to the studs with a caulking gun. Position the drywall sheet, and nail only at the edges and ends where you will be taping anyway. Press the board to check if it's tight to the studs. If it's loose, put a nail or two in the middle. If you're not using adhesive, all nailing should be done from the center of the sheet toward the edges.

Pound each nail into the sheet flush, then dimple the surface slightly with the second stroke. An ⅛-inch depression will hold enough joint compound to hide the nailhead. Do not rupture the paper.

Nail ⅜ inches in from the edges and stay on your chalklines throughout the field of the panel (made from your light floor and ceiling marks, designating the center of the studs). Drywall is nailed in pairs to prevent nail-popping; space each pair of nails 2 inches apart at 12-inch intervals all around the edges and up and down intermediate studs.

Installing Horizontal Panels

Always start from the ceiling and work down. To help support the first panel, drive three 8d common nails partway into the studs, 4 feet down the wall. With the help of a friend, lift the sheet and tilt it in so it butts tightly against the ceiling, then rest the bottom long edge on the nails. Drive nails across the intermediate studs about a foot down to hold the sheet in place, then finish nailing.

Butt the second sheet snugly to the bottom of the first. To keep it in this position as you nail, construct a foot lever by laying a crowbar on the floor and placing a small board over it (FIG. 6-20). Insert the front edge of the board under the sheet and step on the back end.

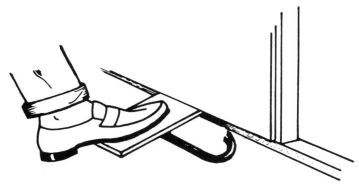

Fig. 6–20. Using a foot lever to raise panels.

Installing Vertical Panels

Butt the first panel tightly into the corner. Check the panel for verticality with a plumb line. Score and trim the panel if needed, so it fits squarely into the corner with its opposite edge ending up on the center of a stud. Use the foot lever to get it into position against the ceiling.

Taping

There are several important things to remember when taping to ensure a good job.

1. Don't attempt to rush the finishing work; there's no way to shorten this 4-day job and do it right because each layer of compound must dry at least 24 hours before the next coat is applied.
2. The more carefully you apply the tape and joint compound, the less sanding you'll have to do later on.
3. Use the proper-sized drywall scrapers for each layer. Don't start with a scraper smaller than 4 inches. Graduate the size of the scraper with each new coat, so you can feather the joints properly. Each layer of compound should extend 2 inches over the previous layer, and each scraper should be wider than the layer of compound you're feathering.
4. Complete one seam before you go on to the next, and scrape the edge of the knife off often. As the compound begins to harden, it will create problems for you, like making lines and grooves in the joints on which you are working.
5. Ladle the compound into a glass baking dish before you start, one that will accommodate your largest knife.

Regular Joints. Take up a quantity of compound on your 4-inch knife and spread a layer over the joint, filling the channel created by the beveled edges. Center the paper tape over the beginning of the "mudded" joint and unroll it with one hand while you press it into the compound with the other. At the end of the joint, hold your scraper squarely against the tape and tear it off the roll. Now go back over the joint once more and cover it with a layer of compound, feathering the edges to make a smooth transition with the wall surface. Work the tape with the knife, so the compound oozes out along the tape's edge, but don't press so hard that you squeeze out all of the compound underneath the tape. If the tape wrinkles, pull it loose and start again. If the tape veers away from the joint, tear it off and start a new strip directly below the torn strip. Apply the compound to nail dimples, feathering the edges the same as you did for joint seams.

Outside Corners. The first step is to apply the metal corner beads to outside corners. Butter a layer of compound over both sides of the corner and press the metal reinforcing strip into the compound to embed it. If you want, you can drive a few nails into the wall to hold it, but the compound should keep the strip flatly adhered to the corner. Apply another layer of compound over the strip and feather the edges. The rounded edge of the metal will show slightly, even after the final coat, but it will be covered by wall-finishing materials.

Inside Corners. Use the 4-inch knife to slather compound into the crack and down each side of the corner. Crease the tape in half lengthwise and press it into the corner with your finger. (It's easier to work with 3-foot pieces.) Draw your knife along each side of the joint to embed the tape into the compound as you feather the edges. Apply another layer of compound over the tape, then smooth and feather it with the corner tool.

Successive Coats. The next day, sand away any encrustations, and even out any irregular areas with medium grade sandpaper and a sanding block. Be careful not to damage or scuff up the paper coating. Dust off the wall. Using the 6-inch scraper, apply the second layer of compound, spreading it 2 inches beyond the sides of the first layer. Do the joints, dimples, and corners, feathering the compound neatly and smoothly.

The third day, repeat the process with a 10-inch drywall knife. This time, thin down the joint compound with a little water until it is the consistency of pancake batter. This final layer should be about 12 inches wide.

When the compound is dry on the fourth day, sand all the joints and nail spots with a fine grade of finishing sandpaper. Work the sanding block in a circular motion with very slight pressure. Go over the walls with a light, shining it along the wall, and look for indentions or depressed spots. If you find any, fill them.

If your walls are to be finished with paint, give them a coat of latex primer when the compound is dry. This will equalize the absorption difference between compound and drywall surfaces and allow the paint to be uniform in color over the entire wall.

Prime the walls with shellac or varnish if you plan to wallpaper them. Then wait three days to be sure your sealer is thoroughly dry before painting or papering the walls.

An End to Dark Passages

Where once stood a solid wall, clean-lined columns open up the hall to light and air without reneging on structural support. Removing walls will transform a dark, small-roomed Victorian-type home into a streamlined contemporary setting, with more accessible traffic patterns and living space.

Innovative Partitions

Many old houses have ample-sized rooms, but the space isn't put to good use. Consider the bedroom below. This pleasantly daylighted corner bedroom had plenty of room for furniture arranging, but was woefully wanting of closet space (opposite, top). A simple, but ingenious, wall screens the dressing area and "stands in" as a headboard, vanity table, and built-in closet supports (opposite, bottom). The whole room takes on a cozier, more pleasing personality and affords the occupant luxuries not previously offered.

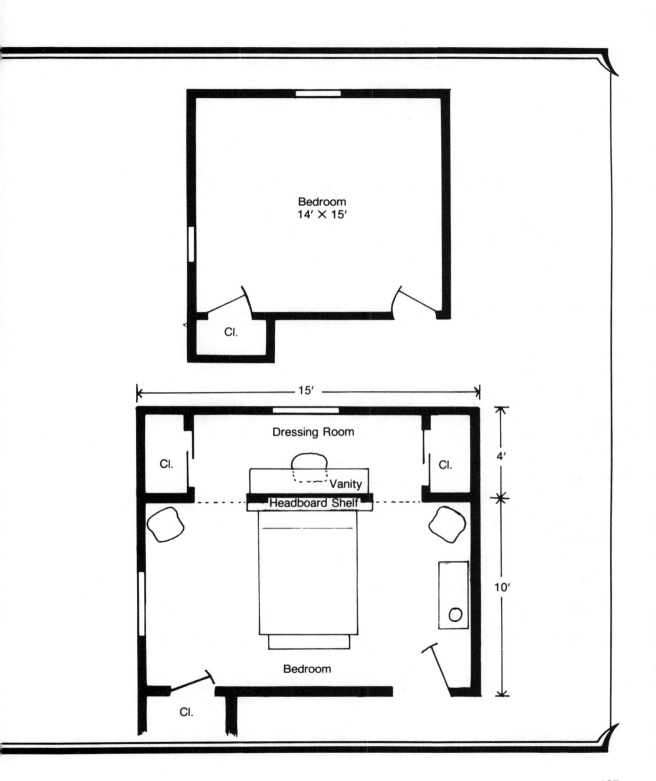

Bedroom
14' × 15'

Cl.

15'

Dressing Room

Cl.

Cl.

4'

Vanity

Headboard Shelf

10'

Bedroom

Cl.

137

Moldings, Trim and Woodwork

You've probably noticed that moldings add texture and definition to a room like no other architectural element. By using imaginative combinations, you can create another whole dimension with which to add contrast, weight, and balance to bland settings. A room with a mediocre background takes on a new personality with the creative use of moldings and trim. And since they come in so many sizes and shapes—solid and filligree—you have endless opportunities to stir up romance or add bold excitement to any room. The trick is to think of moldings as a frame surrounding a beautiful picture that you want to complement or accent. And although they certainly do have a decorative function, their primary purpose is to provide a boundary or meeting point between materials. If you understand this framing function, you have mastered the key to successful selection and placement of moldings.

Selecting moldings can be quite a creative challenge! Your local home center is a virtual treasure trove of decorative borders, moldings, and trims. You can buy prefinished moldings to match paneling, or unfinished moldings that can be stained or painted to harmonize with your walls. You may be one of the fortunate ones who purchased a house full of beautiful, authentic moldings that just need refinishing; but if some pieces must be repaired or replaced, your lumber dealer probably has what you're looking for to accomplish this.

Further along in this chapter, you'll learn how to salvage and restore priceless plaster moldings found in many old homes. These sculptured architectural ceiling adornments can be easily copied and recast. If you have the time to tackle such an interesting project, you can add a hefty equity increase to your planned profit.

MOLDING STYLES

Moldings run the gamut in design, from flat vinyl strips, to multicut or carved wood, to sculptured versions in plaster and plastic. You can purchase them from wood panel dealers who offer matching trim with their products; lumberyards that stock plain and fancy wood moldings in many patterns; and from mail-order companies that sell architecturally correct wood, plaster, and polymer moldings for just about any period or decorating style.

Prefinished Paneling Moldings

Prefinished vinyl panel moldings come in 8-foot strips to match (or contrast with) almost every wood finish. They're meant specifically to cover inside and outside corners, floor and ceiling lines, and seam joints on paneling, so their design is pretty straightforward — no fancy curlicues. But because they have the unique ability to bend and flex to a great degree, they're also used on other wall compositions, often around curves, arches, and various odd shapes (FIG. 7-1).

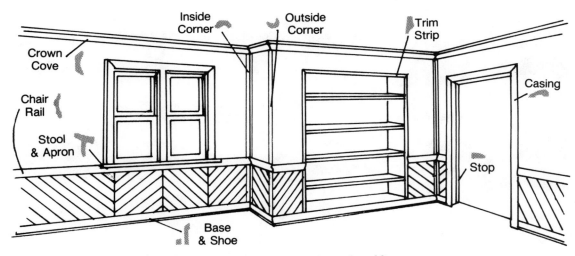

Fig. 7–1. Trim locations for vinyl panel moldings.

Wood Moldings

There is a much wider range in the choice of wood trim (FIG. 7-2). A number of mills make multicut moldings for ceilings, floors, and walls, as well as for doors and windows. By using various combinations of these stock moldings, you can create your own unique trim style. Available also are carved and embossed hardwood moldings, including distinctive profiles like rope, bead, and bamboo, and intricately carved ornaments (FIG. 7-3) that add artistic touches to any room's surface.

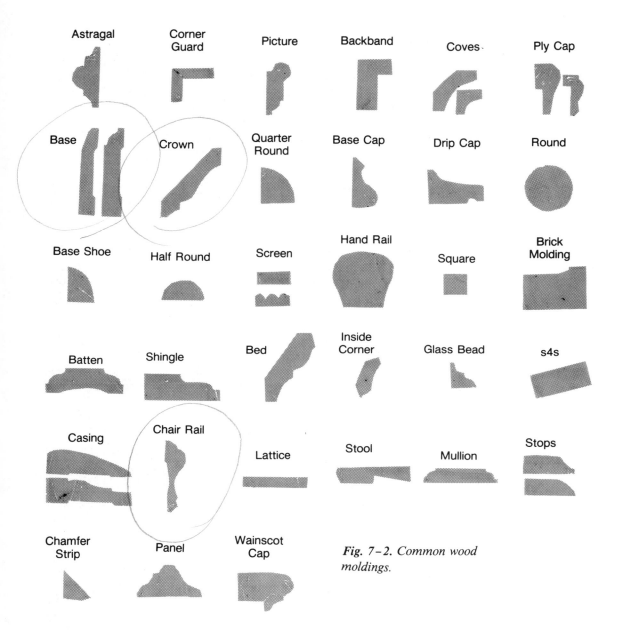

Astragal Corner Guard Picture Backband Coves Ply Cap

Base Crown Quarter Round Base Cap Drip Cap Round

Base Shoe Half Round Screen Hand Rail Square Brick Molding

Batten Shingle Bed Inside Corner Glass Bead s4s

Casing Chair Rail Lattice Stool Mullion Stops

Chamfer Strip Panel Wainscot Cap

Fig. 7–2. Common wood moldings.

Reproductions in Polymer

Several companies sell authentic-looking reproductions in plastic (FIG. 7-4). Their products are molded from direct impressions of the originals and include not only decorative moldings, but ceiling medallions, recessed domes, niche caps, overdoor pieces (*spandrels*), stair brackets, and mantels. These products are extremely tough and lightweight. They can be installed indoors or out and accept any finish from marble to wood. Because they

Fig. 7–3. Decorative wood carvings.

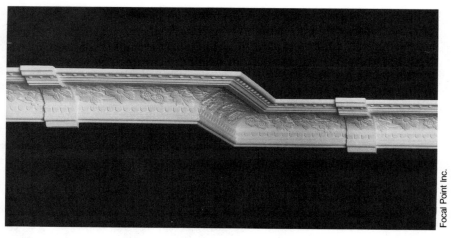

Fig. 7–4. French-style polymer molding.

come in flexible 10-foot lengths, you can use them in oval rooms, curved stairwells, bays, and so forth. They're more expensive than wood, but they are easier to install and offer more design possibilities, especially with restorations.

Specialty Moldings

Although they're not generally stocked, you can order specialty moldings by mail. Such trims, like dentil and bolection moldings, along with columns and pilasters, were popular wall treatments in the late eighteenth century and still are today. (See FIG. 7-5.)

Filigree moldings add beautiful detail that makes a room very special. If an attractive fabric, wallpaper, or contrasting paint is used under the delicate, lace-like wood to accentuate it, the molding will surely be the highlight of the room.

Before you install multiple moldings (one on top of the other), finish both pieces first. For instance, glue the wallpaper or fabric on the bottom piece and paint the overlay, then assemble the two with glue and sparsely placed brads before you miter them. Add more nails after mitering, if necessary.

When painting the overlay, use a 2-inch roller instead of a brush. The roller will cover the fretwork more thoroughly.

Dentil molding is a flat piece with ornamental notches carved or cut out of the bottom. It is used in the classical entablature cornice.

Panel molding is available in strips and matching curved pieces. Rectangles, placed around the room with square-mitered or curved corners, can establish a pleasing, proportionate wall pattern. Add fabric or wallpaper inserts for decorative drama.

Bolection molding projects sharply into the room and is frequently used as fireplace trimming, often in lieu of a mantle shelf.

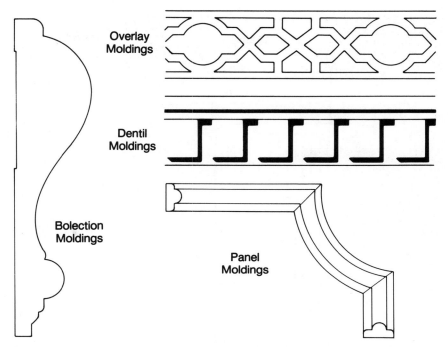

Fig. 7–5. Specialty moldings, such as those shown above, were popular in the late 1700s and are still popular today. Although not generally stocked at home improvement centers, a wide variety is available by mail-order.

Pilaster moldings are used to make rectangular columns on walls and to flank windows and doors. They're often used in conjunction with architectural columns.

Square architectural columns (FIG. 7-6) can be easily made from inch-thick boards, mitered at corners. Apply pilaster molding down the centers, and add stock moldings to top and bottom for a more classical look. The columns can be built around structural support posts for bearing walls or to hide pipes.

Plinth Blocks

Plinth blocks were often used in old house trim, perhaps because they didn't have the mitering equipment we have today, or maybe because they just preferred the look of the squared and butted joints. Here are some easy ways to treat corners if you don't want to deal with mitering and contouring (see FIGS. 7-7, 7-8, and 7-9).

Cut a block from square scrap lumber. Nail it into the corner, and butt square-cut molding against the block for a perfect fit on inside or outside corners. Use it on ceilings, floors, or around doors and windows.

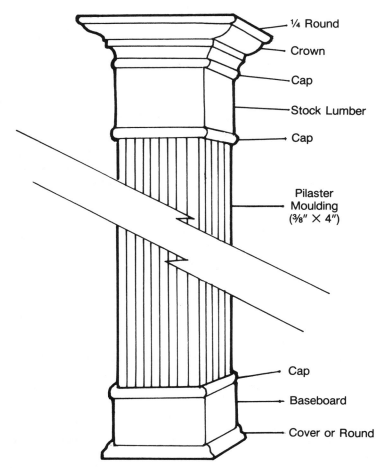

¼ Round

Crown

Cap

Stock Lumber

Cap

Pilaster
Moulding
(⅜" × 4")

Cap

Baseboard

Cover or Round

Fig. 7–6. Square column.

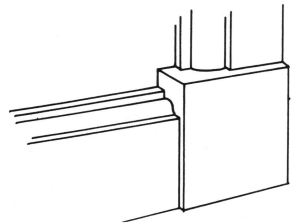

Fig. 7–7. Plinth blocks. Outside corner.

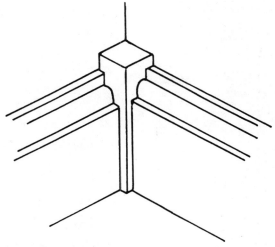

Fig. 7–8. Plinth Blocks. Inside corner.

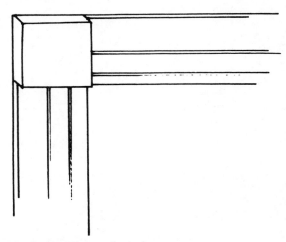

Fig. 7–9. Plinth Blocks. Door and window corners.

MOLDING LOCATIONS

Moldings are commonly placed at chair rail height and at ceiling and floor lines, but they can also be used around windows and doors, or any place where you want to emphasize a shape on the wall (see FIG. 7-10).

Chair Rail Molding

Originally, chair rails were found exclusively in dining rooms and hallways, where they were used to keep the backs of chairs from damaging wall surfaces. Today, they're used in every room because of their design impact (see FIG. 7-11).

Fig. 7-10. *Adding definition to a wall. Window treatment color is used again on articulately-placed molding strips to add contrast and definition to an otherwise bland wall.*

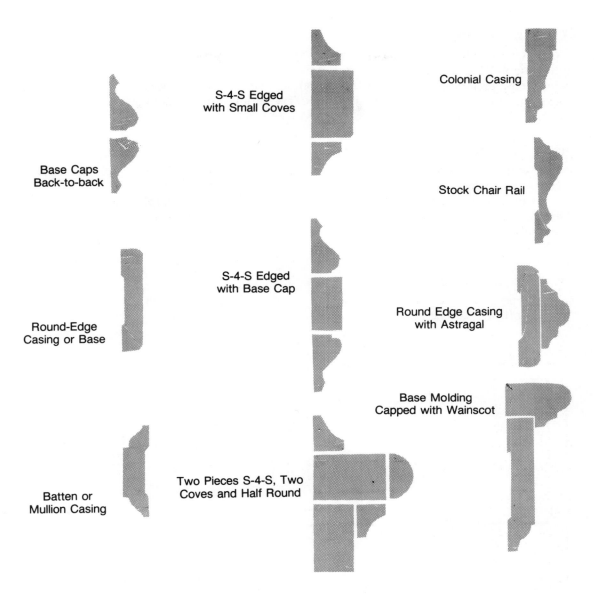

Base Caps
Back-to-back

S-4-S Edged
with Small Coves

Colonial Casing

Stock Chair Rail

Round-Edge
Casing or Base

S-4-S Edged
with Base Cap

Round Edge Casing
with Astragal

Base Molding
Capped with Wainscot

Batten or
Mullion Casing

Two Pieces S-4-S, Two
Coves and Half Round

Fig. 7–11. Chair rail variations.

Chair rails are usually placed from 30 to 35 inches from the floor, or at the height of the windowsill. Sometimes, they are referred to as *dado caps*. Dado (wainscoat) is the wood paneling that's used on the lower section of a wall. For the dado portion of a wall, you can use actual wood, wood paneling, or a wood treillage. You can also create the effect of a dado by substituting paint or wallpaper for the paneling.

Ceiling Moldings

Crown molding (sometimes referred to as *cove molding*) used at the ceiling in any room creates a highly customized look. You can use single 4-inch cove molding for this purpose, but nothing beats the more exaggerated, sculptural effect of multiple moldings. Try various combinations, such as crown and base or crown, S-4-S, and base cap (FIG. 7-12).

Base Moldings

Baseboard used to mean pieces of 1-by-4 or 1-by-6 lumber nailed to the wall at the floor line. Very often, the baseboard had additional molding added to its upper and lower edges. Today, we primarily use the simple 4-inch, ranch-style base with shoe because it's easily obtainable, but there's nothing to stop you from giving the floor line a higher profile with more elaborate moldings (FIG. 7-13).

Window and Door Molding

Casing is used to seal the gap between jamb and wall around the window. It, too, can be used in plain and decorative styles (FIG. 7-14).

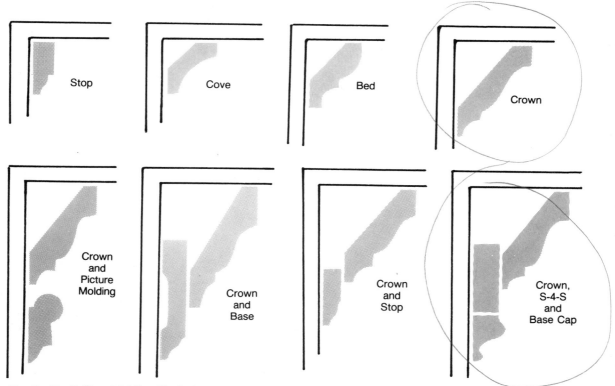

Fig. 7-12. Ceiling Molding Variations.

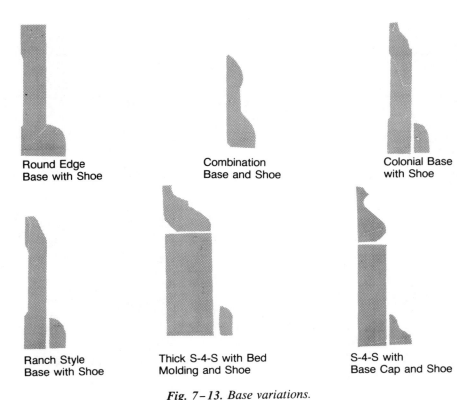

Round Edge
Base with Shoe

Combination
Base and Shoe

Colonial Base
with Shoe

Ranch Style
Base with Shoe

Thick S-4-S with Bed
Molding and Shoe

S-4-S with
Base Cap and Shoe

Fig. 7–13. Base variations.

Fig. 7–14. Casing Variations.

Plate Rail

Another type of molding popular in the 1800s was the *plate rail* (FIG. 7-15). It surrounded dining room walls and was used as a place to show off china collections. It's still very effective today—in kitchens, dining rooms, bedrooms, or dens—for displaying any kind of collection. When you use a plate rail, install a smaller cove molding at the ceiling, then, 10 to 12 inches down, attach the heavier plate rail. If you're decorating with wallpaper,

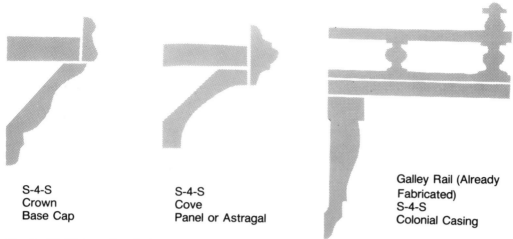

S-4-S
Crown
Base Cap

S-4-S
Cove
Panel or Astragal

Galley Rail (Already
Fabricated)
S-4-S
Colonial Casing

Fig. 7–15. Plate rail variations.

don't use it above the plate rail; instead, paint the area the background color of the paper, so the collection becomes more prominent.

All moldings and trim in a room should harmonize in design and color. Prime, paint, or stain the trim before you install it. Attach it to the wall, then countersink the nails and fill them with putty before you do your final touch-up coat.

MEASURING AND PURCHASING MOLDINGS

Common moldings are usually stocked in pine, but they can be ordered in other woods if you're willing to pay the price. Baseboard and base shoe are quite often available in oak today because of the popularity of oak flooring. Precut wood moldings come in standard lengths of 6-, 8-, 10-, 12-, 14-, and 16 feet.

Measure each piece separately and add a molding width for every miter cut you'll be making. When purchasing, stipulate the length of each cut you need, in case shorter lengths are available. This will help you to avoid excessive waste or having to splice too many cuts. Pick your lengths carefully, so that in the event you have to splice two separate pieces together, they will not be noticeably different after the finish is applied.

CUTTING AND INSTALLING MOLDINGS

Precision is what it takes to do good trim work. Meticulous measurements, painstaking cuts, the proficient use of hammer and nail set, and taking your time will compensate for any lack of experience. It's another job that you can't rush through — if you plan to do it right.

Tools and Materials. You'll need a miter box and backsaw, coping saw, hammer, nail set, rule, 4d, 6d, and 8d finishing nails, putty and #100 sandpaper.

Paint and Finish Molding First. Paint or stain moldings and wait until they're thoroughly dry before you install them. It's a lot easier to finish the strips when they're lying flat on sawhorses—before you cut or miter them—and touch them up after they're nailed to the wall.

Measuring and Marking. Measure each piece of molding separately for the area it will cover. Don't assume that floor and ceiling lengths are identical around the room. As you measure, remember to add an inch or so for miter cuts: on inside cuts for straightening, on outside cuts because the molding will project beyond the corner. Hold each piece to the wall and make a pencil mark where the cut will be made. Be sure the mark is visible when the molding is placed in the miter box. Then, put a number on the back so you don't confuse the order.

Mitering. Mitering is a word that's used often in trim-work. It means to cut at an angle across a piece of molding or trim. We use 45-degree angle cuts at corners (both left and right pieces having opposite 45 degree angles), so when joined, they form a tight right angle. The cuts are made with a miter box and backsaw—an indispensible piece of equipment for accurate trim-work. Wherever you have straight corners and flat baseboard or molding, you can miter both inside and outside corners. (Some inside corners that are irregularly shaped, and moldings like cove, corner, or cap, require special mitering. We'll discuss that later.) To miter:

1. Secure the miter box so it won't slide around.
2. Place the wood in the miter box on its edge with the pencil marks lined up at the appropriate slot. Make sure that you're sawing in the right direction.
3. Hold the molding steady with one hand, then lower the backsaw over the wood on the mark so that its direction conforms with the angled grooves.
4. With the sawblade level to the wood, give it a gentle stroke to begin the cut.
5. Increase the length of your strokes, keeping the saw on course, until the wood is cut in two.

On inside corners, remember that the side of the molding that goes to the wall is always longer than the front, or face side. The piece to your left is cut in the miter box left to right (FIG. 7-16). The molding strip to your right is cut right to left (FIG. 7-17 and 7-18).

On outside corners, the backsides of the molding strips are shorter than the face side. The left piece is cut right to left in the miter box; the right molding, left to right (FIGS. 7-19 and 7-20).

Sometimes, even with accurate mitering, there are gaps between the joints and the walls. Since corners are seldom square in a room, you may have to further adjust the corner joint by shaving the moldings with a sharp utility knife.

If the joint gaps on the wall side, increase the angle formed by the

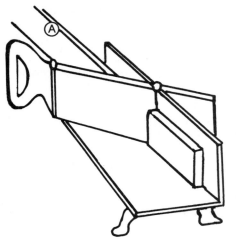

Fig. 7–16. *Mitering inside corner left to right.*

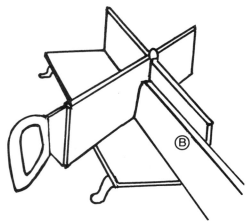

Fig. 7–17. *Mitering inside corner right to left.*

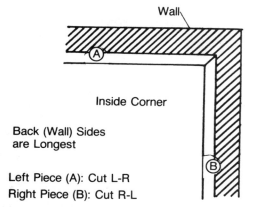

Wall

Ⓐ

Inside Corner

Back (Wall) Sides
are Longest

Left Piece (A): Cut L-R
Right Piece (B): Cut R-L

Ⓑ

Fig. 7–18. *Mitered inside corner installed.*

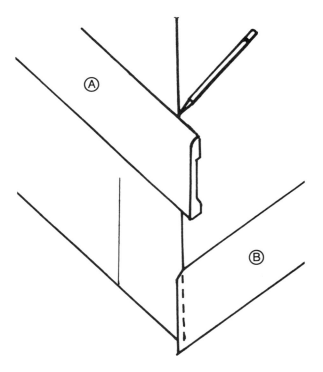

Fig. 7–19. *Mitering outside corner.*

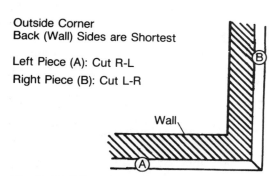

Outside Corner
Back (Wall) Sides are Shortest

Left Piece (A): Cut R-L
Right Piece (B): Cut L-R

Ⓑ

Wall

Ⓐ

Fig. 7–20. *Mitered outside corner installed.*

strip(s) of molding by carefully shaving away the front(s) with a sharp utility knife (FIGS. 7-21 and 7-22).

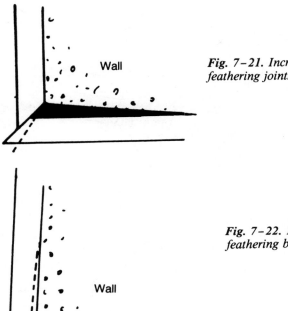

Fig. 7–21. Increase angle of cut by feathering joints.

Wall

Fig. 7–22. Decrease angle of cut by feathering backs of trim.

Wall

Coping. Many joints can not be simply mitered. They must be contoured to fit adjoining, irregular surfaces, or intricately shaped pieces where they meet at corners. This is called *coping.* We cope, rather than miter, for several reasons: 1. it makes a tighter, stronger joint; 2. the joint will not separate as much as a mitered corner if the house settles or the wood shrinks; 3. it's faster and easier because you have only one side of each piece to contour.

When coping, first miter the molding to reveal the face pattern. Then, with a coping saw, undercut along the mitered line (in the opposite direction) to remove the wood in back (FIG. 7-23).

To cope a contoured corner:

1. Install the first piece (A) between two opposite walls with butt cuts on each end (FIG. 7-24) Step 1.
2. On (B), make a 45-degree miter cut on the end that will butt to (A), to reveal the profile of the moulding strip (Step 2). Be sure that you cut in the right direction.
3. Now, undercut the back of the molding (Step 3).
4. Tap or push the coped end into the butt strip so that you have a tight fit (Step 4).

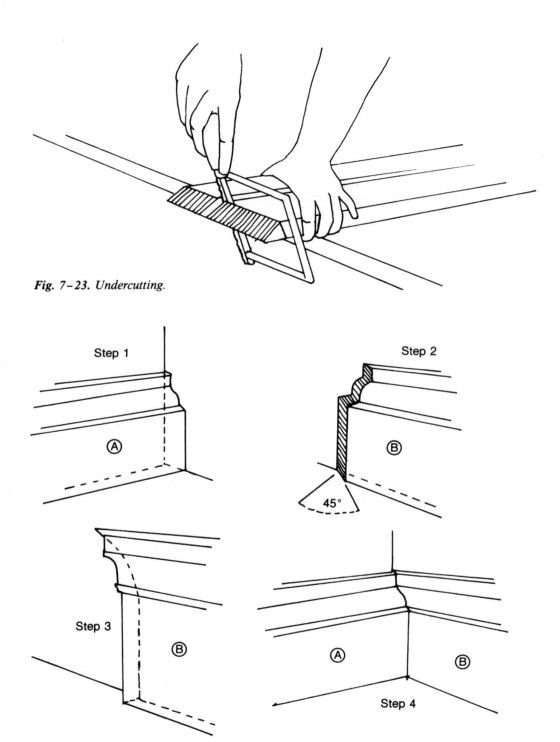

Fig. 7-23. *Undercutting.*

Step 1

Ⓐ

Step 2

Ⓑ

45°

Step 3

Ⓑ

Ⓐ

Ⓑ

Step 4

Fig. 7-24. *Coping. Steps 1 through 4.*

Splicing Moldings with Scarf Joints

If the wall is longer than your molding, or if the length of a strip of molding proves unwieldy, you may have to cut and splice it. Locate a stud near the area you want to splice (FIG. 7-25). Mark the top of the molding where the center of the stud falls and cut it at a 45-degree angle. The cut will bisect the mark. Now, miter another piece of molding at the same angle but at the opposite end. Put a spot of glue on the ends before nailing to ensure their stability. Then position the molding against the wall and drive 4d nails through it and into the stud behind. Paint will hide a splice, but stain will not, so try to avoid splicing if you plan to stain the molding.

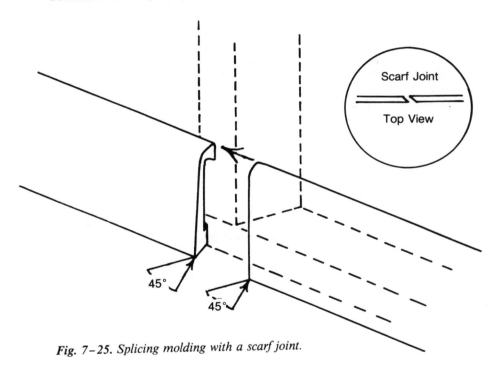

Fig. 7-25. Splicing molding with a scarf joint.

Nailing Molding Strips

Scrape away any irregularities where the moldings will go, like paint buildups or lumps of joint compound that might prevent moldings from fitting tightly against the wall. After you double-check that the joints fit properly, nail the molding in place with either 6- or 8d nails, placing each piece in its proper location according to the marks you put on the back. Begin nailing a strip of molding at one corner and continue across to the opposite end. After the moldings are nailed on, set the nails about ⅛ inch into the wood and fill the holes with wood putty. Touch up with a finish coat of stain or paint.

Installing Door and Window Casing

This type of trim is installed around doors and windows to conceal the gap between jambs and walls and give the opening a more finished look.

Door casings are recessed from the edge of the door opening ¼ inch to allow for hinge movement. Inner edges of window casings may be flush or recessed to match the doors.

To install the casing:

1. Make opposite 45-degree miter cuts on the ends of the head casing (FIG. 7-26). Tack it temporarily in place over the opening. (For window openings without sills, cut and nail a second piece for the bottom. For windows with sills, add an apron to fit under the sill.)
2. Fit the side casing so that the bottom edge rests snugly on the floor; then measure up to the outside corner of the top casing and mark the measurement on the outside edge of the vertical casing. Miter it at this mark to fit. Do the same for the other side, measuring and marking, but miter the cut in the opposite direction.
3. Nail the casing along the outside edge with 6d finishing nails; nail the inside edges into the jamb. Set the nails and fill the holes with putty.

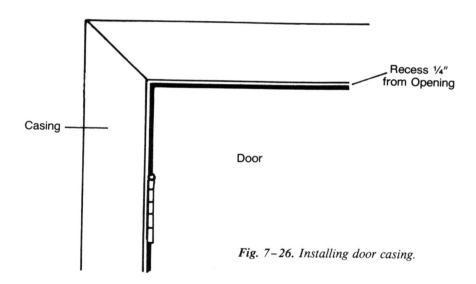

Recess ¼"
from Opening

Casing

Door

Fig. 7–26. Installing door casing.

Installing Base Moldings

Baseboard is added to cover the joint between wall and floor. It's also there to protect the wall from marks caused by vacuum cleaners, tricycles, and the like. Base shoe is added to the bottom of the baseboard to cover any gaps that might be caused by an uneven floor. Together, they add another important finishing touch.

Depending on how square your corners are, or how intricate the baseboard is, either miter or miter-cope inside corners. To install carved baseboard, make sure that you end up on a wall that has an outside corner or door opening. This way, instead of having to cope both ends of the last piece and fit it exactly between walls, you cope only one end and butt or miter-cut to an outside corner, which is a lot easier to do (FIG. 7-27).

To install baseboard and base shoe:

1. Measure accurately between (A) and (B) and butt-cut (square) both ends of the first piece. Nail with 6d finishing nails through the baseboard into the studs along the wall.

2. Facing the corner, take another strip (B–C) of baseboard that will fit to the left; measure, butt-cut both ends, then miter-cut (from right to left) the end (B) that will butt to the installed strip. Next, you must cut the contour of the attached baseboard into the end of the newly mitered one so that it fits snugly over your first strip of baseboard. With a coping saw or utility knife, cut away the wood at the back of the miter, using the face of the strip as your guide. (See instructions for coping.) When you have a snug fit, attach the (B–C) baseboard by driving 6d (or larger) finishing nails through the center of the strip. Remember that plaster is $\frac{1}{2}$ to $\frac{3}{8}$ inches thick and nailing at an angle adds to the thickness, so you'll have to choose the proper length nail to reach into solid wood.

3. Proceed around the room, mitering and contouring each piece to fit over the last square-cut end.

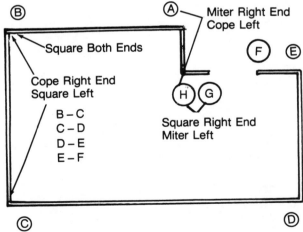

Fig. 7–27. Procedure for installing base and ceiling moldings.

The base shoe is measured and cut after the baseboard is installed. Toenail the base shoe downward with 4d nails, just above the middle of the shoe to avoid splitting the wood.

Set all nail heads and fill with putty. Touch up with paint or other finish.

Installing Baseboard and Base Shoe on Uneven Floors

If the floor isn't too crooked, strips of base shoe will cover the discrepancy between baseboard and floor because they're fairly flexible. But if the floor is extremely irregular, you'll have to scribe the baseboard before installing it. Place the baseboard in position, level it, then tack it in place. Set the scriber to equal the largest gap between the bottom of the baseboard and the floor. With the metal point on the floor—and the pencil on the baseboard—run the scriber along the floor. Remove the baseboard and cut on the scribed line before installing it again.

Baseboards butt into casings, but you'll have to sculpture the obtuse end of the base shoe into a slant for a neater fit (FIG. 7-28). Make a line on the shoe where it meets the door casing, then plane it back from the line. Sand and smooth it before finishing.

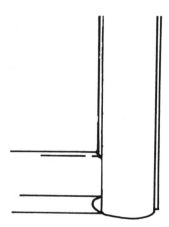

Fig. 7-28. Fitting base shoe to door casing.

Installing Ceiling Moldings

Ceiling moldings are used at the junction of wall and ceiling. They provide a pleasant transition from one surface to another and give the room a finished look. You can use a single molding, or combine several strips for a more elaborate appearance. When joining ceiling moldings at corners, use either a mitered or coped joint.

Any molding that's not designed to fit flat against the wall requires special installation. Crown, cove, and corner moldings are such types. In order to guarantee a snug fit between ceiling and wall (or in the case of corner molding, wall to wall) where you might have crooked corners, the strips are made with hollow backs (FIG. 7-29). This allows the molding to fit tightly against the two surfaces with the face slanting at the proper 45-degree angle.

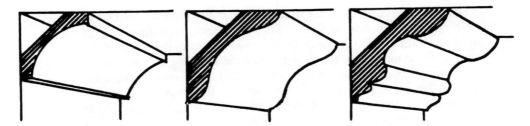

Fig. 7–29. Crown or cove moldings with hollow backs.

Because of their special contour, you don't set crown or cove moldings in the miterbox at the angle you see them on the wall. The rule for mitering ceiling and corner molding is to consider the backplate of the miter box as the "wall" and the baseplate as the "ceiling." This means that you have to place the molding in the miter box upside down.

Mitering Cove Molding. Again, as with other moldings, paint or stain the strips before you cut or install them, and be sure to wait until they are thoroughly dry.

Installing crown or cove molding at the ceiling is very similar to installing baseboard, except for the cutting (see FIGS. 7-30 and 7-31).

1. Measure and cut one full piece of molding for the first wall. Butt both ends against opposite walls with square cuts and nail it to the wall.

2. Facing the corner, take another strip of molding that will fit to the left; measure and square cut both ends. Now, turn the piece end for end and place it in the miter box. Notice that it's upside down and the part that fits to the wall is now against the backplate. Swing the saw 45 degrees to the right and cut your miter.

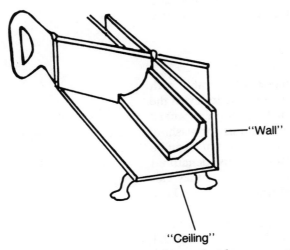

"Wall"

"Ceiling"

Fig. 7–30. Mitering cove moldings. Inside corner.

Fig. 7–31. Mitering cove molding. Outside corner.

3. Next, cut the contour of the attached molding strip into the end of the newly mitered one so that it fits snugly over your first strip of molding. With a utility knife or coping saw, cut away the wood at the back of the miter, using the face edge of the molding as your guide. When you have a snug fit, attach the molding by driving 8d finishing nails, or larger, straight through the center of the strip.

4. Proceed around the room, mitering and contouring each piece to fit over the last square-cut end. On the fourth, or last, piece you might have to miter and cope both ends if you do not have an outside corner from which to work.

5. Set all nail heads and fill with putty. Touch up the strips with paint or other finish.

6. If the ceiling bows, use a caulking gun to fill the gap between ceiling and moldings, then paint caulk to match the ceiling.

SALVAGING EXISTING WOODWORK AND MOLDINGS

Before you begin any large-scale stripping or refinishing process, examine with a critical eye, the worth of the project. Is the wood severely gouged? Can damaged pieces be duplicated with available trim, or combinations of trim, purchased at lumber stores or home centers? Do dark, ugly stains penetrate deep into the wood? Is it hardwood or softwood? Softwoods like pine, are almost impossible to strip, because their porous grains soak finishes deep into the wood fibers. On the other hand, fine-grained hardwood is very much worth the effort. Mahogany, walnut, ash, or cherry would be prohibitively expensive to buy today. Clean away a small patch with some stripper and a sharp scraping tool to find out what's under all of those layers. Raw walnut, by the way, is not brown, but has a grayish cast. Raw mahogany is not a rich, deep red, but ranges from brown to tan (see FIG. 7-32).

Cleaning Old Trim

If shellaced or varnished woodwork has darkened considerably with age, try cleaning away the wax and grime first with turpentine to reveal the wood grain. If this doesn't do the trick, move on to stronger cleaners: trisodium phosphate (TSP), available at paint stores, amonia, or washing soda (sodium carbonate). If the wood has a varnish finish, most of it can be removed with a lacquer thinner diluted with mineral spirits; use denatured alcohol on shellac. Be very careful with the stronger cleaners as they can harm your skin and eyes. Work in a well-ventilated spot and wear rubber gloves and goggles.

If the wood is in good condition at this point, you can restain or paint it after a little sanding. But if too many layers of finish have accumulated over the years, it's best to remove the trim from the wall.

Fig. 7–32. Salvaging authentic moldings. Heavy authentic moldings are restored to their original beauty. Ready-made ruffled curtains and matching bed ensemble enhance the lovely Victorial room design.

Removing Old Trim

The object, of course, is to get the old trim off the wall without splitting or damaging it, and work on it where you can do your finest, without cracking your back. (Sawhorses or a workbench will fill this bill.)

1. First, break the paint seal with a razor or the blade of a utility knife.
2. Now insert a broad-blade putty knife between the molding and wall. Force a second putty knife directly behind the first. Then place a cold chisel or old screwdriver between the knives and pound lightly with a hammer to separate the wood from the wall. As the gap widens, insert a crowbar for greater leverage, leaving the putty knives in place to protect the wall and trim.
3. Draw a sketch of the room on paper. As you remove each piece of trim, label the back with a number and mark a corresponding number at the proper location on your paper plan.
4. Saw through stubborn nails with a hacksaw blade, rather than risk splitting the wood as you free it from the wall. When the strip is removed, don't pound the nails back through the front. File them down, or pull them out through the back with a claw hammer or pliers. Headless finishing nails will offer little resistance.

The Stripping Process

Professional strippers soak the wood in a chemical bath immediately after removing it, but this is risky for the do-it-yourselfer. Follow the surer and safer path outlined below before you move on to the chemical removers.

To Remove Old Paint. Rent a heat gun and a heating iron if you have to remove many layers of old paint. The heating iron is used on flat surfaces; the heat gun is used on rounded areas. The gun looks like a hair drier and melts the old finish by blowing hot air against it. To work it, set the dial at 700 degrees and move it back and forth slowly, 2 to 4 inches away from the painted surface. A heating iron heats the paint itself. Hold the iron flat on the surface just long enough for the paint to bubble. (Don't scorch the wood.) Working in the same direction as the grain, lift off the heated curls of paint with a putty knife or scraper, ever mindful of the fact that each time you gouge or mark the wood with the scraping tool, you'll be left with a dark-colored blemish that will be magnified many times under a new finish.

Chemicals for Removing Old Paint. If the above doesn't work, loosen the paint with a chemical solvent that softens the paint and destroys its bond to the wood surface. Then scrape the paint off with a putty knife or special molding scraper. The best strippers for indoor work are made with methylene chloride. Although they are expensive, they're nonflammable and very effective on oil-based paints, which were commonly used in the past. They're not as effective on water-base (latex) paints.

To cut through latex paint, you'll need a stripper that contains methanol, toluol, and acetone. These chemicals, whether they're combined with methylene chloride or not, are highly flammable. If you use them, keep them away from cigarettes and pilot lights, and don't use soaked pads near electrical outlets. When using any stripper, open doors and windows and protect your skin and eyes. In fact, its best to work outdoors if possible.

Chemicals to Remove Old Varnish. You can buy a varnish remover that's intended for the type of wood you're stripping. Water-base removers are less toxic and less expensive than general purpose solvent-based products, but you shouldn't be using these on plywood, open-grain wood, or veneers, because they'll raise the grain too much. Ask your paint dealer to help you select the right varnish remover. Make sure you follow the precautions on the label, as most removers produce toxic fumes that can be dangerous.

The Stripping Process Using Chemicals. Strippers are sold in both liquid and paste-like forms. For convenience, choose a semiliquid that clings to vertical surfaces. Then follow these steps for best results:

1. Brush the stripper on with single strokes going in one direction. If you move the brush back and forth, the chemicals, which are needed to dissolve the bond between paint and wood, are released into the air, making the stripper less effective.
2. Let the stripper stand about 20 minutes until the paint has liquified; then scrape it from the surface in a continuous curl. If the paint doesn't come up easily, give it another coat and wait again. Be patient. Thick coats of paint sometimes require two or three applications of stripper. Never be tempted to put heaavy pressure on the scraper to hurry up the process; let the stripper do its work.
3. For stubborn grooves and corners, use any scraping tool that'll do the job without damaging the surface: a wood dowel sawed off at a slant with its end wrapped in fine sandpaper or steel wool, an old screwdriver, or a nutpick.
4. Brush away the residue with a scrub brush. Don't wipe it with a rag; this will only work the old finish back into the wood fibers.
5. When the old finish is gone, rinse the wood with denatured alcohol, rubbing it along the grain with a piece of coarse steel wool as you rinse, to remove any residue that might result in a blotchy look.
6. After the surface has dried thoroughly, finish the job by sanding. For large, flat surfaces, you can speed up the job with an orbital sander, outfitted with medium-grit sandpaper. Then, remove all the swirl marks by hand-sanding. Go with the grain, using a fine-grit sandpaper wrapped around a block of wood, until the finish is smooth and mar-free.
7. Sand intricately detailed surfaces or rounded edges with dry steel wool. Or outfit an electric drill with a large flexible-flap sanding wheel or smaller-flapped sanding drum, which are available at hardware

stores. Do not buy the type with wire flaps. For small concave surfaces, glue a layer of felt around a dowel, then hold sandpaper around it to form a sanding block.

8. If you notice some deep stains, lighten them with a fine steel wool pad soaked in oxalic acid or common household bleach. Rub the spot repeatedly until it disappears. You can use this same procedure to bleach woodwork (light-colored woodwork is a new trend in decorating today), but for large-scaled projects you'll get better results with a commercial wood bleach. Most are two-part solutions that are either mixed together or applied in successive steps. Follow the manufacturer's directions.

Filling Gouges

Sometimes you can patch a deep hole instead of replacing the trim. Tap a scattering of holes in the bottom of the gouge with a nail set. This will help the patch to adhere. If you're going to paint over the trim, force vinyl spackling into the nail-set holes with a putty knife, then build upon this layer to the surface of the wood. Use water putty if you plan on staining or varnishing the piece. In areas of heavy wear, like around door casings and window frames, use wood putty. Shape the filler closely to the contours of the molding with a putty knife and your fingers, leaving a slight bulge. When the patch is completely dry, sand it to shape with fine-grit sandpaper.

Applying Paste Wood Filler. If you want a super-smooth "piano" finish on wood, especially woods like walnut, oak, and mahogany, you can apply a paste filler to the pores before applying the finish. The fillers are available in colors, or you can tint a neutral filler to match the stain you've used on the wood. Here's how to apply the filler:

1. Put a quantity of the paste filler in a clean can, and thin it with turpentine or mineral spirits. Blend the mixture until it has the consistency of heavy cream.

2. Brush it on the wood with a stiff-bristled brush, going with the grain. Now, go across the grain to make sure that you're getting it into all the pores.

3. When the filler becomes dull (about a half hour), wipe across the grain with a rough-textured cloth, forcing it into the pores. Now do the final wipes, going with the grain. Let it dry for about 24 hours before applying any finish.

The Refinishing Process

Once molding or other woodwork is stripped, you must apply a finish to it in order to protect the bare wood. If you approach the paint counter unprepared, you'll be overwhelmed by the hundreds of commercial finishes being offered. But if you know beforehand what you want the finish to look like when you're through, you can zero in on the product that will produce the desired results. For instance, if you want to cover up the wood—grain and blemishes alike—use an opaque product like paint, or perhaps, a nonpenetrating wood stain. Both will obscure the blemishes and the grain.

If you want a clear finish applied to bare wood, look for a colorless finish such as shellac, lacquer, varnish, oil, or wax. But remember that no matter what finish you use, you won't end up with the true, natural wood color that you started with. Even the clearest of finishes will eventually turn golden after exposure to sunlight.

If you want to emphasize the grain, or change the color of the wood (example: pine to resemble oak, mahogany, or walnut), use a semitransparent stain.

Here are some of the finishes available to you. The instructions given are general tips. Always read and follow the manufacturer's instructions listed on the label.

Stains. Stains are used to emphasize grain patterns, or change the color of wood, making it look like another species. Besides being available in many shades, you can alter the tone by changing drying time or the number of coats you give it. Wipe the stain on with a rag or sponge until you get the desired shade. When dry, countersink nails, and touch up with a matching putty stick. Finish with a coat of varnish to produce a fine lustre and protect the finish (FIG. 7-33).

Penetrating Stain: The penetrating resin stain is actually a stain with a built-in finish. It's a dye coating that seeps deep into the wood fibers without concealing the grain. When buffed dry, it produces a nice, rich lustre. Then, you apply a coat of wax to protect the finish. The disadvantage of the resin stain is that you can't lighten it. You must wipe off the stain when you deem it dark enough during the application.

Nonpenetrating Stain: This pigment-based stain is more opaque. It rests on the surface of the wood and tends to obscure the grain pattern. A good choice if the wood is blemished or mismatched where mitered.

Oil stain: The pigmented oil stain is the most commonly used. It's durable, long-lasting, and easy to put on. If a section gets too dark while you're working on it, you can lighten it by rubbing it with turpentine or paint thinner, or sand it lighter when it's dry. Before using an oil stain, wipe off the smooth sanded surface with a clean cloth dampened with turpentine or mineral spirits. Many people prefer to apply a thin sealer coat to the bare wood before using an oil stain, which will result in more uniform color distribution. Ask your dealer for a suitable sealer for this purpose. The disadvantage of the oil stain is that it must be given an additional coat, or coats, of a clear finish to produce a lustre.

Latex Stain: This is a water-base stain. It penetrates deeper than the oil stain, and it's easier to apply, but more sanding is required between coats because the water raises the grain.

Fig. 7–33. *Moldings for beauty and budget. You needn't buy expensive milled moldings and casings. Use stained 1 × 2s for contemporary, natural look.*

Clear or Natural Finishes. Clear or natural finishes are colorless, transparent, and they let the wood grain show through. While they don't change the basic color, most of them will give a slightly yellowish cast to the wood. Use a natural bristle brush for applying shellacs and varnishes.

Shellac: Shellac is easy to apply because it goes on without leaving brush marks. It resists moisture but discolors when damp. Expect a limited (6 month) shelf life.

Lacquer: Lacquer is more often used on furniture than woodwork, but if you're looking for a mirror-like finish, this is the finish to use. Don't try applying it with a brush; it dries too fast and will leave brushstrokes. Use a spray applicator instead. Lacquer has a good resistance to wear, but doesn't take moisture well.

Varnishes: There are many varnishes available. The newer ones produce a very pale finish for light-colored, or bleached wood. Most varnishes will give wood a slightly golden look. Ask your paint dealer for assistance when choosing varnishes. Most varnishes dry clear and glossy. They have very tough finishes.

To apply varnish:

1. Be sure the area you're working in is free of dust and lint. The more dust that settles on varnish as it's drying, the more time you will have to spend sanding and smoothing later. Remove all dust particles from the wood with a tack rag before you apply the first coat. To make a tack rag, dampen a soft, lint-free cloth with water, then work a few drops of the turpentine and varnish into the fibers.
2. Thin the first coat with a little turpentine. (All succeeding coats can be used straight from the can.) Make the mix in a separate, clean can. Blend gently with a stick; stirring causes bubbles.
3. Apply the varnish with a new, good-quality, natural-bristle brush or sponge applicator. Dip the end into the varnish and tap it lightly against the inside of the can to remove excess varnish. Don't wipe bristles back and forth across the rim; this only causes tiny, hard-to-remove bubbles in the varnished surface.
4. Brush the varnish on with the grain first; then go across the grain. Finally, holding the brush held at a slight angle, wipe the excess varnish off with the bristles as you pull the brush away. Feather the brush strokes where they overlap, but don't go back and touch up any imperfections in varnish that has leveled and begun to dry. You'll have to sand these spots down and smooth them with the next coat. On large surfaces, work your way quickly and progressively across the whole piece to avoid having to return to an edge that has already dried.
5. Allow the varnish to dry 48 hours. Sand lightly with fine-grit sandpaper and a sanding block. Then wipe with the tack cloth and repeat the process for the second and third coats, using unthinned varnish straight from the can. Let the final coat stand for one week before applying a paste wax.

Polyurethane: Polyurethane (a varnish made from synthetic resins) is generally considered the most durable of all finishes. It comes in matt, satin, semigloss, or glossy finishes. When using polyurethane on softwoods, it's advisable to put a sealer on first to assure even distribution, then apply as you would for regular varnish. Add a coat of wax to improve the gloss and make it shine longer.

Oils. There are two basic types of oil finishes: *linseed* and *tung*. Oils give wood a subtle sheen. Because they penetrate the wood, they do not peel or chip. They are easy to apply, but slow to dry. Although oils are more time-consuming to use they are the most natural finish for wood because they allow the fibers to breathe, which prevents drying and cracking. While they slightly darken the wood, they give it an attractive, mellow lustre. Of the two basic types, linseed is less durable and has no resistance to moisture. Tung oil is both durable and moisture resistant. They are both fairly resistant to scratches. If you decide to stain before using an oil finish, use a water-base stain that will leave the wood more porous than the oil types, which tend to fill pores.

To apply a linseed oil finish, follow these steps:

1. Purchase boiled linseed oil. Mix it in a clean can: two parts of the oil to one part turpentine or mineral spirits.
2. Warm the mixture by placing it inside a larger pan containing very hot water.
3. Use clean, lint-free rags soaked in the mixture to spread it over the wood. Continue rubbing it in until the surface stops absorbing the oil. (As rags become oversaturated, discard them by immersing them in a pail of water to avoid spontaneous combustion.)
4. Next, buff the surface with a clean cloth until the oil stays on the surface and cannot be picked up with your finger when touched. Let dry overnight and repeat the process a second and a third time. The more coats you apply, the more durable and attractive the surface will be.

Wax: Wax is used as a polish over other clear finishes for protection against dirt and wear. It will turn yellow with age and must be periodically stripped and reapplied.

Opaque Finishes. Paint and nonpenetrating wood stains will cover surfaces completely. You can use the less expensive synthetic bristle brushes (nylon or polyester) for latex or water-based paints and stains. Angular sash brushes will get into corners and crevices better. Throwaway pad applicators can also be used. Your choices in paint are as follows:

Latex: Latex paint is odor-free, easy to apply, dries fast, and is a breeze to clean up. But because it contains water, it will raise the grain when you apply it to bare wood. This will require sanding between coats. If latex enamel is used, apply an oil-based primer first. Latex paints are not recommended for doors and woodwork because of their low-wear resistance. they are more commonly used on walls.

Alkyd Paint: Alkyd paint is a durable paint made from synthetic resins and is the most popular choice for woodwork. It's nearly odorless and dries quickly.

Oil: The most durable of paints, oil is the best choice for woodwork in heavy traffic areas. It adheres to bare wood and previously finished surfaces. It's slow to dry and has a strong odor.

If your decorating plans call for painted woodwork, your most difficult job will be choosing the paint color. With a coat or two of enamel paint in such a wide range of colors and glosses, you can make old, unsatisfactory wood trim look like new, and inexpensive "seconds" in new trim look better than new. There are two types of enamel paint recommended for moldings and trim: oil-based and latex (water-thinned). Usually, oil-based enamel produces the best finish and allows you to clean with just damp wipings. The following steps will produce beautiful enamel surfaces.

1. Sand off old finishes with fine sandpaper. Remove old wax, grease, and dirt with a solvent cleaner. Rinse and wipe dry.
2. If the wood is unfinished hardwood, use a paste wood filler to fill

pores; if you're painting softwood, apply a primer or a sealer first. Then rub the wood lightly with fine-grit sandpaper or fine steel wool. Wipe dust away with a damp rag.

3. To avoid drips and runs, try to paint with the wood lying flat. With a good-quality enamel brush, apply an initial coat. When the first coat is thoroughly dry, sand lightly and dust.

4. Brush on the second coat of enamel and let dry. You probably won't need to apply a third coat, but if you do, sand and apply the same as previous coats.

Miscellaneous Finishing Products.

Bleach: Use common household laundry bleach to remove grease and dirt and lighten wood. This will raise the grain of wood, so when the wood is dry, you'll have to sand it smooth.

Primer: An opaque liquid used as an undercoat before applying paint to raw wood to improve the adherence of the paint finish. Use alkyd primer, which does not raise the grain of wood (latex does).

Sealer: A transparent liquid that seals the pores of wood and binds fibers together, without altering the appearance of the wood. Stain, oil, varnish, or paint can be used directly over the sealer.

Filler: Filler is any compound used to fill holes or cover imperfections in wood: wood putty, wood patch, wood dough, plastic wood, vinyl spackling compound or putty stick. Most are available in white, clear, or matching wood tones. Some are applied before finishing and allowed to dry, others are used as a final touch up.

SALVAGING AND RESTORING PRICELESS PLASTER MOLDINGS

Cracks and small pieces that have broken off priceless architectural plaster moldings can be restored or replaced with new plaster and a pointing tool.

Molding plaster can be purchased at most artists' supply stores. Since it contains no lime, it can be handled safely. To mix molding plaster:

1. Fill a bucket half full with water. Sprinkle molding plaster into the bucket until it's almost full, and beat with a paint mixer attached to a power drill. The consistency of the plaster will vary. If you're going to make a shell over a mold, the mixture should be the consistency of thick oatmeal, if the plaster is to be poured into a mold, it can be as thin as honey.

2. Dampen the area around the damage with a spray bottle, then press minute amounts of wet plaster into the crack, or build up the missing part with teaspoonfuls of wet plaster. Then sculpt it back to its original shape with a pointing tool, smoothing the tool lines with a moistened watercolor brush until it matches the original cast.

(Continued on p. 172.)

"Colonialize" a Wall with Moldings

The one most certain way to capture the colonial spirit in a house is to focus on the walls. The charm of colonial interiors is in the attention craftsmen gave to proportion and detail in this area. Nowhere will your work be more scrutinized or more appreciated than on the walls. To "colonialize" your house, use traditional moldings, which are wider and more ornate than contemporary moldings, and use profiles that stand out in their fine detailing, even if you have to double them up to get a more massive effect.

Colonial ceilings always received special attention in downstairs and guest-receiving rooms, so some sort of deep crown molding is a must. Additional moldings and medallions accentuating ceiling fixtures would be a pleasant and rich-looking accompaniment.

Molding rectangles were spaced along the walls in eye-pleasing proportion, determining the relationship between windows, doors, fireplaces, built-ins, and the walls.

Here are some designs for you to try. Let your imagination have free reign when selecting and combining patterns for warm, gracious, colonial Williamsburg interiors.

- ▶ An inexpensive way to produce a rich-looking, yet understated background, is to cover both wall and moldings with white paint (opposite, top left).
- ▶ Stain the plywood dado portion of the wall, along with moldings, a rich, mellow wood-tone; then paint the top section a shade of colonial green, rose, ivory, or tan (opposite, top right). The ceiling molding should match the dado wall.
- ▶ Paint the moldings and bottom part of the wall one color; then use a coordinating wallpaper on the upper section of the wall (opposite, bottom left).
- ▶ Cover the wall with stained plywood paneling and apply matching moldings (opposite, bottom right). Use a heavy ceiling and base molding for this type of "library" wall.

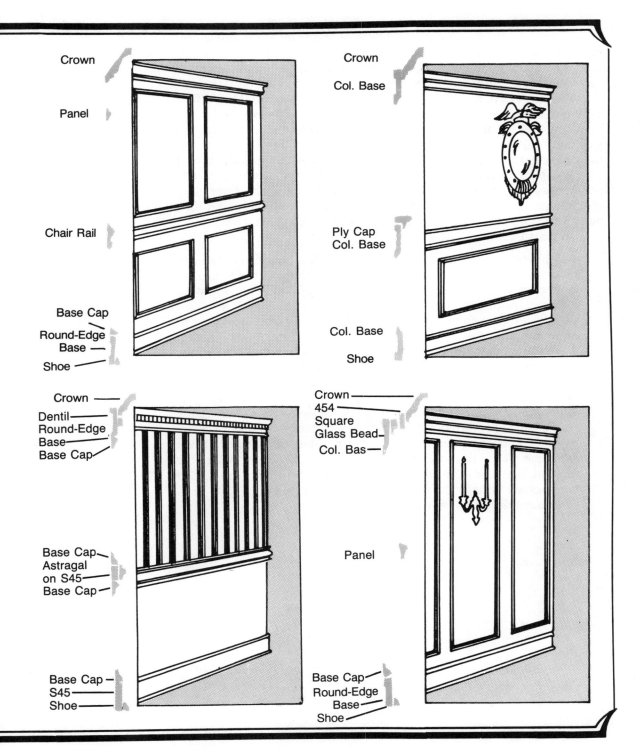

Crown

Panel

Chair Rail

Base Cap

Round-Edge Base

Shoe

Crown

Col. Base

Ply Cap
Col. Base

Col. Base

Shoe

Crown
Dentil
Round-Edge Base
Base Cap

Base Cap
Astragal
on S45
Base Cap

Base Cap
S45
Shoe

Crown
454
Square
Glass Bead
Col. Bas

Panel

Base Cap
Round-Edge Base
Shoe

Larger sections of sculptured architectual ceiling moldings and adornments can be copied and recast. You can replace a small part or an entire section by making a mold of a section that's still intact using a water-based clay available at artists' supply stores.

You don't have to remove the molding to make the cast. Dust off the section of molding you want duplicated, then brush on a clear shellac and let it dry. Make a mixture of three parts kerosene to one part petroleum jelly and brush it over the dried shellac. Press an inch-thick slab of clay over the sculptured plaster, then spread a layer of plaster, $\frac{1}{4}$-inch thick, over the clay. Next, embed a strip of burlap into the wet plaster, then add another layer of plaster over the burlap. Wait about a half hour, then carefully pry the clay and plaster mold from the original molding with a putty knife and pointing tool. Allow the mold to dry thoroughly.

To pour the cast:

1. Moisten the clay with a mist of water. Then pour a thin layer of plaster into the mold. Jostle it so that all the air bubbles rise to the top.
2. Press a piece of cheesecloth over the wet plaster. Wait about 10 minutes, then pour a second layer to fill the mold. After this has set slightly, level it with the edge of a ruler. Let the cast dry hard for about 30 minutes.
3. While the cast is drying, cut and shape the damaged area of the original molding with a chisel to receive the back of the new cast. Shave down the sides and back of the cast to fit the depression you made in the original molding.
4. Score the back of the cast and the depression with a utility knife before you apply the construction or panel adhesive so it will adhere.
5. Apply enough adhesive to bring the molding face flush with the adjoining pieces. Press the new cast in firmly, and let set. When the molding is dry, you can add additional support by driving flat-headed brass screws through the molding into joists or studs.
6. Conceal the joints with plaster and a pointing tool.

[8]

Floors

Perhaps when you first visited the old house and saw its grimy, sagging, and creaking floors, you saw only the natural beauty in them — charm that no other prospective buyer saw. But now the moment of truth has come. Did you really detect a hidden treasure with solid hardwood floors that just need to be honed and polished to their original beauty, or was it fool's gold — worthless old boards in bad repair that need to be ripped up or covered over? Your job could be a labor of love, or it could be an exercise in futility.

Happily, there are ways to salvage floors — even those in the worst shape — and you can do it with style. Some of the alternatives may not last forever, but they will get you through a resale, or give you breathing room until there's enough money in the checkbook again to completely redo them. For instance, you could paint hopelessly blemished floors an opaque color. Or take up old carpeting, salvage an unworn part, bind it, then use it again in the center of the room as an area rug. The exposed perimeter flooring could be painted or stained.

Your alternatives for refinishing or resurfacing range from simple and inexpensive, to extravagant and complex. So take a close look at all the options before you choose.

Whichever method you choose, you'll have to make any necessary repairs first. Sagging floors in an older home are not uncommon. Original posts, girders, joists, and bridging may have shifted or absorbed moisture, which caused them to rot or shrink. Termites may have eaten away at structural members and weakened them. These are not insurmountable problems; repairs or replacements can be made quite easily from the basement or a crawl space. Leveling floors on the second story is quite another matter, however. Since part of the ceiling has to be removed to get at the joists, and aesthetics may prevent permanent jack posts from being installed, you may have to consult with an architect.

Squeaky floors are also quite common in older buildings, but they do not indicate a serious problem. Usually a few boards just need securing.

Both hardwood and softwood floors can be refinished or restored. But if more boards have to be replaced than can be saved, if broken parts can't be matched, or if areas are severely worn into deep valleys, your floors are not sufficiently sound and they should be recovered — not only with a new finish floor, but with a subfloor as well. Usually, this means an underlayment of some sort, like plywood or hardboard sheeting. While it guarantees you a solid new base, it also means extra time and expense.

If you're installing materials below grade, that is, beneath ground level, you must also consider the inevitable moisture problem. Be sure to consult with professionals and flooring dealers on this. Humidity and wet concrete can cause problems; so can moisture evaporating from the ground under crawl spaces. Make sure concrete in basements is well cured; and ventilate and cover the ground under crawl spaces with polyethylene sheets to prevent moisture from getting through to floor coverings.

As far as choosing floor finishing materials, there are so many choices available today that it's sometimes difficult to know what's best. But a few pros and cons on vinyl, wood, masonry, and carpeting will enlighten and guide you toward a better selection for your particular needs, and keep you within safe confines of your do-it-yourself abilities.

REPAIRING FLOORS

A small dip in a floor usually isn't cause for concern, but anything with a more extensive slope may indicate a serious structural problem. If it's a downward sag toward an outer wall, it might have been caused by a settled foundation. Cracked or rotting joists can also cause a floor to sag badly. You can reinforce cracked joists, but termite-damaged ones should be replaced.

For first-floor sags, a telescoping house jack can be installed in the basement to boost the drooping area. In a crawl space, a small bell-shaped contractor's jack can be used. In either case, raise the jacks about a 1/16-inch per day until the sag is corrected. Moving the joists faster than this can cause additional structural damage.

Sag repairs on the second floor are more difficult to fix because of cosmetic considerations. You must remove part of the first floor ceiling to get at the sagging joists. Then you have to devise a way to support the joists from below so the floor stays level. But where there's a will, there's a way. For instance, you could devise a clever decorative column or support that will complement, rather than detract from, the downstair's appearance.

Small floor areas that give or creak when walked on indicate gaps between joists and subfloor. These spaces can be filled with glue-dipped shims. This, of course, must be done from the basement or crawl space. Be sure you don't drive the shims in too far, separating the subfloor from the joists even more. Wedge them in firmly, just filling up the gap.

You can also brace larger gaps with 1 by 4s or 2 by 4s, positioned snugly up to the subfloor and nailed to both sides of a warped joist.

Joists that rack or move can also cause sags and floor vibration. Usually the cause is loose nails, too few nails, or insufficient bridging. Drive in new nails, slightly larger than the old ones. For more rigidity, add solid bridging to the joists. (See FIG. 8-1.)

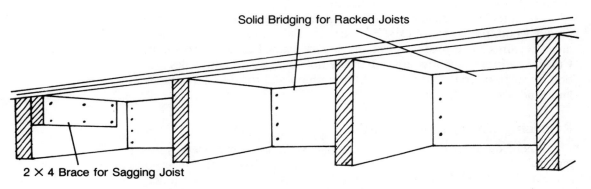

Fig. 8-1. Bracing sagging and racked joists.

Eliminating Squeaks

Squeaks in floors are usually caused by chafing boards. Nails holding the subfloor and finish floor together work loose and cause the boards to rub against each other. Boards also warp and shrink over the years, causing gaps between layers that make noises when you step on them. Floor squeaks can be temporarily silenced by lubricating the edges of loose boards with graphite powder or talc and tapping them so the powder filters down into the cracks.

You can silence squeaks permanently with nails. Locate the squeak by walking around the floor. If the finish floor moves, a few ring-shanked nails driven in at opposite angles next to the joist will fasten loose boards down. Pound the nails about a half inch into the joist using a nail set, then fill the holes with putty or plastic filler. Always drill pilot holes first to prevent the wood from splitting.

If the finish floor does not move when you step on it, but the squeak persists, the problem is probably in the subflooring. Use long screws instead of nails to pull the boards down, penetrating the joist by about an inch.

If you can work from the basement or crawl space, the repair will be neater and less noticeable. Drill pilot holes up through the subfloor and secure the subfloor to the finish floor with no. 10 or no. 12 wood screws that are $1\frac{1}{4}$ inch long.

Filling Cracks and Holes

Most small cracks can be filled with a paste mixture of four parts sanding dust to one part penetrating sealer, tinted the color of the floor. For wider cracks, stuff lengths of felt weatherstripping into the crevice with a wide-blade putty knife, stopping at a level ⅛ inch below the surface of the finish floor. Then mix up a batch of the sanding dust/sealer paste and fill the rest of the crack to the floor surface level.

For holes left by the removal of pipes, the strongest and most desirable plug is wood, preferably of existing floor material. But for out-of-the-way areas, repairs can be made with pieces of cork stained to match the floor. Cut the cork plug slightly larger than the hole and grease both sides and bottom, then pound it into the hole. Smooth off all protruding fragments and sand it level with the floor.

Replacing Finish Floor Boards

When boards are damaged beyond repair, or bare spaces are left by the removal of a wall, you'll have to consider board replacement. Since 90 percent of all wood floors are made of oak, you shouldn't have too much trouble matching your flooring at a local lumberyard. Even if your floors are made of inexpensive pine or fir (commonly found in farmhouses), you should be able to find a decent match. But if your house is more than 50 years old, the original builder may have used something more exotic like walnut, cherry, maple, or pecan. In this case, you may be off on an extended treasure hunt to replace the missing parts. Add to this problem the differences in thickness, texture, and width, and you could also be in for a custom fitting and total refinishing job. Still, it will behoove you to pay the difference—in time and money—to match up the floor with the more expensive wood. Just remember to emphasize the highly treasured floor feature when it comes to selling the house.

Sometimes when we remove a wall, we're left with a space that is unequal to flooring boards; often times the space runs perpendicular to existing flooring. An attractive way to fill in the space is to use one wide board, cut to fit, which will serve as a transition between two different kinds of flooring (FIG. 8-2). Stain the floor all one color to make the wood look alike. Seal with polyurethane.

Where wood flooring meets with another material, treat the floor as you would walls by using molding. Miter the boards to a 45-degree angle and frame the hearth section, or other protrusion, for a professional-looking finish. You will have to remove tongues from boards that run perpendicular to the flooring, or that must butt against hearth stones and other objects (FIG. 8-3).

When patching a strip or plank wood floor, you have two ways to replace the boards. The easiest way is to cut out a square or rectangle that encompasses the damaged area. This leaves a noticeable patch, but if

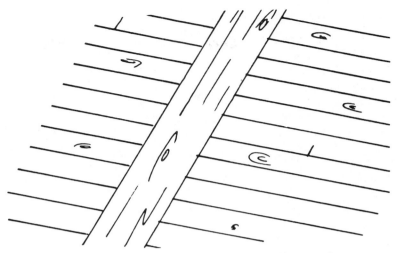

Fig. 8–2. Repairing floors after wall removal.

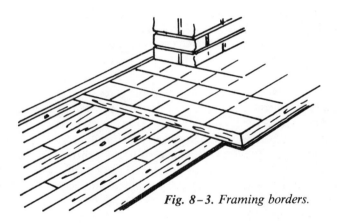

Fig. 8–3. Framing borders.

you're going to cover the area with carpeting or furniture anyway, it won't matter.

Use the staggered method of board replacement where the flooring is visible. Although this process is more difficult and time-consuming, it disguises the patching job more effectively.

To replace boards in a rectangular opening:

1. Mark off a rectangular patch using a carpenter's square and pencil. Keep $\frac{1}{4}$ inch inside the lines on the tongue-and-groove edges so you don't saw into any nailing.

2. With a power saw, score a strip of wood down the center of the rectangle, running parallel to the side edges of the boards. Then saw

around on the rectangular lines. Carefully remove the center strip with a chisel and pry bar; then proceed to remove the rest of the boards working from the center to the marked edges (FIG. 8-4).

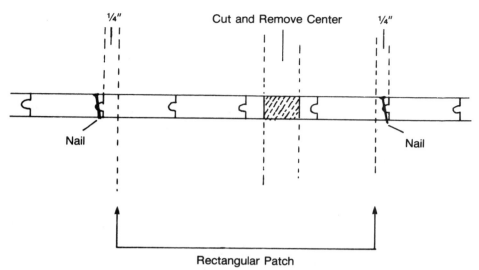

Fig. 8–4. Cutting out floor boards.

3. Use a hammer and chisel to carefully remove the ¼-inch waste pieces attached to the tongue and grooves of the old boards. Set any protruding nails.

4. To lay new boards, make your cuts, carefully sawing on the waste side of the pencil marks so you don't unintentionally make them shorter. Fit the first board into place, sliding it over the tongue of the old board, and pound it snug with a block and hammer. Blind nail with 8d finishing nails, driven in at 45-degree angles through the tongue. Proceed to lay the new boards one at a time until you reach the last board in the patch.

5. Remove the tongue and sand the edge of the last board so it will fit snugly. Then tap it into place. Finally, face-nail the board, set the nailheads, and fill the holes with putty (FIG. 8-5).

To replace boards in a staggered opening:

1. Make pencil lines across each board in a staggered manner, marking off the damaged area to be cut away.

2. Make clean vertical cuts down on the drawn lines with a chisel and hammer, keeping the beveled edge of the chisel facing the damaged area.

3. Next, hold the chisel at a 30-degree angle with the beveled edge still facing the damaged area, and V-cut all the way through the board to the subfloor at the vertical cut line (FIG. 8-6).

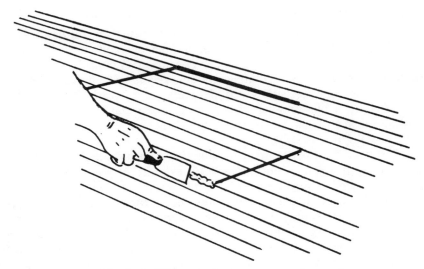

Fig. 8–5. Filling cracks in a rectangular patch.

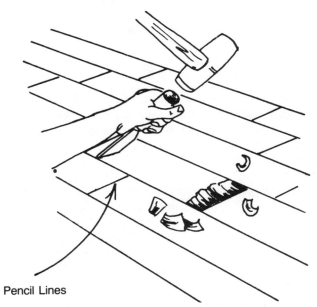

Pencil Lines

Fig. 8–6. Chiseling out old floor boards.

4. Remove the center board by cutting it with a power saw as in Step 2 of the "Rectangular Patch" instructions above. Then follow through, removing the rest of the boards from center to ends.
5. Trim off the tongue on the last board, and face-nail it in place.

Resurfacing Old Floors with an Underlayment

Actually, you can lay new flooring over most surfaces: worn wood, strip flooring, old linoleum, vinyl or asphalt tile, or a concrete subfloor—if the floors are in relatively good shape. Your primary consideration should be that the subfloor is absolutely smooth, clean, tight, dry, and level. If your existing floor meets these requirements, forge ahead. Scrape the floor free of paint or plaster splatterings, check to see that all nails are driven flush, remove base shoe or quarter round, vacuum well, and begin to lay your new flooring.

If the old floor has loose or missing tiles or boards, and you can patch them to form a solid, continuous surface—fine. If you can scrape and remove chipped or torn linoleum down to a level subfloor, well and good. But where irregularities are so bad that the end results are doubtful, you should recover the entire floor with an underlayment. This can be from $\frac{3}{8}$- to $\frac{5}{8}$-inch exterior-grade plywood, or thinner underlayment grade particleboard or tempered hardboard. A water-resistant underlayment should be used in kitchens and bathrooms. Most people prefer the plywood because it's easier to nail into. The subfloor should be installed over the old floor with staggered joints $\frac{1}{16}$ inches apart for expansion and contraction, fastened with $1\frac{1}{4}$ inch annular nails or wood screws that are spaced about 6 inches apart over the entire floor surface. Be sure that all nails are pounded in flush.

Damp-Proofing Concrete Floors

If your installation is over a concrete floor with irregularities such as dips, hollows, and bumps, rent a commercially available grinding machine for smoothing the bumps and fill in the indentations with a quick-setting latex patching compound to level the floor.

In some cases (almost always below grade) a concrete floor may require a membrane of 4- to 6-mil polyethylene to create a water vapor barrier, which will prevent moisture from seeping upward through the concrete and ruining the tile. Such a membrane is also required over "green" concrete, or over concrete floors that did not have vapor barrier installed underneath during construction. A vapor barrier is not required if you are laying the tile over an existing wood or plywood subfloor, or concrete subfloor that is above the ground level.

To damp-proof a concrete floor:

1. Sweep the floor, then mop or squeegee a primer over the entire surface. The manufacturer will probably recommend an organic adhesive. Allow the proper drying time for the primer; then, with the flat side of a tiling trowel, apply a skim coat of adhesive. Allow the skim coat to become tacky.
2. Start at the entrance side of the room and roll a 3- to 4-foot-wide polyethylene strip to the opposite wall. Let the strip roll slightly up the wall and cut it off. Lay another strip alongside of the first one, over-

lapping it about 4 inches. Cover the entire floor in this manner. You'll need to apply only one layer of the film. Ignore occasional blisters or bubbles; they will not impair the film's effectiveness as the tiles, installed over the film, will compress them.

Installing the Subfloor

Store the panels flat with airspaces in between, so they can adjust to the temperature conditions in the room. Do not attempt to install the underlayment if conditions in the room are too humid or unusually dry. Choose a time when room temperatures are normal, or you'll end up with a shrinking or swelling problem later.

Remove the base shoe and lay out the sheets so they overlap existing floor seams. Going by the nailing in the old floor or subfloor, drive the annular nails (or screws) through the underlayment and old floor into the joist below. Nail every 4 to 6 inches apart, keeping ⅜ inches in from the edges of the underlayment sheets. Allow ¹⁄₁₆ inch between sheets for minor expansion. After the subfloor is installed, patch cracks and nail dimples with wood putty. This is especially important if you're laying thin, resilient flooring goods. Sand the putty down after it has dried and vacuum the new floor thoroughly.

WOOD FLOORS

Today's home buyers are focusing on floors, and the wonderful warm feeling of wood ranks high in appeal. Not too many years ago, the rage was wall-to-wall carpeting; but now floor-bored buyers want something with a more enduring quality—and something that will ensure a good return on their investment. Solid wood floors fill the bill.

It used to take a master craftsman to lay a wood floor; today you can do it easily in just a day. Some varieties are installed with mastic, like the vinyl or asphalt tiles; a few brands are made to be nailed in place; and others come with a self-adhesive backing. Follow the manufacturers instructions for each tile installation, use their special trims for finishing, and you will be practically guaranteed of a perfect, professional-looking job.

When it comes to floor finishes, dark floors are considered to be more attractive as a background for fine furnishing—and more practical. But a new chic look is emerging, that of bleached, or pickled wood. And this makes a beautiful background for hand-painted floor designs, or the charming "parquet" stencil borders that one can easily paint around the room. Since the development of polyurethane finishes, we can apply fabric and wallpaper to our floors, and they'll wear—even with hard usage—for over a year before we have to reapply a new finish.

Styles

Whether you choose hardwood strip flooring, planks, or parquet blocks, you can be assured of durability, because wood floors will last the life of your house. Genuine wood flooring is not inexpensive (it costs about the same as a good carpet, installed) and, like everything else, prices vary according to type and quality. Special styles, like random-width planking, ranch planks with beveled edges and walnut pegs, cost more. But each offers a special, stylized look. So shop around. Just remember that what you pay for in product, you'll make up for in labor costs.

Parquet Flooring. A favorite choice today, is the elegant look of parquet, which comes in bundles of 6-, 9- and 12-inch squares, and in thicknesses from 5/16-inch to 3/4-inch. Parquet resembles inlaid wood mosaic with short strips of oak, teak, or walnut laid in geometric shapes that create patterns such as herringbone and basketweave. They come prefinished or unfinished, butt-edged or tongue-and-grooved, and in solid or laminated wood blocks. The thicker parquet tiles are usually laid with mastic and are very durable; but even the thinner, self-adhesive-backed ones offer a decorative and functional floor. These wood floors are not recommended for kitchens and bathrooms, but they are appropriate in any other room in the house.

Strip Flooring. Although wide pine boards typify the traditional "country" look and are probably the cheapest lumber you can buy, they have some major drawbacks. Because pine is softwood, it scars and dents easily. Besides this, pine boards will shrink if not seasoned properly. If you buy green lumber, you'll have to cure it for at least 6 months; if you buy seasoned lumber, you'll pay a premium price. That leaves the hardwoods as the logical buy.

When people refer to "hardwood flooring" they're usually talking about oak strip flooring. Oak strip flooring can be found in houses from 20 to 50 years old; before that they often used pine or fir, and even cypress.

The most commonly used oak flooring is the tongue-and-groove strips, 2 1/4 inch wide by 25/32 inches thick. But it also comes in strips from 1 1/2 to 3 1/4 inches wide, and in 3/8- and 1/2-inch thicknesses. The thinner dimension is not only less expensive, it doesn't raise the floor level as much if you're installing it over old flooring. You can purchase strip flooring in white or red oak, and also in birch, beech, hard maple, and pecan. Most of the strip flooring comes tongue-and-grooved for tight and easy installation. The less-often used square-edged flooring is simply butted together and face-nailed, but each nail must be set and filled with putty before finishing.

Plank Flooring. A hardwood plank is closer to the "country" look of pine boards than any of the other wood flooring products. Planks are wider than strips (3, 5, and 7 inches), and the widths can be combined for a more interesting effect. You can buy prefinished oak tongue-and-groove planks, or ones prestudded with pegs or wrought iron nails.

RESTORING HARDWOOD FLOORS

Does your wood floor need refinishing or just a good cleaning? Layers and layers of wax buildup may make it look like the hard finish is patchy and uneven, but perhaps all that's needed is a good washing, stripping, and waxing.

To wash your wood floor, mix a strong solution of TSP and water (1 cup to 1 bucket of hot water), and scrub it in small sections with a good stiff scrub brush. Remove the water with a sponge or terry towel from each section immediately after scrubbing. Then move on to a new section and repeat the process until the entire floor has been washed. Remember that water left on wood too long can raise the grain and make it rough, so it's important to wipe it up immediately. After the entire floor has been scrubbed, rinse out the sponge and go back over the floor again with clear, lukewarm water. Change the water in the bucket often as you rinse, and use clean towels to wipe it dry.

Removing Blemishes and Stains

Once the floor is dry remove black heel marks with fine sandpaper or steel wool. For water spots, dampen the steel wool in mineral spirits or a solvent-based floor cleaner and rub until the spot disappears.

Scratches can usually be buffed out with a good coat of wax, but dark stains need to be rubbed out with steel wool dipped in mineral spirits and followed by a rinse of vinegar to neutralize the bleach. If the stain is still visible, try sandpaper, feathering out from the stain so that the new finish will blend in with the old. If this doesn't work, try dabbing on oxalic acid (a bleach), until the spot is lightened; use one ounce to a quart of water. (Always wear rubber gloves when using toxic products.) Then rinse with a vinegar and water mixture, and towel dry. When the area is dry, apply a stain that matches the surrounding color.

For burns that haven't penetrated too deeply, sand with steel wool dampened with soap and water.

If small patches of the varnish or polyurethane floor finish has worn off, you can sometimes spot-repair it successfully after the cleaning. Use steel wool to smooth out the affected spot; go an inch beyond. Then wipe up the dust with a cloth dampened with mineral spirits. When dry, brush on one or more thin coats of finish, feathering it into the old finish to prevent lap marks. Allow plenty of drying time between coats. Then apply a good coat of wax to the whole floor.

Don't attempt to spot-repair shellac or lacquer finishes; they're almost impossible to patch successfully. The alternative is sanding the entire room and applying a new finish.

Refinishing Prefinished Flooring. Prefinished flooring should not be sanded. If the floors are discolored by traffic scuffs, use a renovator or reconditioning product put out by the prefinished flooring manufacturer for just this purpose. The product will restore the flooring to its original finish without sanding. Usually, prefinished flooring can be determined by it's beveled edges on each strip or square, or by scratching the surface finish with a coin. If it does not flake off, it was manufactured with a penetrating sealer, which means that that renovating product can be used effectively.

Refinishing Priceless Wood. Priceless wood, such as antique parquet or marquetry, should never be sealed with polyurethane or penetrating sealers. Continuous stripping and sanding would invariably damage and devalue the fine wood. Instead, apply periodic coats of paste wax, by hand, and buff to a protective sheen.

Waxing Wood Floors

Now take another look at your floor. Perhaps all that's needed is several good coats of wax and a buffing.

Stripping. Although you can find products on the market for stripping wax off floors, most waxes can be removed with mineral spirits, fine steel wool, and a soft cloth. Strip the old wax down to the bare finish by pouring a small amount of the mineral spirits on the floor and spreading it around with steel wool. When the old wax is loose, remove the solvent and wax with a rag. Provide adequate ventilation while doing this and dispose the rags in a proper manner. Such solvents can be highly flammable.

Waxing. Wax has been used to protect floors for ages. In the four-teenth century, crude beeswax was melted down and poured over wood and stone floors. The commercially formulated blends of turpentine and beeswax became available in the eighteenth century. Eventually, our self-polishing products were developed. Such products contain high contents of solvents that dissolve and melt away dirt and old wax as they add their own sheen.

Today a host of floor wax products are available—all advertised to beautify, protect, and preserve your floor with a minimum of time and effort. Basically, though, there are only two types of waxes: a solvent-base wax and a water-base wax.

The solvent-base wax contains naptha or turpentine and is recommended for all types of floors—except asphalt and rubber tile. While this type requires buffing, it usually gives the best protection over a longer period of time. You can buy it in either paste or liquid form.

Because the solvent acts as a dry-cleaning agent, the wax cleans as it polishes. With this type, floors should be waxed at least 2 or 3 times a year. It isn't necessary to strip the wax before rewaxing, because the new coat dissolves into the previous one. Paste wax requires about a half hour drying time before buffing. The easiest way to get a hard, polished surface with a paste wax is to use an electric buffer, but if you polish by hand, use a soft cloth and begin while the wax is a bit moist.

The water-base wax is a liquid wax that dries with a shine. It's easy to use but must be removed after several applications to avoid build-up and discoloration. Water-base wax is the only type you should use on asphalt and rubber tile. Apply the wax with a soft clean cloth or lamb's wool applicator to small areas. On wood floors, be sure to follow the grain of the wood. Always keep the coats thin; it's better to apply 2 or 3 thin coats rather than one thick one. Thick ones tend to dry with a smeared appearance.

Sanding the Floor

If your minor restoration efforts don't yield satisfactory results, you might have to sand and refinish the entire floor. In small areas, like foyers, a commercial paint stripper will probably do away with most of the old finish, and you can remove the rest with a small electric hand sander. But where you have large surfaces to finish, or you want to lighten the color or remove some nicks, gouges, and blemishes, you'll have to sand the floor down to the raw wood, and maybe slightly beyond. This will require renting a heavy-duty commercial floor sander and committing yourself to a dirty, tedious, and sometimes back-racking job, but below the marred surface lies beautiful fresh wood that only machine sanding will expose.

Before you sand a wood floor, be sure that it's not one of the new prefinished floors with a veneer face, or that it hasn't already been sanded down so thin that another sanding will expose the nails and grooves at the floor's joints. Check also to see what electric current the machine demands.

Actually, you'll be renting two machines: the drum sander and the edger. The drum sander does the job on the large inside surfaces; the edger sands the places that the drum sander can't reach, like around the perimeter of the room.

The drum sander works like a power lawnmower. It's heavy and unwieldy, and you'll have to keep it under control at all times. If it's allowed to stay in one spot, it will cause a deep impression that you won't be able to repair. The machine must be kept moving across the floor when the power switch is on.

You'll probably have to take each sander over the floor three times with coarse-, medium-, and fine-grit sandpaper before you can expect satisfactory results. Your rental dealer can provide you with everything you need for the sanding process: plenty of sheets of each of the three grades of sandpaper (20-, 40-, and 199-grit) for both machines; a heavy-duty, extra-long extension cord; and full instructions on how to use the machines. You will also need a small hand-held scraper to reach into corners and under radiators, along with a sanding block for finishing off these tight spots.

To begin, clear the room. Open all windows and outside doors. Close all doors to adjacent rooms, and stuff newspapers or rags under them. Sanding produces a highly flammable dust; be sure to turn off all pilot lights and gas appliances. Wear goggles, a respirator, and cover your hair.

Set all nails in the old floor; protruding nails will shred the sandpaper to pieces. Remove base shoe and baseboards to enable the sander to get as close as possible to the wall. Attach the coarse sandpaper to the drum sander, and while it's still unplugged, move it into position along the right wall, close to the corner. Make sure that you'll be sanding with the grain.

Plug the machine in and tilt it up at a 45-degree angle, so that it won't run away when the power switch is turned on. Sling the extension cord over your shoulder to get it out of the way, then turn the switch on. When the motor is at full speed, lower the machine slowly until the sandpaper makes contact with the floor. Then let the sander pull you long, moving slowly forward with the grain (FIG. 8-7). Always keep the sander in constant motion.

When you reach the other side, pull the sander back slowly and tilt it up so you can turn it around. Make a complete turn on the wheels, and face the direction from which you came. Move the sander over about 3 or 4 inches and set it down again overlapping the path you just traveled.

When you reach your starting point, tilt the drum up from the floor again, move the machine over another 3 or 4 inches, and repeat the process. Continue until the floor is completely sanded.

Now put the coarse sandpaper on the edger and sand all around the edges of the room where the drum sander wasn't able to reach. Start at a corner near the baseboard and work outward to blend in with the wood that was sanded by the drum sander. The rotating disk on the edger can be moved in any direction on the wood, but it also has a mind of its own, so you'll have to grasp it securely. To do the edging, you'll have to work on your knees or in a semi-crouch position, with your feet spread about 2 feet apart. Move the edger in a brisk left-to-right looping motion that butts into the baseboard (FIG. 8-8).

After you've edged all around the room with the coarse sandpaper, change to the medium grit, and repeat the drum and edge sanding for the second sanding. Then change to fine grit for the third sanding. Change the sandpaper on the drum and edger as often as needed if it wears down.

In corners, around pipes, and under radiators that can't be moved, you'll have to use a sharp paint scraper. Pull it toward you, working with

Fig. 8–7. Working the sander.

Fig. 8-8. Using the edger.

the grain of the wood. Finally, sand by hand, using all three grades of paper.

Vacuum up the dust and wipe the floor with a tack rag. Don't wet the floor to any degree, and don't use an oily mop. This will only darken the wood and interfere with the finishing process.

Examine the floor carefully for scratches or swirl marks left by the machines and hand-sand them smooth. Fill cracks and nail holes with a paste made from the sanding dust and a floor sealer. Sand the filled areas smooth when dry.

Sanding Parquet, Block, or Herringbone Wood Floors. Sand parquet, block, or herringbone floors on a diagonal with medium-grit sandpaper. Then sand on the opposite diagonal with fine-grit sandpaper. Do the final sanding with fine sandpaper across the width of the room.

Sanding Painted Floors. If an old floor has been painted many times before, use a paint stripper first, to uncover the wood. Old paint requires too much sanding and gums up the sandpaper too often to make removal by sanding feasible.

Finishing Wood Floors

After your floors have been completely sanded and wiped down with a tack rag to remove lint and dust, you're ready to apply the finish coats. The first coat of stain, or other finish, should be applied the same day you complete the sanding to prevent moisture from getting into the pores and raising the grain.

There are actually four steps that result in an exceptional floor finish: 1. applying a color or tone (if desired); 2. sealing the pores; 3. applying a hard protective finish, and 4. waxing to protect the underlying coats. The only short cut you should take is combining Steps 1 and 2, if you wish to use a penetrating sealer that includes a stain. All the rest of the steps should be taken in the proper sequence and executed with care.

Stain. If you want to leave floors the color of sanded wood, you need only to apply a clear sealer and two coats of paste wax. Remember, though, that even a clear finish will darken the wood somewhat.

If you prefer an almost-white finish, one that doesn't obscure the grain, try bleaching or pickling the wood. But if you want the wood colored or toned with the natural grain emphasized, stain it. A stain is simply a pigment in liquid form that gives wood its desired color. Stains are not to be regarded as protective finishes; they are cosmetic. All stains leave the grain of wood partially open, thereby making it vulnerable to moisture and dirt.

There are two types of stains: a wiping stain that stays on the surface of the wood, and a penetrating stain that seeps deep into the fibers. The nonpenetrating wiping stain is usually more opaque than the penetrating stain. It rests on the surface of the wood and tends to obscure the grain pattern—a good choice if the wood is blemished or mismatched. If you want the wood lighter, rub some of the stain off before it dries. To darken it, give it the second coat after the first is thoroughly dry. Follow with a clear penetrating sealer, a hard protective finish coat, and/or two coats of wax.

A penetrating stain seeps into the wood fibers without concealing the grain. This type can't be lightened by rubbing if you've used too heavy a hand in the application, because it's absorbed in the fibers. For the same reason, it fades less. Since stains get their color from dye, and dye fades when exposed to sunlight, the penetrating stain will last a long time.

Sealers. All wood floors are porous, whether or not they are stained. A sealer is required to close the pores and protect the wood from the damaging effects of moisture and wear. Also, without a sealer your finish coat of shellac, varnish, or polyurethane will sink into the wood instead of remaining on top for protection and cause an uneven shine.

The clear penetrating sealer is the easiest to apply. It delivers a low-gloss, satiny finish that wears as the wood wears because it's embedded in the fibers. Some of the penetrating sealers come with a dye already in them, allowing you to stain and seal in one operation. These types of sealer-stains will not fade, chip, or scratch. Even after years of wear you can usually refinish a floor with a clear coat without sanding, because it won't leave lap marks. You can also buy a special renovator or conditioner for penetrating sealers to use where traffic or other conditions caused discoloration or wear spots. (See "Finishing Prefinished Flooring," earlier in the chapter.)

You can use a brush, rag, or squeegee, but a long-handled lamb's wool applicator dipped in a half-full paint roller pan is the easiest and fastest way to apply a penetrating sealer. Apply it generously, using broad strokes with the grain of the wood. Wipe up any excess as you go along; if allowed to puddle and dry, you'll be left with an uneven look.

Wait 8 hours, then buff with a commercial polisher (from rental store). Attach the heavy-duty brush on the polisher, and press fine steel wool pads into the bristles. These will buff out any bubbles that form in the sealer as they rough up the surface for the next coat (FIG. 8-9).

Vacuum and wipe the surface with a tack rag. Apply a second coat of penetrating sealer and follow through as above with the steel-wool buffing. Wait 24 hours before giving your sealed floors a protective, hard-coat finish.

Protective Finishes. After putting on the sealer, you must apply a protective finish to help the floor withstand moisture and abrasive action. Your choices are varnish, shellac, lacquer, and polyurethane—in matte, semi- or high-gloss finishes. The hands-down favorite for floors is polyurethane.

Varnish takes 24 hours to dry, and you must prevent dust and lint from getting into the finish during the drying time. It tends to dry darker, and it yellows with age. It's extremely difficult to touch up without showing lap marks.

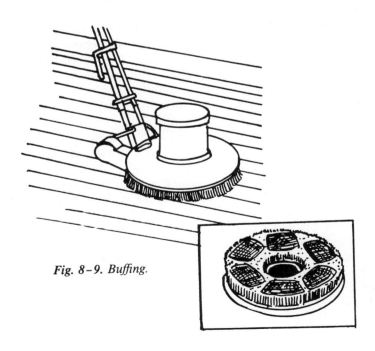

Fig. 8-9. Buffing.

Shellac dries fast (you can apply two coats in a day), but it's easily damaged by water and abrasion. Furthermore, frictional heat will soften the finish and permit dirt to get in. Waxing is absolutely crucial in protecting varnish or shellac finishes.

Lacquer dries so fast that it takes real skill to apply it. While it produces a beautiful shine, the shine is difficult to maintain on floors because of scuffing.

Polyurethane has a definite advantage over the other finishes in ease of application, durability, and appearance. It's available in high-gloss, low-gloss, and matte finishes. Because it's made of a blend of synthetic resins (plasticizers and other film-coating ingredients, which produce a hard, moisture-resistant surface), it's extremely durable. Since the plastic finish coat has a transparent, built-up look, some manufacturers advertise that waxing is not required, but you'll get better wear with little change in the finish if you do.

Polyurethane can be applied over bare, sanded, stained, or painted wood, but the floor must be free of dirt, dust, and grease. If you're applying the finish to a floor that's decorated with stencils, hand-painted designs, fabric, or wallpaper, give the floor three or more coats to preserve the designs.

Bubbles in polyurethane usually remain in the applied finish and, when dry, appear as little white spots. For that reason, don't shake the container or vigorously stir it with a paddle or brush. Blend it slowly with a paint stick. Some types require that the first coat be thinned with mineral spirits or turpentine; read the label. Usually, if the brush drags, it needs thinning.

Wipe the floor well with a tack rag before applying, and try to keep lint and dust from blowing around the room. Use a good-quality brush to apply the polyurethane, and brush with the grain. A lamb's wool applicator will apply too heavy a coat and cause drying problems. Keep the brush fully loaded and apply in long, even sweeps, overlapping and feathering the previously brushed patches. Allow the finish to dry overnight.

Sand as you did with the sealer, enmeshing fine steel wool pads in the bristles of a heavy-duty commercial polisher. Vacuum the floor and wipe with a tack rag. After waiting 24 hours apply a thin second coat in the same manner. If you want three or more coats of finish on the floor, apply each in the same manner, always waiting out the proper drying time. The high-gloss finish especially, will scratch easily under the stress of drying.

Waxing. Waxing over two coats of penetrating sealer or polyurethane is purely optional, but a coat or two of wax will protect the finish coat from scratches and make wiping up easier. In a high-traffic area, any finish will wear, but wax can be reapplied a lot faster and easier than other finishes. (see "Waxing," on p. 184.)

INSTALLING PREFINISHED PARQUET TILE

Since parquet is rigid and unyielding, it won't conform to bumpy or uneven floors. And since wood expands and shrinks with temperature changes, it's not a good idea to lay parquet (or any wood) over a concrete subfloor that's prone to sweat, or over a radiant-heated subfloor. Badly damaged floors, concrete floors, and those with broken or missing resilient tile (if it can't be removed) should be covered with an underlayment. Some tile cannot be laid over no-wax or polyurethane-coated floors—no matter what condition they're in. Be sure to follow the manufacturer's instructions.

Old wood floors, if they're level, can be used as subflooring after removing all traces of old paint, varnish, and wax. Remove all base shoe moldings, doorway thresholds, and floor heat registers. Nail down any loose flooring with ring-shank nails; then set them and fill the holes.

Estimating tile, trim, and materials is a simple task if you use a scaled drawing of your room layout. It will also minimize cutting and eliminate mistakes in ordering and installing.

A few basic tools that you'll need are: a block plane, a tape measure, a sabre or coping saw, chalk line, and a notched trowel (if you are not installing the adhesive-backed style).

Since walls are seldom straight, you'll have to create your own true guidelines for aligning the tile. There are two recommended ways of installing tile. One way is to establish intersecting guidelines two tiles out from adjacent walls. This layout assures that there will be full tiles on two walls. Very often we use this method where we do not wish to have tile pieces as borders at prominent walls.

The other method is to strike intersecting guidelines in the center of the room. If you use this method, you start laying tile in the center of the room at the intersecting lines and work toward the perimeters of all four corners. You will have to adjust the lines before you start, so that you end up with even borders of cut tile at each opposite wall.

Side Guideline Method

Snap two intersecting lines—two tiles, plus ½ inch for expansion—out from adjacent walls in a corner. (The example shown in FIG. 8-10 allows for two complete rows of 12-by-12 tile, plus ½ inch for expansion room.) The expansion space is needed around the perimeter of the room, because wood shrinks and expands with climate changes. The space can be filled with cork strips (optional) or simply hidden later with baseboard and molding trim.

Center Guideline Method of Installing Tile

The center guideline method shown in FIG. 8-17, results in pyramidical or stair-step pattern, starting at the center of the room and working toward the walls.

1. Find the center point of one wall and snap a chalk line across the floor to the opposite wall.

2. Start at the center point on the chalk line and loose-lay a row of tiles to the wall. Measure the space between the last tile and the wall. If the distance is over half a tile wide, proceed to chalk the intersecting line. If the space is less than a half tile wide, move the chalk line over a distance to equal half a tile and snap a new line. This will prevent you from ending up with an extremely narrow cut of tile.

3. Make an intersecting chalk line from center points on the opposite wall and adjust the tiles and center line as you did in Steps 1 and 2 above. Resnap a new chalk line if required, then check with a carpenter's square to be sure that the intersecting lines are at a perfect 90-degree angle. Remove loose tile.

Installing Butt-Edged Parquet Tile

Butt-edged tile are usually made up of several layers of wood that are edge-glued and laminated together. Buckling can occur with this type of block tile as it expands and contracts, if the tiles are lined up with all of the patterns or grains going in the same direction. Instead, turn adjoining blocks at right angles to each other, creating a "checkerboard" effect with the wood grain.

Installing Self-Adhesive Tongue-and-Groove Parquet

These parquet tiles are fitted together as they are laid. Lay one tile, then slide the groove of the next tile over the tongue of the first. For the side guideline method, strike guidelines as shown in FIG. 8-10.

To get started square and true, loose-lay tiles number 1 and number 2 (as shown) and fill in corners with loose tiles A, B, C, and D. If they line up, peel the backing off of number 1, align its grooved edges on the intersecting lines (not the tongues) and press into place. Follow with tile number 2; then numbers 3 and 4, and so on.

If you have to cut the tile to fit at the end of the rows, the quickest and easiest way to do this is to follow the instructions illustrated in FIG. 8-11.

Tile number 1 is the last full tile glued into position. The next tile (number 2) is loose-laid directly over tile number 1. Slide tile number 3 so it butts to the expansion spacer, and using it as a guide, draw a line on tile number 2 for the cutting line. Cut and fit the piece into place for the border tile.

After the first two rows are finished, go back to the beginning and lay a tile adjacent to A, then C; repeat the sequence as you did for the first two

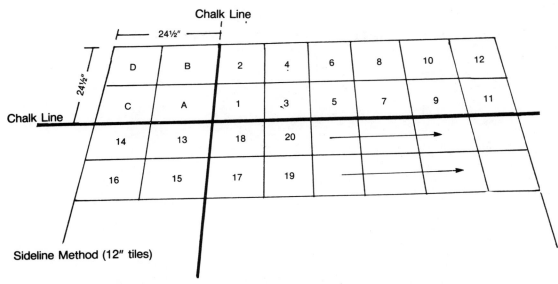

Fig. 8–10. Side line method of laying tile.

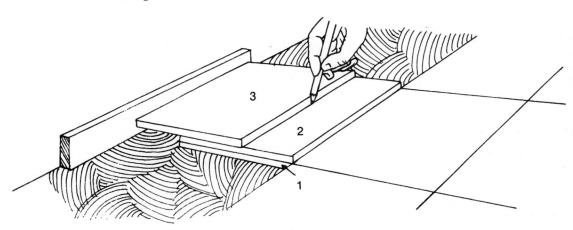

Fig. 8–11. Cutting border tile.

rows. Now you can secure the corner tiles and finish the rest of the floor by duplicating the procedure.

Undercut the bottoms of all existing door casings to enable you to slide the parquet squares under for a tight fit. To do this, rest a tile on the floor to gauge the correct depth of the cut (FIG. 8-12).

Make a paper template (or use the paper backing on the tile) to fit odd-shaped spaces, like round hearths, steps, and so on, then cut the tiles with a fine-toothed saw (FIG. 8-13). Use a block plane or utility knife to trim tongues from tile edges that butt against landing treads and the like.

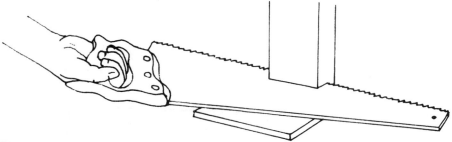

Fig. 8–12. Undercutting door casing.

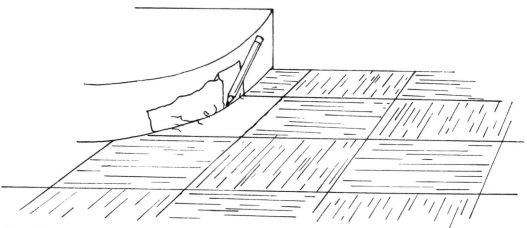

Fig. 8-13. Cutting around odd shapes.

To make a tight fit on outside corners, place a tile A squarely over the last fixed tile on the left side of the corner (FIG. 8-14).

Hold a third tile B over the second tile A, and slide it to about ⅛-inch from the wall. Using the edge of tile B as a guide, mark A with a pencil (FIG. 8-15).

Next, move A, without turning it, to a position squarely over the fixed tile closest to the right side of the border C. Again draw a second line, using the overlying tile B as your guide. Cut the marked tile along pencil lines to fit the corner (FIG. 8-16).

Installing Parquet with Adhesives

To install tile using the center guideline method, strike intersecting guidelines in the center of the room and adjust them so border tiles come out even (FIG. 8-17).

Spread the adhesive with a notched trowel held at a 60-to-80-degree angle. Comb on no more adhesive than you can cover with tile in the

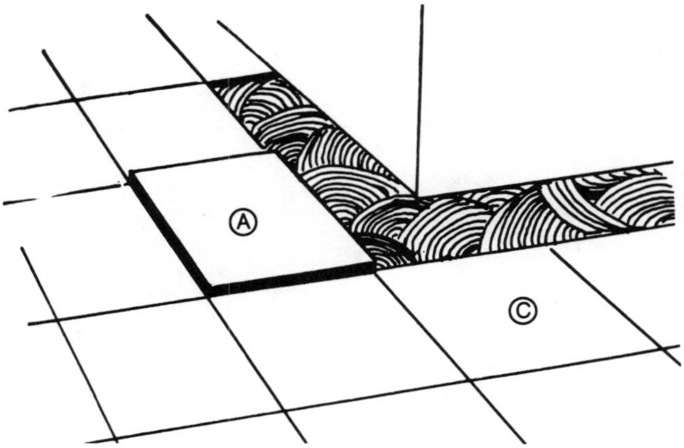

Fig. 8-14. Making a tight fit around corners. Step 1.

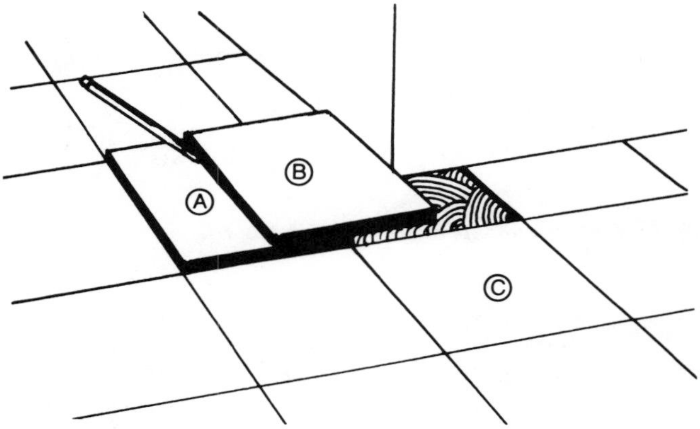

Fig. 8-15. Step 2.

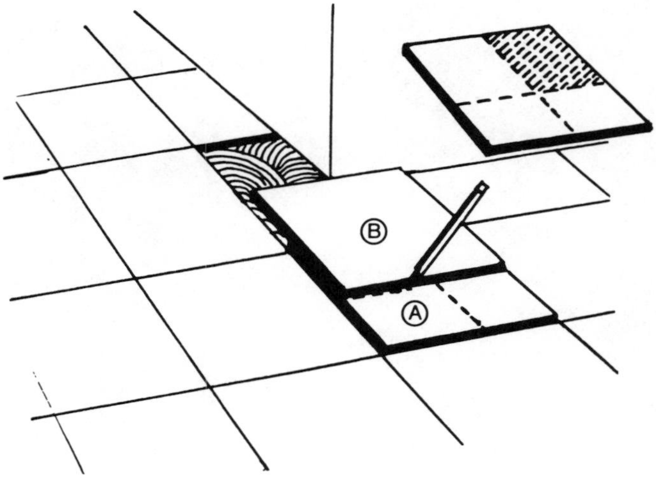

Fig. 8-16. Step 3.

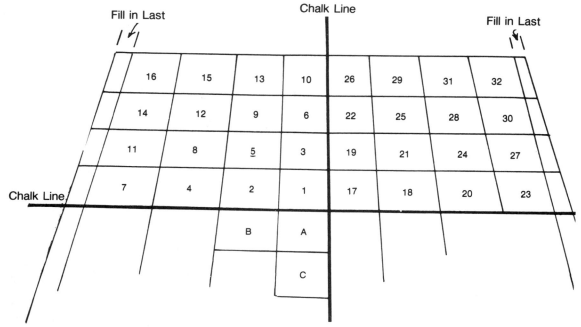

Fig. 8-17. *Center guideline method of laying tile.*

Fig. 8-18. *Begin in upper left quadrant.*

manufacturer's allotted setting-up time; pull off any excess adhesive so it will not come up between tile joints. Be careful not to cover any of your guide lines.

When positioning the tiles, set them lightly into place; sliding them causes excess mastic to pile up on the leading edge of the tile and interferes with the proper fit (FIGS. 8-18 and 8-19). It's a good idea to place a piece of plywood over set tiles if you have to walk on them during the installation. This prevents foot traffic from sliding them out of line.

When the floor is completed, roll it with a 150-pound floor roller (available from rental store or dealer) to ensure mastic adhesion. Let the adhesive set for at least 24 hours before walking on it.

Fig. 8–19. Finish floor with stair-step method.

Trimming Out Parquet Floors

Special moldings are available from the manufacturer for finishing off the room. Reducer strips, combination base-and-shoe, quarter round, threshold, and stair nosing moldings will solve most of your problems easily. Attach all moldings to wall or baseboard, not into the flooring.

Threshold: This molding covers expansion spaces and makes the transition between parquet flooring and sliding doors, and regular doors. It can also be used where adjoining surfaces are at different levels by trimming or planing the bottom surface to accommodate the two different levels. Or, remove bottom portion altogether to make the transition across two floors of the same level but different materials. (See FIG. 8-20.)

Reducer Strip: Use this tapered molding (FIG. 8-21) to bridge the parquet floor and an adjoining floor that is at a lower level (for example, resiliant flooring).

Stair Nosing: Use to trim out stair landings, floors adjacent to sunken areas, or a step (FIG. 8-22).

Shoe or ¾-inch quarter round: Use this molding to cover expansion spaces around counters or steps. Use with existing baseboards to cover expansion spaces (FIG. 8-23). When you replace this molding, nail it into the baseboard, not the floor tile.

Base-and-shoe combination: Where old baseboards can't be reused, this one piece does the job by covering up the expansion space and trimming (FIG. 8-24).

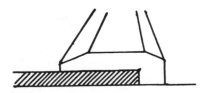

Fig. 8-20. Threshold moldings.

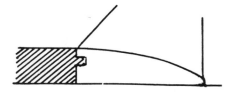

Fig. 8-21. Reducer strip moldings.

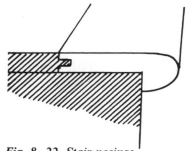

Fig. 8-22. Stair nosings.

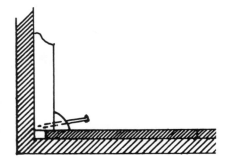

Fig. 8-23. Installing shoe or quarter round moldings.

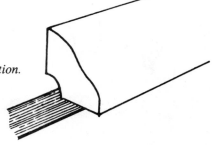

Fig. 8–24. Base and shoe combination.

INSTALLING PLANK AND STRIP FLOORING

Plank and strip floors can be installed over any dry, sound, and level surface. Use the proper underlayments over badly damaged, or moisture-prone floors.

When estimating the standard ¾-by-2¼-inch oak strip flooring, multiple the number of square feet in the room by 1.383 to determine the board feet you'll need, including waste. For other sizes, ask your dealer for help in computing quantities.

Remove base shoe and baseboards. Lay a covering of 15-pound, asphalt-saturated felt building paper over the floor, butting seams tightly and cutting the edges flush with the walls. Nail the edges of each sheet to hold it in place.

For tools, you'll need a chalk line, rule, saw, hammer, nail set, flooring nails, a tube of adhesive, and caulk gun.

Decide which way you want the boards to run. Then lay out your first row with the grooves facing the wall. Allow a ½ inch of space between boards and wall for an expansion joint. You can use wood wedges for the spacing and butt the first row up to it, or snap a working chalk line that includes the board's width and the ½-inch expansion space.

If the wall is out of square, scribe the first row of boards. Face-nail the edge of each board ½ inch from the edge, and blind nail the tongue every 10 to 12 inches apart. Predrill nail holes to avoid splitting the wood. Countersink and fill all nail holes with putty, in case they won't be covered by moldings.

Next, dry-lay another 6 or 7 rows to establish a pleasing pattern of different widths and staggered joints, and to minimize waste. Be sure to leave ½ inch between the end of each row for expansion. Then go back to the second row and continue the installation.

Apply a bead of adhesive all the way down the row, under the tongue at the front edge of the first row of planks. Then fit the groove of the second row of planks to it. To seat each plank, engage the joint first, then use a mallet and scrap of board for a tapping block (FIG. 8-25). This will prevent damage to the protruding tongue.

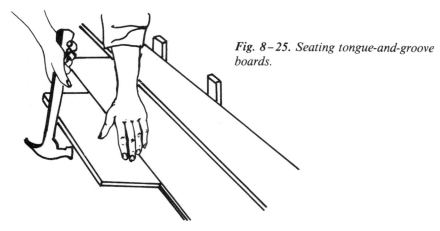

Fig. 8–25. Seating tongue-and-groove boards.

Blind-nail the tongues on each board, and face-nail the ends near the wall. Apply another bead of adhesive under the tongue on the second row and continue installing subsequent rows. If any excess glue oozes up through the joint to the finished surface, wipe it off with a moist cloth or sponge.

More often than not, the last row won't fit. Place a row of boards, unglued, with the tongue towards the wall, directly on top of the last installed row.

Then take a short piece of plank for a marker and turn it upside down on top of the loose-laid boards, with the tongue butted against the wall. Draw a pencil line down the loose-laid row. This is your cutting line for your last row of boards to get them to the proper width so they will fit into the last space. When cut, use a crowbar to hold each board snug against the previously installed one as you face-nail it along the edge near the wall (FIG. 8-26).

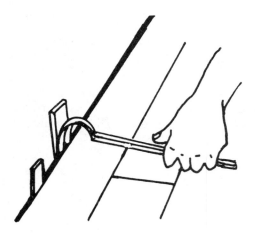

Fig. 8–26. Nailing last board in place.

Remove all wedges and spacers in the room, and cover the expansion joints with moldings. Always attach the moldings to the wall or baseboard —never to the planks. This way, the boards underneath can move freely with temperature changes.

Cutting Around Obstacles. When you get to an obstacle, such as a radiator or pipe, trial-fit the board, measure carefully, and make a cardboard template to transfer the cut onto the board. Use a coping saw for the cutout. If you can't use the tongue, plane it off and sand the edge smooth. Then face-nail the piece in place.

Undercutting Moldings or Door Casings. To provide clearance for the plank flooring to slide underneath door casings and moldings, do as you would for tile in FIG. 8-12.

HARD SURFACE FLOORING

Most hard-surfaced floors found in older homes have survived the test of time because of their unyielding nature to deterioration and damage, including water and fire. Thus, we generally consider concrete, terrazzo, marble, ceramic tile, brick, slate, and stone as permanent flooring. Cleaned and polished, these materials will produce an attractive, new-looking floor that can serve for decades more. Although they don't require additional protection against wear, they're enhanced by a good wax maintenance, which brings out their true color and texture and makes cleaning easier. Sealing is also advised, especially where porosity would cause dirt-catching problems. Actually, all hard-surfaced floors, with the exception of glazed ceramic tile, should be sealed to ward off grease and other stubborn stains.

Laying a new hard-surfaced floor is not an impossible job for the determined, consciencious do-it-yourselfer. Tile used to require a durable subfloor—at least an inch-thick bed of mortar—but today the thin-set mastics make tiling floors a relatively easy, less time-consuming task.

Tile can be installed over most surfaces that are dry, clean, and flat, if some special considerations are observed. When laying ceramic over new floors, use at least ⅝-inch exterior-grade plywood over floor joists; then coat the sheets with a primer recommended by the manufacturer. On existing wood floors, be sure that all loose boards are nailed down securely. If the floor is not solid, cover it with ⅜-inch-thick exterior-grade plywood and prime the sheets.

For concrete floors, remove grease and stains with a chemical cleaner to ensure a tight bond. Smooth the floor with a grinder, or level it with patching compound if needed, then dust and vacuum thoroughly. Sand any old painted surface to roughen it up and ensure that the new mastic will hold.

You can lay tile over resilient flooring if the old material is firmly affixed to the floor and is not of a cushioned variety. If cushioned, an underlayment must be used before installing the tile.

Over old ceramic tile, clean first with a tile cleaner, then roughen up the shiny surface with a rented floor sander, or a portable electric drill equipped with a heavy-duty sanding disk. Then prime the surface before laying the tile.

Many new designs, colors, and textures are available for installing on walls, floors, and countertops—inside and outside the house. Tiles come in sizes from 1-inch mosaics to 12-inch pavers, shaped in squares, rectangles, hexagons, octagons, moorish curves, cloverleafs, hearts and teardrops.

Some tiles come in sheets, conveniently prespaced for grouting and already to set in the adhesive. Some larger ceramic tiles also come in sheet form with built-on spacers to keep grout lines even. Others are available with a special white silicone grout that has been treated with a mildewcide. The flexible pregrouted mosaic sheets allow you to cover curves and odd-shaped areas that larger tiles couldn't otherwise cover.

When buying tile remember that it's important—in terms of safety and longevity—that you make a proper choice. For instance, wall tile is thinner than floor tile and should not be used on floors in heavy-traffic areas. Thicker materials like quarry, pavers, brick, and stone, however, can be used under heavyweight traffic inside and outside.

Glazed, glassy-surfaced tile should not be used underfoot around pool, bathing, or shower areas where people can slip on wet tiles and injure themselves. Unglazed tile is a better choice. Unglazed tile outdoors, however, has a shorter life expectancy due to the porosity of the material and the constant changes in heat, cold, and moisture conditions.

Types

Following is a list of common types of hard surface flooring, the advantages and disadvantages, and some suggestions on their care and use.

Quarry Tile. Usually, unglazed quarry tile is available in the popular earthen-red color and other rich-looking, natural tones. Primarily used as a floor covering, it can be installed indoors or out. Quarry tiles are generally larger than other tiles, from 6 by 6 up to 8 or 10 inches square, in thicknesses from ⅜ to ½ inch. There are a number of shapes from which to choose: square, hexagonal, rectangular, moorish, and octagonal. Some quarry tiles come glazed.

Pavers. Similar to quarry tile in composition, style, and use, but with a more rustic appearance. Highly durable, they're a natural for heavy-traffic areas like walkways, terraces, driveways, and patios that are not subject to freezing conditions. The tile usually comes with a slip-resistant finish to provide for safety. Available in a number of different earth colors, and in sizes from 4 by 8 to 8 by 8 inches. Matching trim pieces are available for both quarry and paver tiles.

Floor Brick. Extremely durable for heavy-duty walkways and driveways. Available in several natural earth tones. Floor brick is made of high-quality shale and can usually be recognized by its scored diamond tread designed for safety.

Swimming Pool Tile. Rugged quarry tile glazed to provide an easy-to-clean surface for pool interiors.

Ceramic and Mosaic Tile. Ceramic tile comes glazed or unglazed. We are most familiar with the 4½- and 2-inch squares. The glazed tile is generally used for wall tile; the unglazed variety is commonly used for floors. There is no limit to the different colors and textures available in the ceramic lines because the glazes, colors and designs are applied and baked on a second time after the fine-grained porcelain tile has been thoroughly cured in the kiln. The tiles come with matching trim pieces to guarantee a professional-looking job. Ceramic mosiac comes in tiny squares (1 by 1 inch, 2 by 2 inch) and rectangles (1 by 2 inch) and many other interesting shapes and colors. Most are ¼ inch thick. This type of tile is impervious to water, stains, dents, and frost. Available in very high-gloss finishes for walls and countertops, and textured finishes for nonslip floors. Mosaic tiles are commonly affixed to a flexible backing sheet of rubber, plastic, paper, or heavy thread, making them a versatile surfacing material for round, curved, or odd-shaped surfaces like fountains, columns, or planters.

Care and Cleaning of Ceramic and Mosaic Tile: Usually, ceramic and grout can be cleaned with an old toothbrush dipped in a household bleach and a special spray-on tile cleaner. But for heavily soap-encrusted tile and chrome fixtures, remove most of the soap and scum from dry tiles, using a dry (non-soapy) steel wool pad, then scrub them down with a mixture of bleach and water and rinse. If soil layers persist, wash the tiles with an old washcloth dipped in kerosene, rinse, and wipe dry. Follow with a polishing using a commercial tile cleaner.

Mildew can be retarded by a vinegar-water rinse after the tiles are freshly cleaned.

Stone and Slate. A hard, fine-grained rock of clay and shale that characteristically splits in layers. It's a very popular flooring choice for entryways, foyers, and hearths. Since it's more available in some areas than others, the price varies greatly. Stone and slate comes in bluish-gray shades and natural earth colors, ranging from black and grays to pinks and reds. Slate can be purchased in boxed sets of mixed colors, but usually, if you want a single color and uniform texture, you'll have to special-order. Stone is more difficult to find at dealers. Most people use native stone found locally.

Because of the weight element, joist support is crucial if not installed over a concrete subfloor. Double joists must be installed, or additional bridging between the joists must be added, before setting the flooring. Slate does not hold up as well as stone outside. Inside, you can lay slate or stone in a bed of ordinary mortar over a concrete slab and let the bed mortar form the grouting between masonry pieces. Or you can put the flatter slate down with ceramic tile adhesive, which has the advantage of adhering well to wood or other surfaces, without adding additional thickness. Grouting is usually done with portland cement mortar.

Care and Cleaning of Slate, Stone, and Brick: Use a vegetable brush and sponge dipped in a vinegar and water solution to scrub and rinse the masonry. For smoked areas around fireplace fronts, use an artgum eraser. For heavy soil, use the artgum eraser first, then wash the area with a strong solution of trisodium phosphate (½ cup to a gallon of water). Apply the solution with a sponge. Scrub with a brush, then rise with clear water and a sponge.

If this doesn't work, dissolve 4 ounces of naphtha in 1 quart of hot water. Cool. Stir in ½ pound powdered pumice and ½ cup ammonia, and mix thoroughly. Apply the mixture to the slate or stone with a paintbrush and let the solution remain on the surface for at least an hour. Then scour with a brush and warm water. Rinse with clean water and a sponge.

Marble. No other tile equals the luxurious look of marble. A variety of limestone, marble is an elegant and durable flooring material found in many colors: gray, black, pink, white, purple, and green. It's available veined or pitted (travertine). Usually the tile is 6-by-6 or 12-by-12 inches square and ¼-inch thick. It can be custom-cut to specific sizes. Although it provides a hard surface, it can be damaged by improper cleaning techniques. Acid will etch or dissolve it. Also, marble absorbs alkaline cleaning solutions that can break down the tiny marble pores and leave the surface dull and rough. There are special marble sealers available that will help protect the marble from serious stains and pitting.

Marble is an excellent choice for fireplace facings or as a base for freestanding fireplaces, as well as for floors that don't get rugged wear and tear. They're not recommended for kitchens or workrooms, even with a sealer.

Care and Cleaning of Marble: First, try cleaning the surface with an ordinary household liquid detergent. Then cut a lemon in half, dip it in table salt, and rub over the entire surface to remove discoloration and stains. Rinse thoroughly.

You may have to bleach out stubborn stains by covering them with an old bleach-saturated towel left on the stain overnight; or purchase a special marble cleaning kit from a marble dealer.

To remove scratches, sand with progressively finer grit sandpaper. Start with 80 grit and work up through 320 grit, sprinkling water over the marble as you sand to reduce friction. Then apply a mixture of rottenstone and water and polish with a felt pad attached to a power sander. Clean the mixture off with water and a sponge, then buff the marble with a soft cloth and a special spray wax formulated for marble.

Synthetic Marble Tiles. These tiles cost about half as much as authentic marble. Marble chips, embedded in a polyester resin, allow this material to be manufactured in many colors. Day-to-day maintenance of synthetic marble is less of a bother than the real stuff, although it doesn't last as long as true marble. Like marble, it scratches and mars more easily than other stone or masonry materials.

Terrazzo. A high content of marble chips in a cement base is ground and polished to a very smooth, hard finish. Although it's highly durable and resistant to moisture, terrazzo is subject to staining.

Masonry Sealers and Waxes

Sealers should be applied to all types of stone and masonry floors to protect the grout from discoloring and prevent adverse effects from alkaline cleaners. Sealers also protect the floor's surface from scratches and soil and help bring out the natural color and beauty.

Special sealers formulated for stone and masonry are available from flooring dealer and builders' supply stores. Check with builders and contractors who usually apply sealers to new floors. Before sealing, test to be sure the appearance is satisfactory. Then apply a sealer, and a coat or two of wax.

A solvent-base buffing wax gives masonry floors a satiny luster, which most people prefer. It's particularly recommended for darker colored stone floors, but this type of wax is practical only when an electric floor polisher is available for buffing. Water-based polishes can also be used on these floors. Generally, they provide a higher luster, and they're easier to use, but the wax must be removed after several applications to avoid build-up and discoloration.

INSTALLING WALL AND FLOOR TILE

If you're doing both walls and floor, install wall tiles first to prevent adhesive from dropping on the newly installed floor tiles and hardening. It's easier, also, to apply the cove trim if the walls are finished first.

Tile requirements are usually figured in terms of square feet. Multiply width times length and add 5 percent for breakage and waste. If your floor plan is drawn on graph paper, however, you can get a much more accurate estimate. Let each square represent a tile, or half-square for a rectangular tile. If you're creating a tile design, use colored felt pens to represent the different colors in the design. Multiply the horizontal row of tile by the number of vertical tile, then subtract the tiles that go into the design to get the total number of background tiles. As before, add 5 percent for waste.

There are several kinds of adhesive that you can use to install the tiles, but it's always better to use the one recommended by the manufacturer. Most do-it-yourself tiles are set with a thin-set adhesive rather than a heavy mortar. Thin-set adhesives come with an organic, cement, or epoxy base. Organic adhesives, usually called *mastics*, are premixed, water-resistant materials that are usually recommended for flat tiles, installed on floors, walls or counters over properly prepared surfaces, such as concrete, gypsum board, backer board, plaster, cement, asbestos board, wood, plywood, brick, ceramic tile, marble, plastic laminate, or terrazzo.

Cement bases are excellent for applying tiles to concrete or masonry subfloors that are not quite smooth. Or for tiles that are not flat, like the more rustic, warped tiles.

Epoxy creates the strongest base and has the best bonding power, but it hardens so quickly that it is often very difficult for the do-it-yourselfer to handle.

Tools: Chalk line, straightedge; tape rule, square, abrasive stone (carborundum or whetstone), the properly notched trowel (recommended by adhesive manufacturer), rubber grout float, tile cutter, tile nippers, rod saw, and masonry drill bit. You can rent a tile cutter from most dealers. While the cost is a little high, you'll get a professional-looking job with minimum waste.

Preparing the Floors

Prepare the floors so they are sound, dry, and clean. Some adhesives require that a sealer be laid on concrete before they can be spread. Be sure to read the label.

Check for plumbing leaks and repair them. If you are tiling a bathroom floor, you'll have to remove the toilet. Refer to the how-to section in Chapter 4.

Since the level of the floor will be raised slightly with the new tile, be sure that you are able to trim doors to the proper clearance. Stack two tiles, one on top of the other, and draw a line across the door bottom above the top tile. Then saw or plane the door flush with the line.

Remove all shoe molding in the room.

Spacers

Usually, wall tiles come with built-in spacers attached to the sides of each unit to form even grout lines. If tiles don't have spacer lugs, as in quarry tile, you'll have to make or buy some in the recommended width for the grout you're using and place one spacer at either end between each tile. Some spacers stay in place only until the adhesive has set, others can be covered over with grout. You can make your own removable spacers, using strips of wood battens, toothpicks, or dampened cords or rope that is stretched between nails on the grout lines.

Establish your working lines, intersecting them in the center of the room, and loose-lay the tile along one working line, allowing for grout space (FIG. 8-27). Make necessary adjustments so that you cut as few tile as possible. Lay the tile in a pyramidical pattern as you would for laying resilient or wood floor tile.

Applying the Adhesive

Apply no more adhesive than you can cover with tile in 30 minutes. Hold the trowel at a 60 to 80 degree angle and spread the adhesive with the notched edge of the trowel, pulling off excess adhesive so it will not come

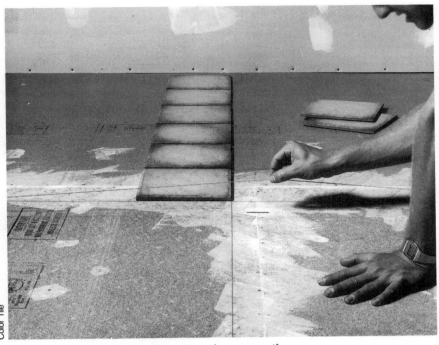

Fig. 8–27. Establishing working lines for quarry tile.

up through the tile joints. If the tiles have deep ridges on the back, butter the backs with adhesive before you set the tile.

Set the first tile in the center of the room at the intersection of the two lines and proceed to tile one quarter of the room at a time. Place the tile in position with a slight twisting motion. Do not slide the tiles; wiggle them into alignment. Then seat the tiles firmly in the adhesive by tapping on them with a hammer and beating block covered with a piece of old carpeting. Make sure that all joints stay uniform. When you are using 4¼-by-4¼-inch or larger ceramic tile, built-in spacers will gauge your grout lines. When setting quarry tile, place one spacer at either end between each tile as shown in FIG. 8-28.

When finished with each section, remove excess or smudged adhesive before it sets. Do not walk on the tiles until they are thoroughly dry. After all the full tiles have been set, cut and fit the remaining pieces.

Cutting Tile

You will be using the following tools to cut the tile.

Tile Cutter. To fit an irregular contour, cut a template and use it to transfer the shape to the tile with a felt pen. If you're using ceramic or quarry tile that has a ridged back, make cuts parallel to the ridges. Mark the face of the tile with a felt pen before you cut. Set the tile cutter angle gauge

Fig. 8–28. Setting quarry tile with spacers.

to the size of the cut desired and insert the tile glazed-side-up. Score the tile with the cutting wheel. Then press the breaking wings of the cutter near the edge of the tile or on an edge next to the angle gauge. Press down on tile cutter firmly and break the tile (FIG. 8-29).

Nippers. For small, irregular cuts like those around pipes and fixtures, use tile nippers (FIG. 8-30). Nibble off small chunks at a time. If you take too big a bite, you could break the tile. Smooth the rough edges with a rubbing stone or coarse file. It's not necessary to smooth edges that will be covered by trim or fixture rims.

Rod Saw. This tool, like a hacksaw, is used to cut out half circles for faucets and pipe outlets and for enlarging holes started with the masonry drill bit.

First, use a masonry bit on an electric drill to drill small holes in tile, then enlarge the small holes with the rod saw.

Since all walls are not perfectly plumb, you should not cut half tiles beforehand. Cut them as you get to the end of each row to ensure a perfect fit.

Apply remaining trim and allow tile and trim to set for 24 hours before grouting.

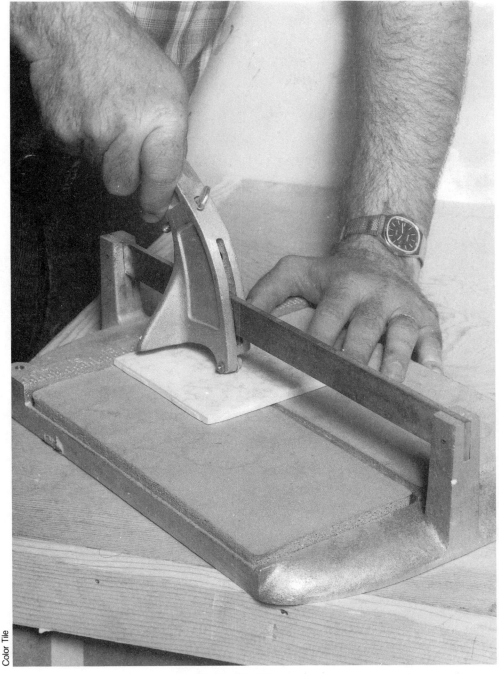

Fig. 8–29. Tile cutter.

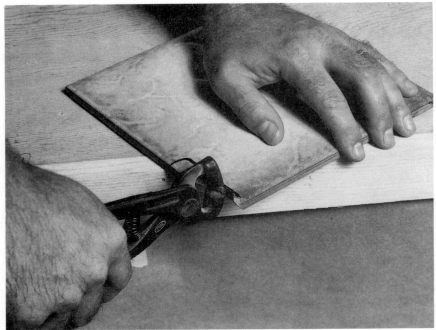

Fig. 8–30. *Tile nippers.*

Grouting

After a 24-hour waiting period you can begin the grouting. If you are using unglazed tile, apply a grout release product, following the instructions on the label. Grout is available today in white, gray, and many other colors to help hide dirt and create a contrasting color for a design feature. Today's grouts are also waterproof and mildew-resistant and a lot easier to clean. You can prevent dirt buildup in the grout lines by spraying on a silicone sealer after the grout has set.

Always wear rubber gloves when grouting, and use the grout recommended by the manufacturer. Spread the grout with a wide rubber float (FIG. 8-31). Work diagonally across the tiles to force the grout into all the joints. After the grout is worked thoroughly into the joints, draw the float across the tile surface to remove the excess. Wait about 10 minutes, then carefully wipe the tile off with a damp sponge.

Strike the joints with the handle of an old toothbrush or another round-edged tool. Wipe the surface down again, rinsing the sponge often. Wait 30 minutes until a haze appears on the tile then wipe it off with a soft, dry cloth. Dried grout cannot be easily removed so do not allow it to dry before cleaning.

You should use a silicone-rubber grout for shower and bathroom floors. Apply the silicone with a caulk gun; follow the tube directions for clean up. Let the grout dry for 24 hours.

Fig. 8–31. *Applying the grout.*

Finishing the Tiled Surface

Let the tile and grout cure for 72 hours before you caulk around the corners, tub, or shower pan areas, or faucet and spout openings. Allow the caulking to dry thoroughly before sealing.

Seal the grout with two coats of silicone tile sealer applied with a spray applicator or foam brush. Wait one hour between coats. After the second coat dries, buff the tile with a clean towel to remove any film and restore the luster to the tile surface. Shower or tub can be used 24 hours after the grout is sealed.

LAYING A MASONRY FLOOR

Masonry floors are usually of brick, flagstone, slate, or stone. Because of their weight and bulk, they're best laid over a concrete slab. If you're not going to lay masonry over a ground-level, concrete slab, consult with a building expert on how to reinforce the subfloor.

The concrete slab must be clean and dry, but a few irregulars can be eliminated with the mortar. Bricks and stones can be cut by scoring them first with a brickset or stonemason's chisel. Then, with the scored line placed over the edge of a board, strike off the excess with a hammer.

Bricks

Lay out your working lines, intersecting them about two bricks away from opposite walls. If your walls are plumb, you can use the wall or baseboard as a guide. Loose-lay one complete row for a trial run. Then begin by soaking the bricks in water for a few minutes as you apply a spread of mortar over a manageable area along your work line. Place the first brick in the center on the line and work toward each end. A wood spacer, placed between the bricks as you lay them, will assure equal mortar joints. Tap the bricks even and check them often with a masonry level. Keep the runs straight by snapping new working lines every two coarses.

After allowing the bricks to set in the mortar for 24 hours, do the joints. Pack mortar tightly in the spaces with a small trowel. When the mortar has set sufficiently, strike the joints with a jointer or wood dowel to make them slightly concave. After several hours, rub the surface with a piece of rough burlap to knock off any mortar chunks.

Stone

Stone is a bit more tricky to lay. You must place the pieces in the mortar, jig-saw fashion, varying the amount of mortar they're set in to raise or lower their surfaces to keep them level with their neighbors. The spaces between should be as equal as possible. Before you lay stone, sprinkle the concrete slab so that it's damp. As with brick, tap the tops of the stone to keep them level and to seat them. Check with a level frequently.

After the stones have set 24 hours, prepare the grout (three parts sand to one part cement) and mix it to a soupy consistency. Since the grout has to run between and under the stones, it cannot be as stiff as brick mortar. Pour the grout from a coffee can into the spaces and pack it firmly with a trowel. Then wipe up the excess grout with a wet sponge. Smooth the grouting before it hardens.

Finishing Brick and Stone. Since all masonry flooring has a porous surface, it should be sealed with a sealer recommended by your building supplier. A coat of wax will further enhance the texture and color of the masonry.

RESILIENT FLOORING

As long as the appeal for casual living continues to grow, so will the expanded use of resilient flooring. These smooth-surfaced, easy-care floors allow food and drink to be taken out of the kitchen without fear of liquid and grease spills ruining floor coverings. Not only do they provide accident-proof surfaces, they also offer low maintenance and durability. At a reasonable cost, you'll find just about any color, pattern, texture, or design you desire to go with all types of period furnishings.

Resilient flooring falls into two categories: tiles and sheet (roll) goods. Tiles usually come in 9-by-9-inch or 12-by-12-inch squares, in vinyl, vinyl asbestos, rubber, cork, leather, and asphalt. Sheet types include vinyl and linoleum in 6-, 12-, and 15-foot widths. Some resilient tile can be installed only above grade, but most can be installed both above and below. Read the manufacturers instruction for each product.

Vinyl sheet flooring is the successor of linoleum, which has a felt-type back that attracts moisture. Now vinyl sheet flooring has a moisture-resistant back and can be used from basement to attic, but it's not the best choice to lay directly over below-grade concrete floors. Since concrete has to "breathe" to release moisture buildup, covering the entire floor with sheet flooring may seal moisture in and create damp pockets that will cause blistering. Tiles are a better choice on a below-grade concrete floor—installed according to the manufacturer's instructions and with waterproof cement.

All resilient floors have a tendency to take on the bulges and bad contours of the floor underneath, so before you start, make sure that the existing floor is smooth and level. It must also be free of dust, grease, and wax to ensure a proper bonding. Don't hesitate to enlist the help of your flooring dealer if you have additional questions about underlayment or the type of bonding you should use on your floor. Some of the rules of thumb are:

▶ You can lay new floor tile over old asphalt or vinyl asbestos tile in good condition, but not over cushioned vinyl, rubber, or solid vinyl.
▶ If the floors have been previously painted, fill all cracks with the appropriate compound and roughen up the surface with a floor sander. Then vacuum up all sanding dust.
▶ Never try to sand or scrape up an old resilient floor. It may contain asbestos fibers that are harmful if inaled. For these floors, and floors that need numerous repairs, add a subfloor or underlayment.
▶ In kitchens or bathrooms, remove furniture and appliances and check for plumbing leaks. Shut off the water supply valve in the bathroom, remove the supply line and draining tanks, then unbolt and remove the toilet. Use a water-resistant underlayment board to prevent bulging in the event of water seepage. After the new floor is installed, reset the toilet over a new wax seal.

Types

Before you shop for resilient flooring, review the following to determine which will be best for your particular installation.

Linoleum. Linoleum, one of the first man-made resilient flooring materials, consists of a mixture of ground fillers (cork dust and/or wood flour) bound together by a linseed base and laid over a burlap, canvas, or felt backing. Originally the patterns were printed on the surface, but today they're usually inlaid. Although its use has somewhat declined, linoleum is still a practical choice for resale properties because of its low cost and easy installation. It must be installed above grade, however, and it should never be put over concrete floors, even above grade, because of its moisture-prone backing.

Usually, linoleum does not come with a high-gloss finish. Like all smooth-surfaced floors, a good waxing will enhance and protect the surface and greatly prolong its life. Linoleum has a fairly low resiliency, and it's easily damaged by heavy weights or abrasive action. Also, strong alkaline cleaners may melt-run the pattern.

Sheet Vinyl. Because it's made from thermoplastic resins, sheet vinyl is extremely durable and highly resilient. It's available in clear, bright, fade-resistant colors and in many high-style patterns with smooth or embossed surfaces. Special depth effects are achieved by combining translucent and transparent vinyl materials. Usually inlaid, the pattern goes all the way through the thickness, so it wears for years. A clear polyurethane top coat gives vinyl its no-wax finish. The thickness of the top coat, and the sheet goods, itself, affects both the price and quality of the flooring. Vinyl resists abrasion, indentions, stains, grease, acids, and bleaches, and it's usually not harmed by strong cleaners. Sheet vinyl will retain its high-gloss finish, even without waxing, but like all smooth floors, a good coat of wax is beneficial.

Some sheet vinyl is so flexible and easy to handle that you can cut and lay it in a few hours. Over wood floors, you simply staple the edges and reinstall base and moldings over the staples; other types are cemented down. Some come with felt backs, others with foam cushioning that springs back when walked on, making it very comfortable underfoot.

Rotovinyl. There is a growing popularity for a high-style flooring with a photographic design called *rotovinyl.* It's produced through the use of photographs and rotograve printing. After the design is printed on the sheet, a heavy coat of clear vinyl is applied, providing an exceptionally durable and easy-to-clean surface. Sometimes, it's available with a foam cushion backing. Cost is dependent on the thickness of the layers, but it's usually less expensive than inlaid vinyl.

Asphalt Tile. Asphalt tile, precursor to modern resilient tiles, is an all-purpose tile about ⅛ inch thick. Asphalt tile tends to be harder and more brittle than other tiles, and it's more susceptible to stains and scuffs; however, it has excellent moisture resistance, making it one of the few that can be used safely on concrete floors. It's inexpensive and resists alkalines, but it has a low resiliency and dents easily. It must be waxed regularly to overcome these limitations. Never use an oil-based sweeping compound on asphalt tile, as the oil softens the asphalt. Consider it when the budget is an important item and if you are prepared to keep it well waxed.

Vinyl Asbestos Tile. This tile is similar to asphalt in appearance, but it's more flexible and resilient. Currently, it's the most popular choice for do-it-yourselfers because it comes in a wide variety of distinctive designs and colors and is well within the range of most budgets. It can be laid over concrete, strongly resists stains, alkali, grease, and mildew, and can be cleaned with any type of cleaner. It's available with a no-wax finish — in both self-adhesive and adhesive-installed styles.

Solid Vinyl Tile. Vinyl tile is similar to vinyl asbestos tile but more expensive. It's flexibility is greater, so it's easier to cut and install. Available in a wide color selection, homogenous vinyl tile is extremely durable and long-wearing because the colors and patterns run through the entire thickness, withstanding the wear of heavy traffic. Although it can be installed on all grade levels, the proper adhesive must be used. Check with the manufacturer for the recommended adhesive.

Rubber Tile. Rubber tile has excellent resiliency; it cushions footsteps and muffles sound. It's easy to maintain and has fair resistance to grease. The muted colors make it one of the most beautiful floor coverings, but it must be waxed regularly to ward off scuffs and scratches and maintain its appearance. It can also be damaged by grease, oil, and strong alkaline cleaners. Originally, it was made from natural rubber. Today, a synthetic rubber is often substituted to make the tile. It's expensive, thus not widely used.

Cork Tile. Cork has characteristics similar to wood—a rich, natural texture, and warm, unadulterated coloration—but it doesn't have much resistance to grease or average soil. Because of its resiliency, it's one of the most comfortable floors on which to walk. Add to this excellent sound and thermal control, and you have the reason why cork is often chosen over other floor coverings. Its porosity, however, requires that it be treated with a penetrating floor sealer and a perennial coat of wax to prevent flaking, gouging, as well as grease and water damage. Only solvent-based buffing waxes and cleaners should be used on cork.

Leather Tile. Another beautiful, resilient floor tile is pigskin leather. It has all the exemplary qualities of cork, plus one more: an ultimate look of luxury. So perfect for the den, study, or library, leather tiles come factory-finished with a special coating to protect from scratches, scuffing, and stains. Like cork and wood, its longevity depends on maintaining a good top coat of wax.

Laying Resilient Tile

Prepare the floor so it's smooth, level, and free of wax, soil, and grease. Do a layout on graph paper, so you can figure tile quantities and discern how and where you'll place the tile to achieve the best design with the least amount of cutting.

The tile is usually laid in a pyramidical pattern, starting from the center of the room. The starting point is established by snapping intersecting chalk lines on the floor.

1. Find the center point of one wall and snap a chalk line across the floor to the opposite wall.
2. Start at the center point on the chalk line and loose-lay a row of tiles to the wall. Measure the space between the last tile and the wall. If the distance is 2 or more inches, proceed to chalk the intersecting line. If the space is less than 2 inches—or more than 8 inches—move the center of the line 4½ inches (one half tile) toward the wall and remark

the center point. This will prevent you from ending up with an extremely narrow cut of tile.

3. Make an intersecting chalk line from center points on the opposite wall and adjust the tiles and center line as you did in Steps 1 and 2. Resnap new chalk lines as required and check with a carpenter's square to be sure that the intersecting lines are at a perfect 90-degree angle (FIG. 8-32). Remove loose tile.

4. Open all cartons of tile and check for noticeable color variation. If there is a variation, work from the cartons on an alternating basis to assure even color/pattern distribution. You may want to run the grain or pattern in the same or opposite direction. Some tiles come with arrows on the back to indicate which way they should be placed. Plan in advance what you will do before applying the adhesive, as this can influence the selection of your starting tiles.

Installing Adhesive-Backed Tiles. If you are using adhesive-backed tiles on a plywood or hardboard underlayment, brush on a coat of sealer and let it dry before installing the tile. This will prevent the thin layer of glue on the back of each tile from being absorbed by the wood. Strip off the backing paper and proceed to lay the tile, beginning at the right angle formed by the intersecting chalk lines in the middle of the room (FIG. 8-33).

Applying Cement for Dry Tiles. Read the instructions on the can carefully. Cement for regular vinyl asbestos tile can be applied with a brush. Cement for embossed vinyl asbestos should be applied with a trowel. Do not apply too much adhesive. Too much adhesive will ooze up

Fig. 8-32. Establishing working lines for resilient tile.

Color Tile

Fig. 8–33. Installing self-stick tiles.

between tiles, or form a soft layer underneath that will allow heavy objects to dent it. Too little will result in loose tiles. Press the trowel firmly against the floor so that the adhesive passes only through the notched holes. Hold the trowel at a 45-degree angle for the best results.

5. Spread on an even coat of tile cement over one fourth or one half of the room. If the room is fairly small, you can fill in one half of the floor space at a time; larger areas should be divided in fourths. Do not cover your working chalk lines.

In most cases, the cement will dry to proper consistency in about 15 minutes. Exact time will vary, depending on humidity and room temperature (around 70 degrees Fahrenheit is best). In any case, the adhesive should be tacky and not stick to your thumb when pressed.

There are several layout patterns that you can use. Your choice will depend on the design and the amount of drying time required for the adhesive to set up. Follow one of the sequences shown, unless otherwise instructed by the manufacturer.

6. Start in the center and place the first tile in the cement flush with two intersecting chalk lines. Press down firmly, then lay the rest of the tiles in sequence. Do not slide the tiles; drop each tile into place and press it firmly into the cement after butting it tightly to the previously installed one.

Laying a Masonry Floor   217

7. When you get to the end (border) tile, place a loose tile exactly over the last installed tile. (See FIG. 8-34.) Then take a third tile and slide it across the two until it's about ⅛ inch from the wall. Mark the middle tile as illustrated·and cut with scissors or a utility knife. It sometimes helps to warm tiles slightly with a lamp before making the cut. This makes them more flexible. Fit and glue the pieces in the border space.

Pipes, Door Jambs, and Obstructions. To fit tile around pipes, door jambs, and other obstructions, make a pattern with heavy paper, or use the backing paper on the self-adhesive tile. If a tile must be slipped over a pipe, cut a slit in from the back of the tile before you cut the opening (FIG. 8-35).

You can also use a contour gauge or compass to trace around irregular shapes on a tile (FIG. 8-36).

An even neater way to fit tiles around a door jamb is to undercut the door frame at its base about ⅛ inch. Then slide the tile underneath to hide all ragged edges.

Rolling the Tile. To assure a tight bond, you should roll the tile. Do this after all the tile has been laid and excess adhesive has been cleaned from the floor. Rent a 150-pound floor roller to apply weight to the tile, but don't push the tiles, or cause them to slide out of position. You can also

Fig. 8–34. Cutting and fitting the border tile.

Fig. 8–35. *Cutting and fitting around pipes.*

Color Tile

Fig. 8–36. *Using a contour gauge for fitting.*

Color Tile

Resilient Flooring 219

roll your floor with a more accessible device like a rolling pin, if you have the time and are willing and able to expend the elbow grease.

Reinstall old baseboard and shoe, or use vinyl wall base molding that matches the new tile floor.

Vinyl Wall Base. Vinyl wall molding completely seals the joint where wall meets floor, eliminating dirt and dust accumulations while providing a smooth, tough surface that won't chip and never needs painting. Use a notched trowel to apply the adhesive to the wall, keeping ¼ inch from the top of the base so the adhesive won't ooze above the molding. Press the molding to the wall with the long side of a 2-by-4, then roll with a hand roller or other smooth, cylindrical object (FIG. 8-37).

Feature Strips. You can incorporate your own designs and patterns with contrasting feature strips. Plan your checkerboard, striped, or border design on graph paper first. Feature strips come in a multitude of colors and widths to accommodate tile sizes. Don't put feature strips down first and tile to them; lay them in place in the proper sequence, going by your graph paper design. Butt the edge of the strip firmly against the laid tile and lower it into the adhesive. Start the next row as you would for a regular row of tile.

Installing Resilient Sheeting

The most common types of roll goods used for floors today are vinyl sheeting, rotovinyl sheeting, and linoleum. Some of these materials are

Fig. 8-37. Installing vinyl wall base.

slightly stiffer than others, but all can be applied in basically the same manner. Order your sheet goods to arrive at least three days before you install, so it can adjust to the temperature conditions in the room, which should ideally be no lower than 70 degrees Fahrenheit.

Make a scaled drawing to include all irregularities like closets, alcoves, cabinets, and doorways. If you must have a seam, determine where it should go. It's best not to put a seam in a high-traffic area.

Again, the first step in laying any type of flooring is to properly prepare the base floor. It must be smooth, level, clean, and dry.

1. After removing moldings and trimwork, unroll the flooring in a large, open space and transfer the floor plan from the graph to the roll goods with a felt pen. Make a rough cut leaving about 2 or 3 inches of excess around the felt-pen boundaries.

2. Lay the longest edge against the wall first. Position the entire piece, making sure the excesses curl up the walls on every slide. Use the long side of a 2-by-4 to crease the goods on the first long wall, then scribe it. When you finish-cut the vinyl, always leave an ⅛-inch gap at the walls for expansion. This will be covered by the molding. If you are fitting the vinyl goods to a cabinet or other place where no molding will go, cut it flush to the obstruction or cabinet. Trim away the excess using a sharp utility knife and a metal straightedge. Make relief cuts at the corners so that the sheet goods will lie flat.

If the goods are to be seamed, snap a chalk line on the floor to establish a long straight guideline where the two pieces will meet.

3. *Cutting Around Doorways or Other Irregular Shapes*: Use a template made of heavy paper, or a compass. To make a template, first place pieces of paper on the floor fitted or cut to fit around the odd shape. Tape the pieces together so they will not shift out of position. Make several loops of tape (or use double-faced adhesive transfer tape) and stick them to the face of the paper pattern in several areas. Next, gently lower the sheet goods onto the paper pattern, press hard, and lift it up so that the template sticks to the back of the vinyl goods. Cut around the template to get the exact shape (FIG. 8-38).

If you prefer, you can undercut doorjambs by resting a saw on a piece of flooring.

Where you encounter pipes or posts, mark the exact location of the pipe. Use a compass to draw the circular shape that's to be cut out. Make a slit in it from the back edge to the circle; cut out the circular opening.

4. After the entire piece is cut and fitted, you are ready to cement it to the floor. Remove the roll goods, or turn it back on itself to apply the adhesive.

Spread the adhesive evenly across the floor according to the manufacturer's instructions. You may be instructed to lay the vinyl back over on itself and spread a thin coat over half the subfloor. Or you may be instructed to apply a band of adhesive around the perime-

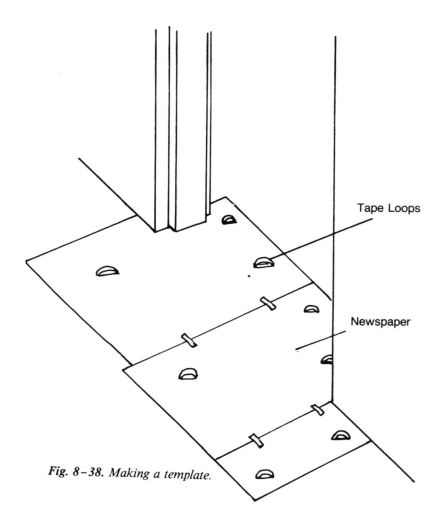

Tape Loops

Newspaper

Fig. 8–38. Making a template.

ter of the room with bands 12 inches apart over the rest of the floor. Whether you apply the adhesive in bands or cover the entire floor, be sure to apply it evenly and allow the proper time for it to set up. In most cases, you spread the adhesive about 36 square feet ahead of the already-laid covering.

5. After you have laid the roll goods firmly into place over the adhesive, clean the floor according to the manufacturer's instructions. Then roll it with a rented linoleum roller or rolling pin so that it sets firmly in the adhesive. Always start in the center of the room and roll to the walls to remove air bubbles. Clean the entire floor again, then replace the base and shoe moldings.

Feature Strips. You can add a contrasting feature strip to outline the room and tie colors together with sheet goods, too. Decide where you want to place the strip and loose-lay it over the installed flooring. Carefully trace its location on the newly installed sheet goods with a fine point felt pen. With a metal straightedge and a sharp utility knife, cut out the strip from the flooring and insert the feature strip. Borders of contrasting color should be carefully mitered at corners. For a mitered joint, overlap the two border pieces at the corner and cut through both pieces diagonally. Remove the excess and press them into position in the adhesive.

Vinyl cove moldings are available for sheet goods, as well as for tile goods.

Installing Flooring With a Seam. Allow an additional 2 inches on each piece for overlapping the seamed joints in the center. If you're using adhesive, spread it on the floor under the first piece, but stop short about 10 inches from the chalked seam line. Lay the first piece in the adhesive, allowing it to overlap the chalk line 2 inches and run up the walls 3 inches. Cut and fit the opposite wall. Position the second piece of flooring, allowing it to run up the walls 3 inches and overlap the center seam at least 2 inches.

After you have cut and fit the second piece, spread the adhesive on the floor, stopping 2 inches from the chalked guideline. Position and align the second piece, allowing the centers to overlap. Cut half-moon shapes at the end of each seam where it runs up the wall, so the ends butt to the wall. Trim excess on end walls as you did on the first two opposite walls. Snap a new chalk line over the lapped seam and cut with a straightedge and utility knife through both sheets. Lift up both halves and apply adhesive, then press the seam in place. Use pressure to roll the seam. An object like the head of a hammer run along the seam works well.

CARPETING

Carpeting used to be considered a luxury item. Today it makes for a good-looking, economical, quick coverup. If you're in a hurry to sell your house, you'll probably be wise to choose carpeting for all of your floor coverings. There are so many styles and colors available today that you're almost guaranteed of finding everything you'll need at your first stop to fit your decor and budget.

Basically there are two types of carpet installations: wall-to-wall carpet over padding, and a cushioned-back carpet that is glued directly to the floor. The wall-to-wall carpet and pad installation is a little more complex for a beginner, but it affords the more formal, custom look, which is usually preferred in "company" rooms by most people. The cushioned-back variety is very easy to install, and generally, less expensive. While it usually does not give the luxurious look of plush carpet, it is appreciated for its wearability and cleanability. Your best bet is to use both types—in colors that blend and coordinate with one another.

Select carpet type for room performance. Heavy traffic areas like kitchens, family rooms, and halls call for a durable carpet that is crush-resistant and easy to clean. This will usually mean a low-level, tightly constructed loop. In light traffic areas, like bedrooms, you can use less expensive cuts of plushes, shags, and loops. For value, check pile density. When you bend the sample back, does it expose too much backing? If so, it's probably too thin for even moderate-traffic areas like dining rooms and living rooms. When buying carpet remember that the more fiber that's packed into a square inch, the better the carpet will wear. Here's a run down on different fiber characteristics.

Nylon–Looks like wool. Cleans and dries more easily than most fibers, but soils more readily. Nylon is the most durable of all fibers, but it tends to build static electricity.

Polyester–Although not as resiliant as nylon, it has a softer, more lustrous texture.

Acrylic–Looks and feels like wool but does not resist abrasion well.

Polypropylene–A tough, stain-resistant fiber most often used in commercial carpeting.

Wool–The most luxurious and long-wearing fiber available. One that resists crushing and soil. It's also the most expensive.

Today's carpets are constructed in such a way that they have varied appearances. The plush carpet is a level-surfaced, cut-pile carpet that has a velvety look and feel. Cut piles are offered in many different heights and thicknesses, which give varying looks (FIG. 8-39). A low, or medium-cut pile carpet, relatively dense, is probably the best choice today for a more formal room because it will retain it's original appearance longer.

A nubby, more casual look is created with the same level, cut pile when a heat-set twist is applied to individual fibers. The heat-set twist gives a carpet more resiliency and tends to hide footsteps.

Long, level-surfaced cut pile produces a shag look that goes every which way for the casual look. While shags hide dirt well, the dirt is more difficult to get out from deep within the fibers. Not a good choice for rentals.

The tight, low level-loop carpet makes a hard, smooth surface for a sleek, contemporary look. It cleans more easily but tends to show soil and stains faster, even in the darker colors. Still it is the best choice for heavy-duty traffic areas because it will outwear all other styles.

Multilevel carpets produced from a mix of cut and loop fibers create

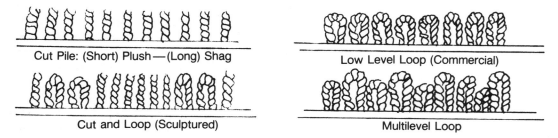

Cut Pile: (Short) Plush—(Long) Shag

Low Level Loop (Commercial)

Cut and Loop (Sculptured)

Multilevel Loop

Fig. 8-39. Carpet types.

an interesting sculptured look. The tend, however, to be more difficult to vacuum and lose their shape quickly in heavy-traffic areas.

Carpet backing, because it adds stability, is also an important consideration when buying carpeting. Usually, it's made of jute or polypropylene. All tufted carpets have secondary backings of jute, rubber, latex, foam, or polypropylene beneath the primary backing. But don't choose jute if you plan on putting the carpet outdoors, in the basement, or other damp areas. Jute will mildew and rot.

Foam backing makes padding unnecessary, and it's the most popular choice for do-it-yourself carpet installers.

How Much Carpet to Buy?

It is virtually impossible to buy carpeting without some waste—which you pay for. Since carpeting is sold by the square yard and usually comes in rolls 12 feet wide (15-foot widths are rarely available anymore), unless the floor you're covering is a square or rectangle exactly 12 feet wide with no irregularities, waste is inevitable. You can't cut down on the coverage, so the trick in saving money, is to cut down on the waste. When you order, order the smallest amount of carpeting needed to do the job, even if it means piecing and seaming.

Professional-looking results, however, should not be expected unless an accurate floor plan is drawn on graph paper and the installation is preplanned, so the pieces are put in the least visible areas. If you're willing to take the time to do your own measuring, planning, and fitting, your estimates will come in much lower than the carpet people's figures who shy away from piecing and seaming whenever possible. Remember, too, that if you decide to hire someone to do the installing, he will charge by the total amount of yardage on the roll that you purchased—including the uninstalled remnants and waste. So it's important to keep this figure at a minimum.

Measuring and Sketching. Start by carefully measuring around the room with a steel tape 50 or 100 feet long—include insets, protrusions, and door openings. Carpet should stop under the door when it's closed; always add an extra inch to this measurement for trimming, squaring, or turning under. Record accurate measurements on a room sketch and make pertinent notes.

Planning and Estimating. Transfer your measurements carefully to graph paper. When your floor plan is finished, cut a strip of paper, or even better, see-through acrylic, in a width that equals 12 feet on your graph paper. Mark the strip with arrows to help you to remember the direction of the pile.

Place the strip of paper over your floor plan, decide on seam placement, and cut the strip off to cover one whole side of the room. Next, move a 12-foot wide remnant around until you can place pieces and seams where they will be least noticeable and out of high-traffic areas. Mark each carpet section. Finally, put the strip back together again and figure the total lineal feet and square yardage. Keep these points in mind when you piece and seam.

▶ Seams should be placed in out-the-way places; down long walls without doors, or in areas where there is no thoroughfare traffic.
▶ Seams are less visible if they are run parallel to the brightest light rays coming in a window.
▶ Carpeting must always be laid in the same lengthwise direction; you cannot butt and seam pieces with the nap going in opposite directions.
▶ Always allow 6 inches for inside thresholds.
▶ Round off inches to next foot when figuring the total run of a width. Then figure the square footage.

Figure 8-40 shows how to figure the best coverage arrangement for

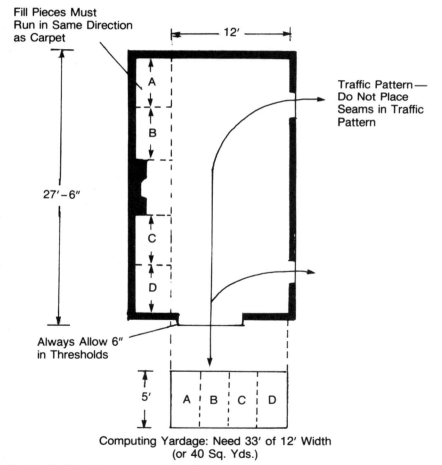

Fig. 8-40. Figuring seams and yardage.

each room. If you piece or seam, label all sections (A through D, and so on) and use your scaled drawing for installation instructions.

Installing Foam-Back Carpeting

1. Roll out the carpeting so it overlaps all walls 3 or 4 inches; then fold it back on itself to expose one half of the floor.
2. With a piece of chalk held at a 45-degree angle to the floor, mark the floor and wall junction simultaneously by drawing a line all around the room, including protrusions, insets, and doorways.
3. Roll the carpet back down again and press it into the chalk marks so they transfer to the back of the carpet. Be sure you do not shift the carpet as you do this.
4. Cut the carpet on the chalk line with scissors or utility knife.

For larger rooms, where you have to seam the carpet, first place a strip of double-faced carpet tape on the floor over the planned seam line. Loose-butt the carpet pieces together at this point, making sure that the carpeting will cover the whole floor evenly and lap up the walls about 4 inches. Lift back the carpet edges and pull off the protective paper on top of the tape. Press the carpet down on one side, then do the other side, being careful to butt the edges tightly together. Then continue fitting the carpet to the room's perimeter as above.

Installing Bathroom Carpeting From a Kit

Even if the kit includes heavy paper for making a pattern, it's sometimes easier to use newspapers, taping them together as you go along. Start on the fixture side of the bathroom and snug the first sheet up into a corner. Cut slits in the paper from the backs of the fixtures to the wall, then trace the outline of the fixture on the paper and make the cutouts. When the fixture wall is finished, tape the newspapers securely together and anchor the entire section to the floor so the pattern won't shift. Now butt more newspapers to the opposite wall, overlapping them on the pattern that you just cut. Tape all sheets together and lift the pattern carefully from the room.

Lay the pattern facedown on the reverse side of the carpet. Tape it securely, then cut it out with scissors or a utility knife. Remove the pattern and lay the carpet in place anchoring it around the edges with double-faced tape.

Installing Wall-to-Wall Carpeting

To do a professional wall-to-wall installation, you'll need to rent a few specialized tools: a knee-kicker, a power stretcher, a serrated spreader for pushing the edge of the carpet into the gully, and a seaming iron and porcupine roller for joining carpet pieces or widths. Other tools you'll need include: a standard hammer, tack hammer, rubber mallet for installing binder bars, chalk line, awl, and a sharp carpet hook knife. Supplies will include: tackless strips for anchoring the carpet and binder bars, which are metal edging strips, for doorways and other areas that don't end in a wall. Also, you'll need hot-melt seaming tape for joining carpet pieces. (See FIG. 8-41.)

Fig. 8-41. Carpet tools.

Start with a properly prepared subfloor. Remove all shoe molding. Usually a room with wall-to-wall carpeting does not need shoe molding, so you don't have to save it unless you have another use for it.

Tackless carpet strips are available in 4-foot lengths, prenailed for either a wood or concrete subfloor. These 3-ply exterior plywood strips have specially designed zinc-plated steel pins embedded in them with their points facing upward at a precise 60-degree angle. Buy enough of the stripping to go around the perimeter of the room, including cupboards, cabinets, and other abutments. Install them with the steel pins slanted toward the walls (FIG. 8-42).

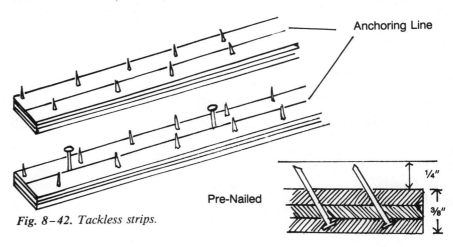

Fig. 8–42. Tackless strips.

Place the strips on the floor a distance from ³⁄₁₆ to ½ inch from the wall, depending on the thickness of the carpet.

The gully between the strip and the wall is always less than the carpet thickness. If there's too much gully, the carpet will have a drooping effect around the perimeter of the room; too little gully will not receive and hold the carpet edge securely. (See FIG. 8-43.)

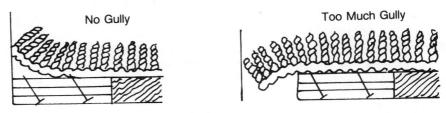

Fig. 8–43. Improper tackless strip placement.

If the strips are not prenailed, nail them down with 3d lath nails, 6 to 9 inches apart on hardwood floors, 5 to 7 inches apart on softwood floors. Drive the nails through the "anchoring line" printed on the strip; this will prevent the strip from tilting when the stretch is made. If you're laying the strips over ceramic or terrazzo, use the contact cement and nailing system recommended by the manufacturer. For concrete floors that have been subjected to oil, dust and moisture, anchor the strips with concrete nails driven every 6 inches along the anchoring line. For some types of hard-surfaced flooring, a combination of cement and nails can be used.

Binder bars, whether metal, plastic, or rubber, give the carpet a finished look whenever the carpet edge meets with another type of flooring. Binder bars make an attractive transition from one surface to another and reduce tripping hazards (FIG. 8-44).

Attach the binder bars between doorways or in open spaces with either nails or cement. Binder bars should be installed so they are directly under a door when it's closed.

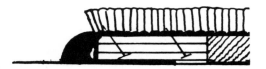

Fig. 8-44. Binder bars.

Rough-cut the padding so it covers the entire floor. Butt pieces together at seams, then tape them. If the padding has a waffle pattern, turn face it up. Padding should be trimmed so that it comes right up to the edge of the tackless strip. Staple the pad down at 6-inch intervals around the perimeter. On hard-surfaced floors use the adhesive recommended by the carpet dealer to secure the adding.

After the padding is down, roll the carpet out in a large, clean, flat area (driveway, basement, or garage). With accurate measurements taken from your floor plan, make your cuts, allowing at least 3 inches overlap around the perimeter of the room and for seams.

Bring the rough-cut carpet into the room and lay it out so the selvage on two adjacent sides (A–B and A–C) laps evenly up walls approximately ⅜ inch (FIG. 8-45).

Stretching and Hooking Carpeting

Again referring to Step 1 in FIG. 8-45, start at corner A. Hook, using the "compressed edge starting technique" (Instructions on p. 232). After corner A is compressed and hooked, stretch carpet with knee-kicker or power stretcher to corner B and hook; *don't cut off surplus on wall B–D.*

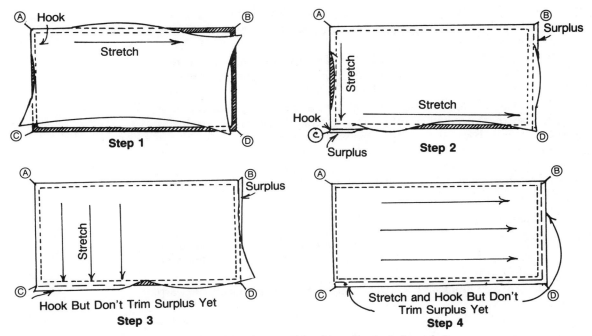

Fig. 8-45. Stretching and hooking. Step's 1 through 4.

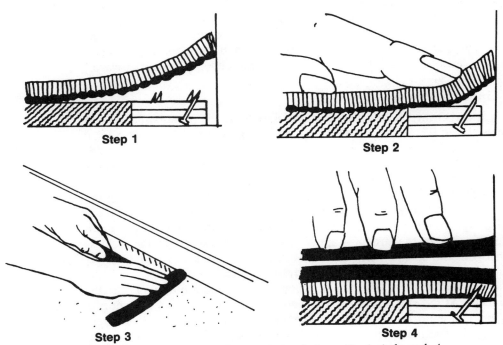

Fig. 8-46. Compressed edge starting technique. Step's 1 through 4.

(Selvage edge on carpet along wall A–B and A–C should remain approximately ⅜ inch.) Now, using the hand compression starting technique, finish securing wall A–B.

Stretch A to C and hook corner C (Step 2). Next, stretch carpet from C to D and hook corner D temporarily. Secure carpet on pins at Corner C. Then, go back and secure along wall A–C.

Starting at corner C, work to D, stretching and hooking in direction of arrows. Use the knee-kicker or power stretcher (Step 3). If surplus is excessive, trim it back to *flush* with the wall—no less.

Starting in corner D, so you can keep your weight on the stretched portion of the carpet, stretch and hook to B (Step 4).

When all adjustments have been made, you are ready for the final trimming along walls B–D and C–D.

Compressed Edge Starting Technique.

1. Referring to Step 1 of FIG. 8-46, lay out the rough-cut carpet in the room so that selvages (A–B and A–C) lap up the wall approximately ⅜ inch.
2. Rub fingers along carpet edge at wall so pins will penetrate the warp (Step 2).
3. "Iron" the edge of the carpet with a tack hammer to compress the carpet and cause full penetration of the pins (Step 3).
4. Hold the hammer face flush to the wall (Step 4). Don't tilt in downward; this will cause the edge to roll in the gully resulting in loss of compression. Keep the hammer shank flat on the carpet. With a firm, downward pressure, run the hammer head along the carpet selvage. This contacts the warp to the tackless strip pins and causes the back row of pins to start the penetration of the warp.

Using the Power Stretcher

A carpet mechanic's two most useful tools are the power stretcher and knee kicker. These can usually be rented from a carpet dealer or a local rent-all. The power stretcher stretches the carpet across the room and holds the stretch until the end can be hooked over the pins. The knee-kicker is used for small jobs to give the carpet a bump over the pins.

To operate the power stretcher, work in a kneeling position with the stretcher on your left side and your weight on the stretched carpet. Keep the power stretcher's head approximately 4 inches from the wall. The main idea is to make the stretch—apply downward pressure over the tackless strip with the spreader as you release the stretch and let the natural rebound of the carpet hook the warp over the pins.

Lift the stretcher handle with your left hand (assuming you're right-handed). At the same time, lift the head block with the tips of your fingers of the right hand. Now firmly drop the head block on the carpet to securely engage the teeth. The stretcher handle should be at an approximate 60-degree angle from the floor (FIG. 8-47).

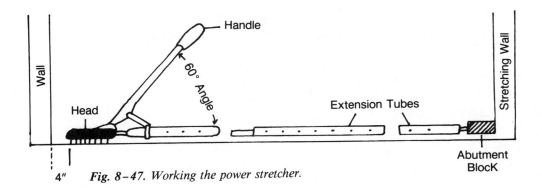

Fig. 8–47. Working the power stretcher.

Now apply pressure to the stretcher handle, using a slight pumping action. You will notice the carpet move forward. Apply pressure until the handle is in a downward and locked position (FIG. 8-48). At first, the tendency is to take too big a bite, but you will quickly learn to adjust the amount of bite to the amount of stretch that the carpet will take.

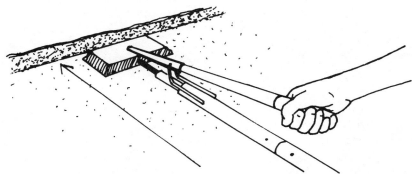

Fig. 8–48. Locking the handle.

When each stretch is made, apply pressure with the spreader over the tackless strip. Hold the pressure until you release the stretch, allowing the natural rebound of the carpet to hook the warp over the angle of the tackless strip pins (FIG. 8-49).

Use the awl to hold the penetrated pins in place after each stretch, so the hooked section doesn't come loose when you power stretch the next section.

Move the awl to the left of the stretcher and secure the newly stretched section; then release the stretcher and move the stretcher head over for a new stretch, repeating the process.

Using the Knee-Kicker

To work the knee-kicker, adjust the teeth to the depth of the carpet fabric. The teeth should reach through the pile and grip the backing, but not the padding.

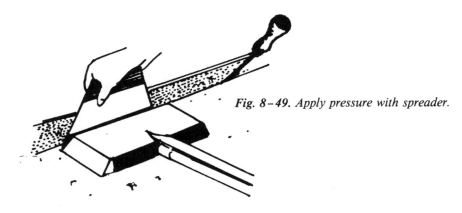

Fig. 8–49. Apply pressure with spreader.

Apply downward pressure to the neck of the kicker. The warp will slide over the pins and secure itself when your kick reaches the peak of its forward movement. Give it one or two good bumps with your knee (FIG. 8-50).

After the carpet is stretched and hooked all around the room, it's ready to be trimmed. At this stage, you will have surplus carpet at walls C to D, and B to D. Inspect your work carefully before you do any trimming. Are seams straight? Do the patterns match? Is the carpet evenly and tautly stretched? At this point, you can still unhook, make adjustments and rehook the carpet.

Fig. 8–50. Using the knee kicker.

Trimming the Carpet

You can rent a carpet trimmer or use a sharp-bladed hook knife to trim the carpet. Hold the blade of the knife against the baseboard or wall as you trim and cut downward between the wall and tackless strip (FIG. 8-51).

Then, with an awl or screwdriver, push the carpet edge into the gully. The carpet edge should not reach the floor if the cut was made right (FIG. 8-52).

If it bunches up, trim a little more off the edge. Using your fingers and the knee-knicker, give the carpet one last kick, moving the selvage deeper

Fig. 8–51. Trimming the carpet.

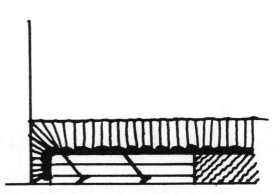

Fig. 8–52. Tucking the carpet in the gulley.

into the gully where it will barely touch the floor. Finally, smooth the edge by ironing it with the hammer head as in Steps 3 and 4 of FIG. 8-46.

Clamp the carpet to the binder bar at doorways and other open areas. First, trim the carpet so it fits under the lip of the metal bar, then tap the top of the bar with a rubber mallet or hammer and wood block to secure the carpet.

Seaming Carpets

When installing carpeting over padding, seams are usually made before the carpet is laid. Use your scaled drawing to gauge the proper widths and pieces and do your seaming beforehand. Cushioned back carpeting is easier to seam as the carpet is being installed.

To make a nearly invisible seam, you have to have selvages that match. Sometimes this means retrimming the edges.

On a low-cut pile, place one edge over the other about a half-inch and make a cut through the two pieces with a sharp utility knife and straight-edge. Remove the remnant strips and check the match.

On deep-cut pile, overlap the edges, but use the top piece's edge for the cutting guide, moving the tufts out of the way as you cut through the second, or bottom, piece.

1. Stay-tack one piece to the floor about 6 inches back from the selvage edge, parallel to the edge. Overlap the second piece ½ inch over the first piece and stay-tack it so that the two pieces "tent" up when butted (FIG. 8-53).
2. Unroll hot-melt seaming tape down the entire length of the seam, making sure that the adhesive side is up and the printed line is centered where the seam will be made. Heat the seaming iron to 250° Fahrenheit. (*Continued on p. 238.*)

Do-It-Yourself Marquetry

One of the prettiest and most unusual floor decorations that you can do resembles priceless, inlaid wood, not unlike that of fine marquetry. It's created with stencils, stains, and varnishes, and looks best in a border pattern around a room. (See stencil patterns on opposite page.)

1. Start with a freshly sanded floor of raw wood and draw your border pattern around the room. Score the shapes in the wood with a sharp utility knife. This will prevent the stains from creeping over the lines and bleeding into the neighboring design.

2. Apply a clear penetrating sealer with a small brush, to that part of the design you want to be the lightest color. When dry, sand lightly and go over the sealer with a coat of polyurethane varnish. Be careful not to get the polyurethane on any of the raw wood.

3. When the polyurethane is dry, hand sand. After wiping the entire floor with a tack rag, apply an over-all oil stain with a soft, lint-free cloth. Because the stain cannot penetrate the first application of sealer and varnish, it will bring up the border design in the natural wood color.

4. When the stain is dry, give it a light sanding. Wipe with a tack rag, and apply the darkest stain to the appropriate part in the stencil.

5. Seal the entire floor with a clear, penetrating sealer. Then apply three or more coats of polyurethane varnish, sanding lightly after each coat. This type of floor looks best when a satin varnish is used.

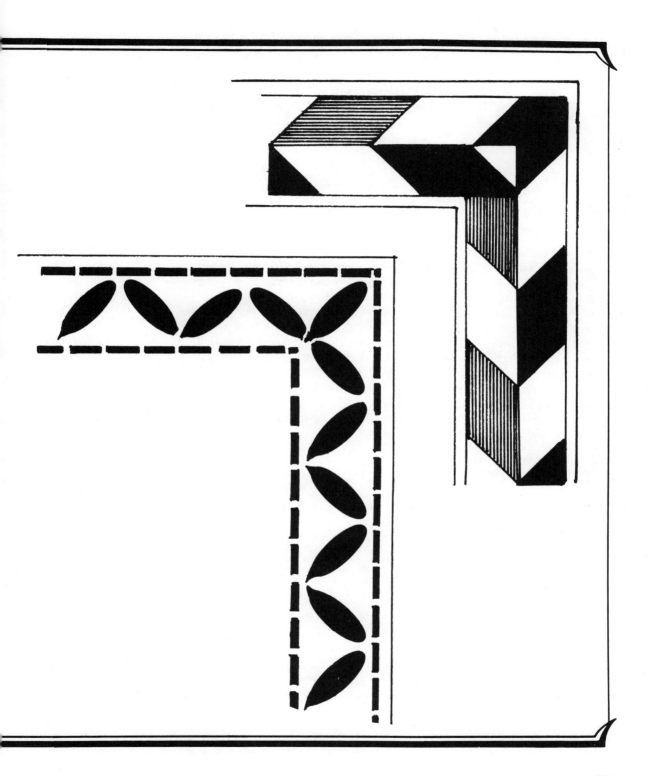

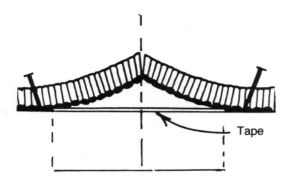

Fig. 8–53. "Tenting" carpet edges over the center of the tape.

3. Fold back the edge of one side and weigh it down to get it out of your way. Hold back the other edge with one hand and heat the tape with the seaming iron with the other hand. Move the iron slowly over a foot or two of the tape to heat the adhesive.

4. Now, with both hands, butt the edges of both pieces together directly over the heated section and press them down on the center line. The fullness of the tented carpet will allow you to get a tight bond. Push excess carpet to the right and left up against the stay-tacks. Apply pressure and let the seam set. Repeat the procedure until the entire length of the carpet has been joined. Remove stay-tacks and let the seams bond thoroughly before you begin to install the carpet.

5. Use the porcupine roller to move the tufts or loops over the seam line until the seam is nearly invisible.

Ceilings

Interest in ceilings is hardly new. Old World artists almost always used this surface as a "fifth dimension" for their work — another wall to embellish with their artistic skills. There's probably no room in your home that even resembles the proportions of the Sistine Chapel — and a Michelangelo, you're not; but that doesn't mean you should paint your ceiling white and forget about it.

Besides, from a purely practical standpoint, you should consider this an opportunity to add light and height to a dark room by visually, or structurally, raising the ceiling; or make a too-grand room cozier by lowering the ceiling. And if just looking up at a hopeless mess makes you shutter, there are many creative coverups that you can employ for a few dollars and a couple hours of your time.

Here are some lofty ideas for your ceilings.

PAINT

If the problem is one of peeling or flaking paint, and the drywall or plaster underneath is in relatively good shape, a good scraping, followed by a prime coat of sealer or stain-killer, and then repainting will usually solve the problem. Of course, cracks and holes must be repaired before applying the sealer or paint. The one drawback about a big flat surface is that any unevenness shows up glaringly; even if there are no holes or cracks, old paint lines and lumps and bumps are very obvious when painted over. Unless you remove every speck of old paint, or take the time to sand the demarcation lines smooth with the ceiling, a new paint job won't be a satisfactory solution. In this case, you may opt for another alternative.

Textured Paint

One popular method of camouflaging old, uneven ceilings is to paint them with a heavy-bodied texture paint. Textured paint won't help, if the old drywall is badly sagging or large pieces of plaster are missing. However, for covering cracks, and small holes and smoothing bumps and lumps, it's perfect. Patching later can be a problem, as textured paint is difficult to match. Also, once applied, the textured ceiling is permanent. You can no longer go back to a smooth ceiling unless you cover it with drywall.

Textured paint is applied the same as for walls, except that you press the paint-ladened trowel to the ceiling and more or less pat it on. You then swirl it to add more pattern by turning your wrist, while still applying pressure to the ceiling.

DRYWALL

Drywall is the least expensive and most adaptable surface that you can use as a base for paint or any other decorative material. You can install the drywall directly over an old ceiling—if it's flat—by nailing it into existing joists. If it's uneven, install furring strips over the joists to level the drywall. If additional nailing space is needed for the drywall ends, install 2-by-4 nailing blocks between joists. Always install the sheets perpendicular to the joists and be sure the ends land on the center lines of the joists or furring strips.

Installing drywall on ceilings requires more labor than installing it on walls. You should have another person help you get the heavy panels into place and nail them up. But if you have to work alone, make T-braces by nailing 2-foot lengths of 1 by 4s to the end of a 2 by 4 that is cut an inch longer than the reach from floor to ceiling. After the panel has been raised, you can wedge the braces securely under them to hold them in place while you nail.

Build a scaffold on which to work so that your head is about 3 inches from the ceiling. The scaffolding should be placed directly under the area where you will be putting up the first sheet; rest your T's close by so that they are within easy reach. Pick up the first piece of drywall and place the center of the panel on your head. When you get on the scaffold, grab a T-brace and wedge it in front of you; then wedge the other T-brace behind you. Adjust their positions and begin to nail.

Sometimes it's easier to nail a few 1-by-6 boards to the joists to make a ledge for the drywall (FIG. 9-1). Then you can rest the panel on the ledges while you nail. Use 8d nails to secure the ledge boards to the joists, but don't nail the boards tight to the joists. Leave a space in between so the drywall can slip in. Place the nails in the center of the boards so that the next sheet of drywall can be supported by the opposite edge of the board.

Start in a corner and butt the first sheet tight. Drive nails in at the edges to hold it temporarily, then nail all the way across, 16 inches apart at each joist, and drive nails in each corner ½ inch in from the edges. After all the panels have been installed, finish the joints with tape and compound and sand smooth.

If you use a combination of drywall adhesive and nails, you'll reduce the amount of nailing. Driving nails in from an awkward position, then

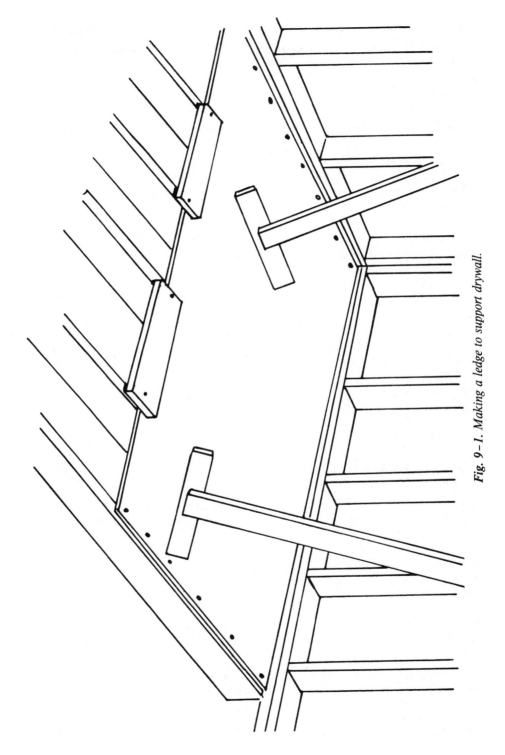

Fig. 9-1. Making a ledge to support drywall.

241

covering, taping, and sanding them can be very stressful on the arms and neck. Lay straight beads of adhesive with a caulking gun down the joists where they will make contact with the drywall panels. On joists where drywall panels join, zigzag the adhesive so that both edges will adhere.

PANELING

You can create a handsome, warm-looking ceiling with veneered plywood and still hide flaws. Thin plywood sheets should be nailed onto furring strips attached to the ceiling if the surface is bumpy or wavy.

Solid board panels and tongue-and-groove flooring planks can also be used on ceilings. They should be nailed into furring strips or directly to the ceiling joists.

Old Victorian ceilings were often wainscotted. If your ceilings are wainscotted, you'll want to restore instead of remove them. Oak wainscotting today is prohibitive in price, so you'll be offering the buyer a unique feature.

CEILING TILE

A more expensive alternative to drywall and paint is ceiling tile. Ceiling tile, made from either cellulose or mineral fiber, is designed with tongue-and-groove construction and usually sold in 12-inch squares. These tiles, available in a wide range of textures and colors, also help to muffle sounds and provide extra fire protection. Some do-it-yourselfers are tempted to simply cement them to an existing ceiling; but if the paint peels, the tiles drop. You're better advised to staple them to a furring strip grid that's anchored to joists.

A basic rule for a neat job is that partial tiles go around the room's perimeter. These cut border tiles should all be the same size and never less than half a tile wide. To determine the width of the border tiles, measure the length of one side of the room. If the measurement comes out in exact feet, you'll have no border tile for that direction. If the tiles come out uneven, add 12 inches to the number of inches remaining and divide by two. The resulting number is the width of your border tile. (Example: For a wall measurement of 10-feet, 6 inches. 12 inches + 6 inches = 18 inches. Divide by two = 9-inch border tile width.) Determine border tiles for both directions. Now snap chalk lines on the ceiling equivalent to border tile widths. These will be your guidelines for installing the first rows on both the short and long side of the room.

Cut the first tile to fit in the corner. Since the dimensions of the border tiles going in both directions may not be equal, measure carefully before you make the cut. Cut the tile on a flat surface with a sharp utility knife, using a straightedge as a guide. If you're gluing the tile directly to the ceiling, place dabs of adhesive in the center and all four corners of the tile, press it to the ceiling, and place a staple or two in the flange. After you've installed the two rows of border tile, fill in the center with full tiles. After completing the installation of the full-sized tiles, measure and fit each border tile carefully on the opposite two walls.

To fit tile around posts, pipes or ceiling fixtures, cut the tile in half and contour the center to the desired shape with a utility knife. Fit the halves around the obstruction and staple them back together.

Install a molding at the ceiling-wall junction to give the job a nice finished appearance.

Installing Furring Strips

Attach the first furring strip to the ceiling next to the wall that runs at right angles to ceiling joists. The second furring strip should be positioned so the distance between the center of the furring strip and the wall is the width of your border tile. Be sure to measure the remaining strips and place them so that the distance from the center to center of each strip is exactly 12 inches. To minimize measuring mistakes, cut a scrap board exactly 12 inches, minus the width of the furring strip, and use it as a space marker between successive furring strips. Nail through the furring strip at each joist, making sure the grid stays level; add shims if needed. Place scraps of furring strips at the wall edge between the full length strips to provide nailing space at this location.

Snap your chalk lines over the furring strips and continue attaching the tile with staples.

SUSPENDED CEILINGS

Sometimes you want to hide unattractive overhead joists, new air ducts, and ugly plumbing, wiring, and junction boxes, yet you still want to have easy access to them. A suspended ceiling will allow you to accomplish this and give you the additional advantages of reducing heating/cooling costs and insulating against sound. If your ceilings are high enough to permit lowering, you can easily install a commercially packaged suspended ceiling system.

Basically, the system consists of lightweight fiberglass panels that are laid into a metal interlocking grid dropped from the ceiling with wires. Individual components are: L-shaped angle strips that form a ledge around the perimeter of the room to support the gridwork; the gridwork, itself, which consists of metal main runners connected at four-foot intervals by 2-foot cross tees; and, of course, the 2-by-4-foot (common), or 2-by-2-foot fiberglass panels in many colors and textures. Although the main runners come 12-feet long, they'll span only 11 feet, because the slots designed to hold the cross pieces start 6 inches in from each end. They can, however, be joined for longer lengths. Be sure to order accordingly.

Planning the Gridwork

To assure a symmetrical arrangement of panels, plan the design on paper, so you'll end up with a neat installation and a minimum of waste.

Your plan will also allow you to more accurately estimate the amounts and costs of the materials.

First, take exact measurements of the room, carefully measuring alcoves, bays, and other odd shapes, and draw the dimensions to scale on graph paper. The main runners are positioned 4 feet apart across the ceiling, perpendicular to the joists. The panels at the room's edge should be spaced in such a way that the borders are equal on both sides and not less than one half the panel length. Adjust the first and last main runners to accommodate border panels. Space the cross tees so that their borders, are also equal at the ends of the room and as large as possible.

If recessed lighting is to be installed, mark where the panels of light will be located. Install the fixtures before any of the following steps are taken.

To install the ceiling:

1. Determine the exact height at which the suspended ceiling is to be placed. If recessed lights are to be used, a minimum clearance of 6 inches is required; otherwise you can get by with a minimum of 3 inches.

Add an extra inch to the chosen height to allow for the width of the perimeter angle strip. Use a level to draw a plumb line around the room indicating where the wall angle is to be attached. Fasten the wall angle securely to the wall, positioning it so that the bottom flange is on the level line. Nail it firmly to studs, or use screw anchors. If the walls are masonry, use the appropriate wall fasteners. Overlap the wall angles on inside corners; miter them with a hacksaw on outside corners.

2. The main runners should always be at right angles to the joists in the room. Mark joist location on the ceiling, then indicate the planned position of each main runner by stretching a taut reference string across the room to the opposite wall. Secured the strings with nails anchored into the walls at the top edge of the wall angle.

3. Hang suspension wires every 4 feet from the ceiling to the taut guideline string. Cut the suspension wires 12 inches longer than the actual distance between the ceiling and string. The first suspension wire for each main runner should be located directly above the point where the first cross tee meets with the main runner. If you have border panels, refer to your scaled plan for this location. Fasten suspension wires securely with screw eyes, screw hooks, nails, or by drilling small holes through structural ceiling members. Make a 90-degree bend in the wire where it crosses the level guideline, and install the main runners. If you need longer main runners, splice them, but be sure to align them in such a way that the holes for the suspension wires will be correctly positioned.

4. After the main runners are in position, insert the cross tees into the slots provided in the main runners. This locks the grid system together. (*Continued on p. 246.*)

The Tudor Look

The room shown was paneled with 4 × 8 sheets. Then two-inch strips were ripped from an extra sheet of the wood paneling and installed on the walls and ceiling above, covering the drywall joints. This created the interesting Tudor effect.

5. To install the panels, tilt them slightly and raise them above the metal framework, then let them drop into place. Start at the room's perimeter and work inward.

Fluorescent Fixtures

Fluorescent fixtures are often used with suspended ceilings. One type is completely recessed into the ceiling and sits flush on the main runners. Supporting wires should be nearby to hold the extra weight, and there must be at least 6 inches of overhead clearance.

Another type projects below the suspended ceiling and is attached to the grid with mounting clips. It, too, must be placed near a supporting wire, but it does not require overhead clearance. Fluorescent fixtures can often be hooked up to each other end-to-end and run in a row the length of the ceiling. These fixtures are available at electric supply stores.

[10]

Stairs

Since first impressions count, the tone and character of your house will be established as soon as the front door is unlatched. If you have a main staircase, it could possibly be the single most style-setting element in your home. Whether it's a magnificent colonial sculpture with striking angles and winding curves, a traditional restrained straight-run, or a contemporary space-saving spiral, try to make the stair the star attraction of the house. Aside from simple repairs and replacement parts, major design changes in a stairway are possible for do-it-yourselfers. (See FIG. 10-1).

For instance, you can open up the compartmentalized walls of a stairwell to allow more free-flowing space and light. With today's stock-milled steps and ready-to-finish newel posts, balusters, and rails, you can change the plain, rough carpentry appearance to a more finished old-time cabinetry look. You can even change the location of a stairway if you do your homework and find that conditions are favorable. Installing prefabricated stairs are not beyond the do-it-yourselfer's expertise because they come almost completely put together with clear and explicit instructions for installation.

If you're one of the lucky ones with an impressive staircase that needs only to be tightened up to eliminate squeaks, have a few repairs made, or replacement parts added, then the following instructions will get you through your chores posthaste. For extra equity, however, do consider changing a "plain-Jane" staircase into a "bell of the hall." Utilize waste space underneath with good-looking built-in storage closets, shelves, sleeping nooks, or entertainment bars. Always make sure, though, that your prime consideration is given first to safety and function. Your stairs should not only be attractive, they must allow for the easy and safe passage of people and furniture.

Fig. 10–1. *Stock-milled moldings and parts can change a rough carpentry appearance of a stair to a more finished old-time cabinetry look.*

STAIR STYLES

The style of a stair is not always determined by aesthetics; it's often the only solution for a space problem. Since imposing, winding staircases are specifically built to impress visitors, whole rooms are given to this feature, but most stairs are designed for function and compactness—to get from one floor to the other using up the least amount of living space. In such cases, L and U designs are common. The straight-run stair, which goes in an uninterrupted diagonal from one floor to another, is the simplest to build but takes up a lot of space. In remodeling, special problems are also encountered: bearing walls, plumbing, fireplaces, and chimneys may block the path of a stairway, thus, a space-saving spiral may be the only choice. (See FIG. 10-2).

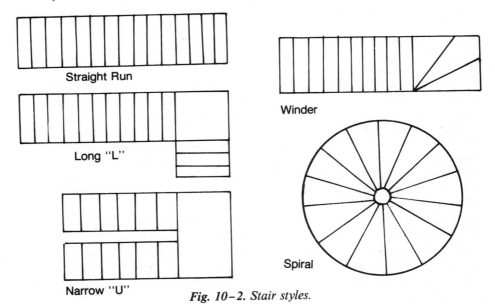

Fig. 10-2. Stair styles.

PARTS OF A STAIRWAY

The main parts of a stair are the *treads, risers, carriages,* and *stringers,* and of course, for an open stairway, the *newel posts, balusters, railings,* and *moldings.* (FIG. 10-3).

The treads are the "foot" part of a stair. Each tread projects beyond the vertical riser beneath it about 1¼ inches and has a rounded edge called a *nosing.* The nosing gives each tread more foot room than the typical rise-and-run ratio might allow. Ideally, each tread will be at least 11 inches wide. You can buy stock replacement treads (with nosings) that come from 9½ to 11½ inches wide. Treads should be at least 1¹/₁₆ inches thick for carriages or stringers up to 30 inches apart and 1½ inches thick for treads that span up to 36 inches.

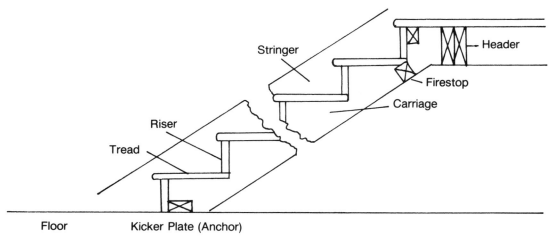

Fig. 10-3. *Main parts of a stair.*

The risers are the vertical boards between treads. They are usually cut from 1 by 8s or 1 by 10s that are ¾ inch thick. For a common main stairway, which has about 105 inches between the first and second finished floors, 14 risers would be required. This gives the ideal 7½- to 7¾-inch riser height (14 divided by 105 inches equals 7½ inches); however, in some older houses, builders had to increase the height of the riser to the maximum 8¼ inches or more to accommodate ceiling heights. Today, stair construction, like everything else, is governed by building codes, and all stock parts reflect these dimensions in width, length, and thickness. In very old houses, however, you may have to custom-cut and fit all replacement parts.

The carriages or stringers are the side boards that support the risers and treads. They are fastened to the wall studs on each side, or in the case of an open stair, supported by short walls below. The carriage-riser-tread assembly is attached to a double header at the top of the stairway and fits over a 2-by-4 kickplate anchored to the floor at the bottom. If the header at the top of the stairs rests on a bearing wall, a single header may be used, as in FIG. 10-11.

Structurally, there are three types of stairs: those with notched carriages, those with cleat carriages, and those with a combination of both. Usually the main stair is constructed with a more finished-looking cleat or cleat-and-notch system. Basement stair carriages are usually made from rough-cut, notched 2-by-12 planks, which support the riser and treads. In all cases, where stairs are wider than 30 inches, an intermediate notched carriage is installed in between.

Two-by-twelves are used for the notched carriage. This leaves at least 3½ inches of unnotched plank below the cutouts for stability and strength. The carriages are anchored to side walls, or to a full stringer attached to the side wall, then the risers are nailed to the carriage, and finally, the treads are attached to the carriage and risers. (FIG. 10-4).

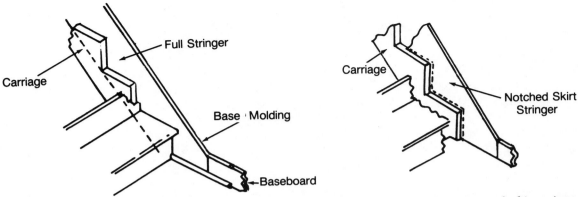

Fig. 10-4. Notched carriage with full stringer.

Fig. 10-5. Notched carriage with skirt stringer.

A more finished stair combines the rough notched carriage and a finishing baseboard called a skirt-stringer (FIG. 10-5). The notched carriages, with treads and risers in place, are nailed to wall studs on each side. Then skirt stringers, scribed to accommodate the ends of treads and risers, are fastened over them to hide nail holes.

After the risers and treads are marked on the stringer, a line is drawn below each tread line at a distance equal to the thickness of the tread. A 1-by-3-inch cleat, cut to the unit-run length of the tread, is then screwed (with 5 countersunk screws) to the inside face of the stringer (FIG. 10-6).

In a modern prefabricated stairway, the stringer and carriage, called a *housed-stringer,* are one and the same. The housed stringer has ½-inch routed grooves cut into its face to receive the ends of the treads and risers (FIG. 10-7). Wedges are then glued into V-shaped spaces between risers and treads underneath the stairs to secure them tightly to the housed stringer. All treads and risers are rabbet-joined with glue blocks added at the inside joints for reinforcement. On enclosed stairs, this type of carriage is used on both walls. On open-sided stairs, notched carriages are used with wall

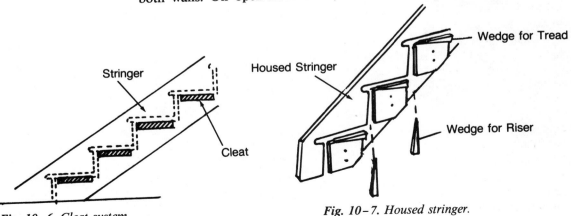

Fig. 10-6. Cleat system.

Fig. 10-7. Housed stringer.

studding below for extra support. All riser-carriage joints are mitered to form finished outside corners, and return nosings are used at the ends of the treads. Moldings installed under the nosings finish off the stairway.

STAIR REPAIRS

Repairs may range from fixing a simple squeak, to replacing broken or missing parts, or to installing a whole new stairway. In any case, you'll need to know how your stair was built. To find out which type you have, inspect the underside. If you can't get beneath the stairs, push a thin knife blade into the joint between stringer and stair tread. If it penetrates only about ½ inch, the stairway has a housed stringer. If the blade goes all the way through to the wall, it's a notched carriage with a skirt stringer. The cleat stair is easily detected by its vertical joint between tread and abutting stringer.

Squeaks

Squeaks may be annoying, but they're easy to fix. Most often they're caused from treads separating from adjoining risers, usually because nails or screws work loose under heavy foot traffic, or because boards warp or shrink. They're more often a problem in carriage-supported stairways than in housed-carriage construction. Treatment varies according to whether the staircase is opened or closed.

On an open staircase (one where you can get underneath) have someone walk slowly up and down the stairs so you can locate and mark the faulty step. If you find gaps between the tread and riser sides, tap in small, glue-coated wood shims (FIG. 10-8). If old glue blocks are loose, install new ones between them, or scrape off the old glue, apply new glue, and refasten them with screws.

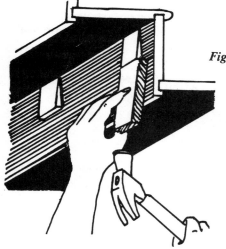

Fig. 10–8. Tap in wood wedges from below.

If gaps aren't apparent, and there are no reinforcing glue blocks, glue and screw several 1-by-3-inch blocks of wood into the area where tread and risers meet. Use wood screws that don't go all the way through riser and tread boards (FIG. 10-9).

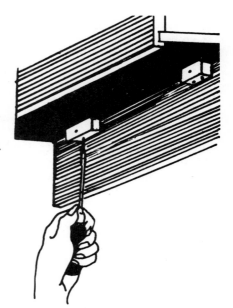

Fig. 10–9. Install wood blocks.

Although squeaks in a housed stringer are rare, occasionally wedging comes loose between the tread and riser. Try nailing it down, or rewedging the gap.

On a closed staircase, you'll have to work from above. If the stairs are carpeted, remove the carpeting, and locate the squeak by walking up and down. Mark the spot. Treads that are loose at the nose can be secured with ring-shanked flooring nails driven through the tread into the riser at slight angles to each other. If the gap is too large to close with nails, use no. 8 wood screws 2½ inches long driven through pilot holes. Coat the screw threads with paraffin first so they will turn easier in the hardwood. Countersink the screws or nail heads and fill the holes with putty; or glue pieces of dowel into the countersunk holes and sand them off level with the tread. If screws or nails will cause the front edge of the step to bow, use wedges, instead, under the nosing to level the tread and stop the squeak (FIG. 10-10). This is not possible, of course, with a tongue-and-groove joint, unless you can get to the underside to drive the wedges in. Cut wedges off flush with a sharp knife in front and cover with scotia molding.

Loose joints at the rear of the tread can be treated in several ways. One option is to force a bead of graphite (available in hardware stores) in the tread-and-riser joint. Another option is to drive small hardwood wedges or

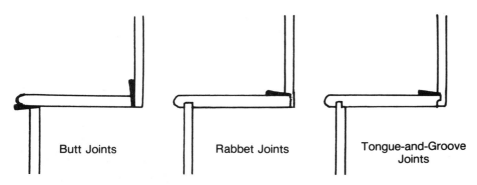

| Butt Joints | Rabbet Joints | Tongue-and-Groove Joints |

Fig. 10–10. Eliminating Squeaks from above with wedges.

shims into the joint crack after dipping the wedges in glue. Use a hammer and wood block to drive them in, then trim away excess wood and cover the joint with shoe molding. A third option is to nail quarter-round molding in place against the riser and tread, alternately nailing into both the riser and tread along the moldings length.

Sagging Steps

If the steps sag or bounce when you walk on them, it may be a signal that the house has settled and the stairs are now out of plumb. Jack up the floor from underneath and see if you can realign the stair joints. If all the stair parts are in otherwise good condition, all that's needed is a little scraping, regluing, and adding a few nails.

Worn Treads

To replace worn treads, you'll first have to remove the old ones. If the stairway is an open one, you'll also have to remove the balusters. Always remember when working with treads and risers that you're working with hardwood, which will split unless pilot holes are drilled in first for screws or nails. Also, since new glue will not adhere to old glue, all joints must be scraped well to remove residue. Your job will be easier if you can disengage the glue blocks and pound the tread up from underneath. If you have to work from above, pry the tongued or butted front edge up first, then pull the tread away from in under the riser at the back. If the tread doesn't come up easily, cut it in several sections using drilled starter holes, then carefully remove the tread pieces. Going by the original installation procedure, replace the treads by reversing the process. Spread a generous bead of glue over the carriage before nailing the treads down with 8d finishing nails. Replace balusters, return nosings and moldings where applicable. Countersink nails and fill holes with putty. Let the step dry thoroughly before you allow foot traffic on it again.

REPLACING OLD STAIRS

The easiest and best solution for replacing an entire staircase is to purchase a factory-built one. The mill or manufacturer will make the stairway to your specifications and deliver it to your door. You need only install the stair unit and add the balustrades, which are purchased separately from stock parts.

Accurate measurements, of course, are crucial. Take careful measurements of the staircase that you're replacing. If you're planning to make some changes, take precise measurements. In many cases, local builders or manufacturers' representatives will help you measure and choose a stair; some will even write the specifications for you. But it's up to you to comply with local building codes.

Information the stair builder must have includes:

▶ Whether the stair is closed, open, or partially open
▶ Whether the open side will be supported by a wall (A free–standing side must have extra support.)
▶ Whether it will have a balustrade
▶ The total rise, total run, and width of the stair

If you're involved with new construction or opening up a floor to add a new stair in a remodeling project, you'll have to take accurate measurements and make the proper allowances according to code. On new construction, spacer boards are usually nailed to the sides of the carriages before they are attached to the wall studs. This ⅝-inch space allows you to insert the drywall when you finish off the stairwell walls (FIG. 10-11).

Stair Width

Building codes specify minimum widths for clear passageway and headroom. These factors will determine the total width and length of a stair and stair opening. If the code stipulates that the minimum width of a stair should not be less than 32 inches between handrails, the opening must actually be wider to accommodate finger space between the rail and wall, the rail itself, and any new finishing materials that will be applied to the wall like, drywall, paneling, or plaster (FIG. 10-12).

Vertical Clearance

Headroom, measured from the finished ceiling height down to the nose of a tread, is important too. Usually codes dictate a minimum clearance of 76 inches for basement stairs and 80 inches for main stairs. Of course, greater headroom clearance is an advantage for tall people and furniture movers. To be safe, make sure that there is at least a clear vertical distance of 6 feet, 8 inches from each tread on the main staircase to the ceiling, and a 6-foot, 4-inch clearance for basement stairways.

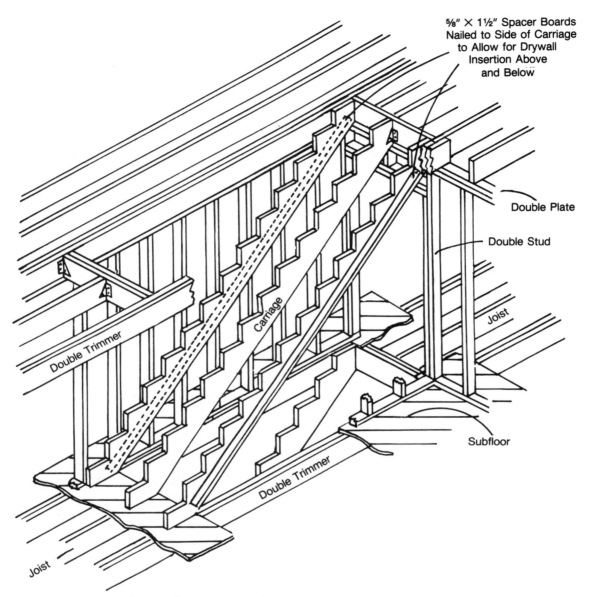

Fig. 10–11. *Interior framing for new construction.*

Other Stair Clearances

No stair run should be longer than 16 steps without a landing. If landings are required between the top and bottom of a stair, they should not be less than 2 feet, 6 inches wide between handrails. Landings at the foot and head of stairs should allow adequate room for the opening of

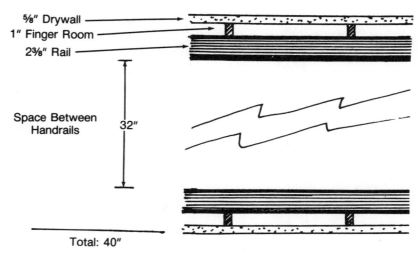

⅝" Drywall ⎯⎯⎯⎯⎯⎯
1" Finger Room ⎯⎯⎯⎯
2⅜" Rail ⎯⎯⎯⎯⎯⎯⎯

Space Between Handrails   32"

Total: 40"

Fig. 10–12. Figuring actural stair width.

doors and for turning corners while moving furniture. This usually requires a 3-foot-square area of free space.

No stair should be steeper than 35 degrees.

Figuring the Rise and Run

You can measure the rise and estimate the run of the stair by the following method. The total run of the stair you receive from the builder might be slightly longer or shorter than your estimate, but your calculations will tell you roughly where the bottom step will go.

1. Measure between the upper and lower *finished* floors. If a floor on a level is not yet finished, add the estimated thickness to this figure. If there is no stair opening yet, drill a hole through the stairwell area and drop a plumb bob to measure the depth from above. Convert the distance from finished floor to finished floor to inches (FIG. 10-13).

2. Proper stair height and tread width is required for safety and comfort and is well governed by established rules. In order to keep the unit rise between 6 and 8¼ inches (usual code stipulation), divide by 7 or 7½ to get the number of risers. (Example: 105-inch finished height, divided by 7½ unit rise = 14 risers). If your measurements end up in fractions, round them up for a slightly shallower stair, down for a steeper one. The result in the example is 14 risers with a unit rise of 7½. Fifteen risers for the finished height would result in a 7-inch riser height.

3. For any kind of stairs, carpenters make sure that the unit rise and the unit run total 17 or 18 inches. Thus, if we add 10½ inches for the unit run to our 7½-inch rise, we will get 18 inches. The total run will be 13 (there is always one less tread than riser) times 10½ inches, or 136½ inches (11 feet, 4½ inches).

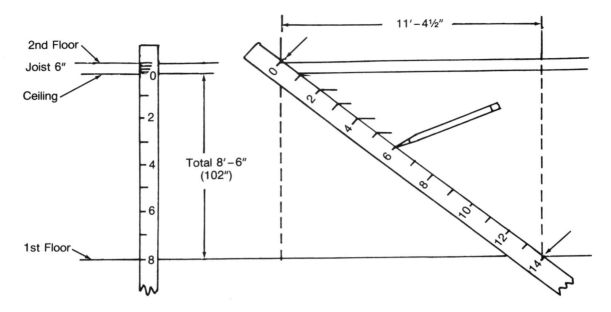

2nd Floor

Joist 6"

Ceiling

0

2

4

6

8

Total 8'-6"
(102")

1st Floor

11'-4½"

0

2

4

6

8

10

12

14

Measure from 2nd Floor Line
to First Floor Line

Set Scale for 14 Equal Spaces (Risers)
and Mark Risers Accordingly

Fig. 10–13. Laying out a stair.

4. With a plumb bob, mark the floor where the stringer will rest at the head of the stairs. Then, from this mark, measure off and mark the total run on the floor.

The builder will provide a landing tread at the top of the stair that will make the transition from the stair to the finished floor that it will join to. If you are using a balustrade, specify a bullnose starting tread, which will simplify installing the starting newel post. (See FIG. 10-14).

Opening Up the Floor

Replacing a stair in an existing opening shouldn't pose much of a problem for most do-it-yourselfers — providing they have enough helpers to assist them. But where an entire new stairway is to be erected and installed through a new access opening in an upper floor, a reevaluation of carpenter skills is in order. The job may be simple or complex, depending on the following.

First, some sort of framing is necessary to reinforce or replace the structural members that you cut into. This isn't an insurmountable task if the stair's long sides run parallel to existing joists. But where the length of the stair runs perpendicular to the length of the joists, and where you'll have to cut into six or more of them, the project becomes a little more complicated because the opening will have to be reinforced with long

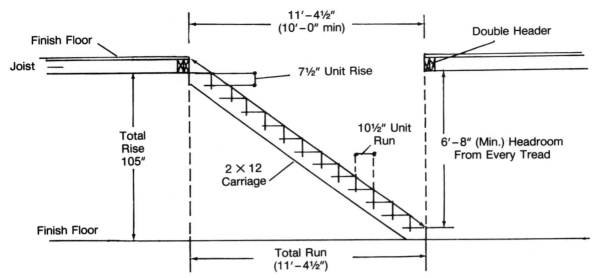

Fig. 10-14. Common stair construction

double headers and may require a supporting wall underneath. Without a supporting wall, the opening cannot be more than 10 feet in length.

If, however, the size and planned position of the stair meets all codes; has at least 3-foot clearances at both head and foot of the stair; and doesn't interfere with chimneys, plumbing lines, electrical wiring, heating ducts and the like — have a go at it! Especially, if — as luck will have it — the long sides of the openings run parallel to existing joists and your stairway is a simple straight-run against an adjoining wall. But if you foresee other problems, you should honestly admit to your carpentry limitations and hire a professional to do the job.

Making the Stair Opening. To locate the opening above the stair, you'll have to make sure that there is a minimum headroom (6 feet, 8 inches) from every tread. Using the total run measurement you marked on the floor, and starting with the bottom step, mark the riser positions on the adjoining wall. (If the stair is to be in the center of a room, you'll have to measure riser heights from the floor.) When you locate a step that does not allow the minimum vertical clearance, go back to the next lowest tread that does, and mark the ceiling above it with a plumb bob. This point indicates the other end of your stair opening. With a chalk line and precise measurements, mark off the rectangular opening of the stairwell on the ceiling.

Cutting a stair opening requires removal of finish flooring, subflooring, joists, and some ceiling material. But before you do this, you must provide adequate support for each side of the hole. (See p. 126, FIG. 6-19.)

1. After the joists on each side of the proposed opening are supported with jack posts or temporary 2-by-4 frame supports, drill holes up through the corners of the planned opening. On the upper floor,

extend the length of the opening 3 inches to allow for the thickness of the double headers at the ends. Snap chalk lines and saw through the finish floor and subfloor. Remove obstructing ceiling material and hand-saw the joists flush with the new opening.

2. Cut two lengths of joists to fit between the trimmer joists at each end of the opening and nail them together with 10d nails.

3. Nail 3-inch joist hangers to each end of the double header, and butt the header against the ends of the cut joists between the double trimmers. Then nail the joist hangers to the trimmer joists, using all the nail holes in the hangers.

Framing Stair Openings

Next, slip joist hangers on each of the cut joists and nail securely. Nail the other end of each hanger to the header. Install the opposite double header in the same manner. (See FIGS. 10-15 and 10-16).

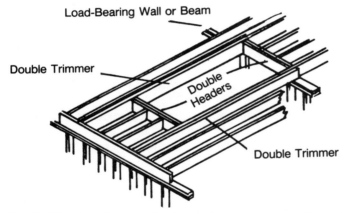

Fig. 10–15. Framing: Length of stair openings running parallel to joint.

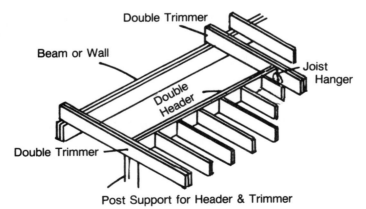

Fig. 10–16. Framing: Length of opening running perpendicular to joists.

Installing the Prefabricated Stairway

You are now ready to install the new stair. With one helper on the upper floor and another assisting you in maneuvering the stair from below, position the housed-stringer flush to the wall with the top riser against the double header, even with the top of the subfloor, and the bottom stair held in place behind wood blocks temporarily nailed to the floor. Fasten the riser to the double header securely with 16d finishing nails in vertical rows. Make the rows about 10 inches apart and space each nail in the row 2 inches down from one another. You may have to shim both bullnose step and riser to get them plumb before nailing. Make sure each step is level. (See FIG. 10-17.)

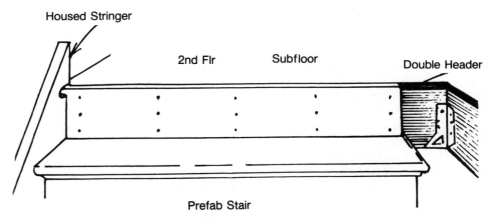

Fig. 10–17. *Nailing the top riser.*

Locate the wall studs on the adjoining wall underneath the stair and fasten the housed stringer to the center of each stud with two or more 16d common nails.

To build a supporting wall underneath the open part of the stair, nail a top plate to the underside of the stairs. Start the plate at the floor on the bottom and nail it to the risers, allowing a half inch of space between the stringer and top plate for drywall insertion later. Install the sole plate on the floor directly under the top plate and complete the partial wall with stud framing (FIG. 10-18).

The Balustrade

On an enclosed stair, the handrails are screwed to wall framing. Open stairs that go beyond three steps should have a balustrade for support and safety. A balustrade usually consists of a starting and landing newel post, balusters, and a handrail. In some cases, where a rail makes a sharp pitch to an upper newel, a curved gooseneck is required for the transition. All parts are ordered separately, along with the hardware to install them, which

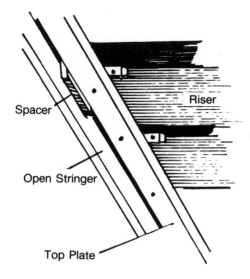

Spacer

Riser

Open Stringer

Top Plate

Fig. 10–18. Building a partial wall under a stair.

include rail bolts (lag bolts), hardwood plugs to fill access holes for the rail bolts, and trim to cover the hardware.

Balusters. The balusters are the vertical posts between tread and railing. Since handrails should rise 30 to 34 inches above the tread, balusters should be ordered accordingly. They usually come with dowels on each end, which are fitted into holes drilled in the treads and underside of the handrail. Some types are installed with dovetail joints on the bottom.

Railing. A rail should be narrow enough (no more than 2½ inches) so that it can be grasped firmly; it should be securely anchored to the newel posts. Usually, the ends of the rails are attached to the newel posts by rail bolts. The rail bolts are inserted through shank holes at each end of the rail. A bored hole under the rail that intersects with the shank hole allows access to the machine-threaded end of the bolt, which is fitted with a washer and nut. The nut is tightened by a nailset pounded against the notches on the nut. Then a wood plug is inserted into the access hole to conceal it.

Newel Posts. Starting and landing newels give structural support to the railing at the bottom and top of the stairs. Newels can be carved or plain posts that are mortised on the bottom to receive the ends of the riser and stringer. Starting newels usually extend through the floor and are bolted to joists beneath.

A more easily installed starting newel post is attached to a *bullnose tread,* a wider bottom step that has a rounded end. The traditional bullnose has several balusters encircling the main post, all of which are capped by a spiraling rail end, called a *volute.*

The main post is set in a hole drilled through the center of the rounded tread end. A thick dowel on the end of the post extends down to the floor, passing through two wood shelves that create additional support for the post. This system eliminates the complicated fitting, drilling, and mortising of the landing newel mentioned above.

Gooseneck. Where a railing rises sharply to an upper newel post, a curved piece, called a gooseneck, is inserted to make the transition.

Spiral Stairs

Where there is not enough space to accommodate a full flight of stairs, a spiral stairway can be installed. Spiral stairs are available in kit form and are made of hardwood, aluminum, or steel. These prefabricated stairs require openings from 3½ feet to 8½ feet in diameter, but widths less than 4 feet are not recommended. You can order a full spiral (360 degrees) or a three-quarter turn (270 degrees).

The stairs are assembled prior to shipment. Finished assemblies of stringers and treads are shipped in a single unit; you install the balusters and handrails.

To order, include a sketch and scaled drawing of the room. Specify exact height from finished floor to finished floor and indicate the diameter of the opening. Also indicate the preferred entry and exit directions for each floor. The manufacturer will help you decide the number and size of the treads and include comprehensive instructions for installing the stairs.

Unlike other staircases, the opening for the spiral stairway must be finished before stair installation. If scraps of the ceiling material cannot be reused,you'll have to finish the exposed edges with new drywall, plaster, plywood, or decorative moldings.

CARPETING STAIRWAYS

The quickest way to cover stairs in disrepair is to carpet them. You can do this by simply adding a runner, precut and bound, in 18-, 22½-, 27-, or 36-inch widths. Or you can custom-install your own strip of carpeting with a margin on either side of the step, or, from stringer to the edge of the balusters. However, if you want carpeting around each baluster and tailored over the end of each open step, hire a carpet installer, as this job is difficult and time-consuming.

To measure for the carpeting, start under the nosing of the top riser and continue on down to the bottom riser, measuring every tread, nosing, and riser. Never assume that all risers and treads are equal, especially in older houses. This could be a fatal mistake. If the hall carpet can drop over and include the top riser, so much the better. You will eliminate a seam and a tacking job at the head of the stairs. Add a full inch to each step for pad take-up, then add an extra foot to the total overall measurement to allow the carpet to be shifted when it begins to show wear at the nosing. The extra length will be folded under against the top and bottom risers.

If you're laying a cut-pile carpet, be sure that the nap (the smooth stroke) runs down the stairs so that you get maximum wear from the carpet.

You can rent the tools you'll need: a knee kicker to stretch the carpet and a stair tool to tuck the carpet into the crotch between riser and tread.

For anchoring materials, use either tackless stripping (metal or wood strips that have angled nails or teeth to grip the carpeting), or pressure-sensitive tape (which must be additionally reinforced by tacks). You can also employ the old-fashioned "tack-and-turn" method, using only tacks and a hammer.

Tape Method. The tape method is usually used on runners, foam-backed carpeting which won't be glued down, or where the carpeting is installed without padding. When using tape, place it on both sides of the tread-riser joint and around the nosing. With both the tack-and-turn and tape methods, the carpeting's position should be reinforced with tacks placed 5 or 6 inches apart in the crotch. (See FIG. 10-19).

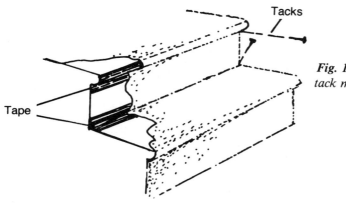

Fig. 10–19. Tape and tack method.

Tack-and-Turn Method.

1. Mark guidelines on the treads and risers to indicate the finished carpet line (A), and where the padding will stop (B), ¾ inch inside the finished carpet line. Don't use padding that's too thick; it will "roll" over the nosing and create a safety hazard.

2. Cut pieces of padding for each tread to the width measurement (B), long enough to completely wrap the nosing and overlap the riser by about a half inch. Cement the padding down, then tack every 6 inches along the back of the tread and under the nosing (FIG. 10-20).

3. Fold under ¾-inch on each side edge of the carpet. Then, lay the carpet on the floor, pile side down at the foot of the stair, and run an extra 6 inches up the riser. Nail a wood strip over the carpet at the base of the riser. Then fold the carpet over the strip for an invisible bottom anchor. (See FIG. 10-21).

4. Use the knee kicker to stretch the carpet taut over the nosing and tread. With the side edges folded against the finished carpet lines, place

(Continued on p. 266.)

An Under-Stair Niche

A stairway with unused space under it has the potential for becoming a sleeping niche, extra storage space, entertainment center, or even a telephone booth. One possibility is shown below. An awkward space under a stair is an ideal place to nestle a cozy sleeping compartment and extra storage space. Add storage drawers under the bed and doors to make optimum use of nook-and-cranny space. Other possibilities include a cozy reading room or convenient lavatory. With a little ingenuity, you can transform wasted space into useful space.

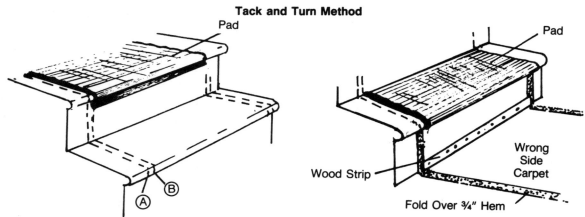

Tack and Turn Method

Fig. 10–20. Mark guidelines for carpet and pad.   *Fig. 10–21. Installing the carpet.*

one tack at each side of the carpet in the crotch. Do this all the way up to the top riser. Fold under 6 inches of excess carpet against the top riser.

5. When the entire carpet is stretched and anchored in place, work back down the stairs, nailing tacks every 4 inches apart across the crotch on each step.

Tackless Strips. When fastening the carpet with tackless strips, nail a strip (teeth facing down) to the bottom of every riser except the bottom one, up ½ inch from the crotch. Nail another strip (teeth facing crotch) at the back of every stair tread, ½ inch from the crotch. Then glue padding to each tread as you would in Step 2 of the tack-and-turn method, except butt it to the stripping at the back of the tread. Follow Step 3, and proceed up the steps, stretching the carpet over the tread nosings and anchoring it into the teeth of the tackless strip. Keep the folded edges aligned with the finished carpet guideline. With a stair tool and hammer, drive the carpet into the crotch, further tightening the carpet. For further help, follow the directions for carpet installation in Chapter 8.

[11]

Fireplaces

It's true. The hearth is the heart of the home. It creates a mood of warmth and coziness that seems to draw people to it. A crackling fire makes a room come alive with a charm and vitality that no other decorative or architectural feature can equal. Even one safe, working fireplace in a home will increase its market value considerably. If your house does not have a fireplace, there are many energy-efficient, easy-to-install, inexpensive models available today that would qualify as justifiable expenditures when remodeling for resale.

STYLES AND TYPES

Fireplaces can be grouped into five main categories: the built-from-the-ground-up masonry fireplace, the built-over-a-form masonry fireplace, the prefabricated freestanding fireplace, the prefabricated zero-clearance fireplace, and electric or gas models.

A masonry fireplace that's built from the ground up is the most expensive kind. Unless it's already in the house you're remodeling, your budget probably won't take the $3,500 to $5,000 that it would cost to build. This kind of masonry fireplace is installed on an inside or outside wall over a solid foundation.

If a masonry fireplace is still what you want, however, and you think you can afford from $2,500 to $3,500, consider one that's built around a manufactured form. The form will limit you to conventional size in width and depth, but it's faster and easier to install than the custom masonry fireplace. This type will also require a foundation and masonry work for the face.

The prefabricated zero-clearance fireplace costs from $400 to $2,000. It can be positioned directly against a wall or in a corner and does not require a foundation. The flue extends through the wall and rises outside to a point above the ridge on the roof. Made of galvanized steel plate, this type of fireplace radiates heat into the room instead of absorbing it as masonry does. It does not necessarily require a masonry face; many use paneling or other standard building materials. If you select a combustible material, however, hold such material a distance of 5 inches from the sides, and 7 inches from the top of the opening. Mantels should not be installed less than 12 inches from the top of the opening.

A prefabricated, metal, freestanding fireplace stands clear of the house's walls. It throws off heat in all directions—not only from the firebox, but from the metal chimney as well. Therefore, it's more energy efficient than any of the other types. It's also less expensive, starting at $300. A do-it-yourselfer can easily install this type in a day or so. Installation entails cutting through the ceiling and roof and putting in the stove-pipe and chimney. Follow manufacturer's directions on flue sizings and installation.

A gas or electric model fireplace might be the perfect solution for apartment dwellers. They look like wood-burning models, but they are considerably cheaper, running from $150 to $500. Available in many materials, including simulated brick, these fireplaces are primarily decorative and do not give off substantial amounts of heat. A gas fireplace must be connected by a gas company employee. Check to see that gas fireplaces are allowed in your community; some are restricted by code.

Installation of an electric fireplace is simple; you merely take it out of the box and plug it in. This type of "instant" fireplace will cost dearly on the electric bill and may be a negative feature when it comes time to sell the house. Fake logs that look like real logs contain an electric heater. Some even "project" flames onto a black background, giving the illusion of wood burning.

EXISTING FIREPLACES

Fireplaces were used as a sole heat source years ago, so it's not uncommon to find one in every room in an old house. If you're lucky, they'll still be intact; but more likely than not, you'll find them faceless, or buried behind layers of old paint wallcoverings or walls. If you want to preserve them, you'll have to unearth them carefully in your own archaeological dig.

Cleaning the Chimney

Chimney fires cause millions of dollars in damage each year and take hundreds of lives, so before you light a fire in the fireplace, be sure the flue is clean and the chimney masonry is sound. Creosote is a highly flammable by-product of combustion, and it doesn't take more than a quarter-inch of a creosote-soot buildup inside a flue to fuel a fire. The easiest way to get the job done, of course, is to hire a chimney sweep. This way you can get the chimney cleaned along with an accurate assessment of its condition. Chimney sweeping is something of an art because of the infinite shapes, sizes, and types of chimneys. You can, however, clean and check your own chimney, if you have a steady pair of legs and don't mind climbing around the rooftop.

Determine the diameter of the brush needed to clean the flue properly. You can rent wire brushes and scrapers to fit specific chimney sizes. The basic procedure is very simple, as well as dirty; you must scrape away the heavy encrustment from the chimney's inner surfaces, then use the brush to remove the rest of the soot and creosote. The brushes and scrapers come with long extension handles. You may get some friendly advice on ways to save money cleaning chimneys—like pulling old burlap bags filled with sand up and down the chimney's interior or whacking an old tire chain around the inside. Don't be tempted. You'll probably knock out the bricks and your problems will really begin.

Relining the Chimney

Once the walls of the flue are clean, check for cracks, holes, and missing mortar with a trouble light. Should you find deficiencies, your options are: 1. tear the chimney down and rebuild a safe one; or 2. reline it. Many old chimneys lack liners to protect the brickwork from extreme temperatures, which cause deterioration. Even if they were lined with tile, a previous chimney fire could have cracked the lining, which will permit smoke and flames into the house. Chimney relining costs are approximately one-third of what a mason would charge you to tear down the old stack and build a new one in its place. Many people consider a relined chimney safer than a tiled one.

There are two ways of relining chimneys: with a column of stainless steel, or by the Insulcrete bladder method. In the stainless steel method, a baseplate with a hole in it to accommodate the liner is installed on the smoke shelf above the fireplace opening. A tube of stainless steel is threaded down the chimney and attached to the baseplate; then it's centered with clamps and stabilized. The area around the liner is then filled with the appropriate insulation. Usually the first few feet of the void consist of a vermiculite and masonry cement mixture to seat the tube firmly. From that point on, it can be filled with insulation alone, as long as the chimney is sound. Since vermiculite absorbs water, the top of the flue must be carefully sealed with either a masonry cap or fabricated stainless steel lid.

With the Insulcrete method, a 6-inch rubber bladder tube is dropped down the chimney and inflated by an air compressor. Insulcrete is then poured by bucket brigade down the chimney, filling the space around the bladder. The form is left in place 24 hours, then deflated and removed. The top of the chimney is pointed out with regular mortar.

Once the chimney, flue, and firebox are in good condition, check the fireplace's performance to see if it draws properly.

Correcting Fireplace Deficiencies

There are a number of reasons why a fireplace will fail to draw properly: 1. it needs to be cleaned; 2. there is a horizontal run built into the chimney that causes a poor draft; or 3. there is an improper, or deficient, smoke shelf in the fireplace opening. Assuming that it's none of the above, here are some more probable causes: a chimney too low to catch the wind from all directions may prevent a proper draft; neighboring buildings, a hill, or a large tree may be the culprits. In this case, you will have to extend the rise of the chimney. (See FIG. 11-1 for the parts of a fireplace).

A faulty damper or a missing part will also prevent the fireplace from drawing properly. If you find that it's necessary to replace the damper, hire a qualified mason to do the work.

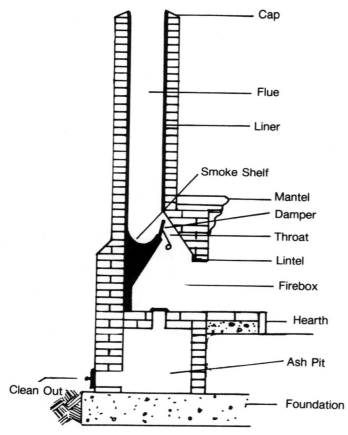

Fig. 11-1. A typical working fireplace.

Another external problem may be caused by low indoor air pressure. *Chimney backdraft* is what happens when air flows down the flue and into your house instead of up and out to the atmosphere. And it can be a very serious health hazard. Where you have numerous fireplaces and exhaust fans operating in a house, and the house is exceptionally tight, an imbalance may be created between air exhaust and air supply. Instead of natural gases within the house rising and helping to maintain an updraft, the house is depressurized. The depressurization creates an opposite force and sucks the air down the chimney and into the house. Fireplaces are responsible for most of the serious backdraft incidents in a house. A problem fireplace is one with an open front. You can solve this by installing glass doors on the fireplace front.

In order to get the oxygen a fire needs for combustion, the fire must draw room air into the fireplace. In cold weather, the warm air leaving the house up through the fireplace chimney is replaced by frigid air seeping into the house via cracks and holes. Drafts and cold floors are caused by this infiltration. A better way to provide oxygen for combustion is through a direct air supply duct or inlet kit, which is sold through heating supply stores. Inlet ducts fit into holes drilled in back of the floor of the fireplace and come with doors and baffles to feed outdoor air directly into the fireplace.

Fireplaces often take more heat out of a room than they put in. While a fire will emit a lot of heat, fireplaces don't. Most of the heat from a fireplace never reaches you, it goes right up the chimney. About 80 percent, in fact, is pulled up and out with the gases; the walls and floors of the fireplace intercept some more of the heat. All told, you probably end up with only 10 to 15 percent of the fireplace's heat to warm you.

When you install glass fireplace doors and inlets to a fireplace, you improve the efficiency of the fireplace. Glass doors not only control intake drafts, and reduce excessive airflow up the chimney, they also reduce wood consumption and offer safety from flying sparks. Choose doors that fit snugly, and caulk the gap between the frame and masonry.

FREESTANDING STOVES AND FIREPLACE INSERTS

Another very popular and aesthetically acceptable method of keeping the house heat in the house today is by installing a fireplace insert or hearth stove. By doing this, you increase your energy efficiency by 3 to 5 times over the standard fireplace, even one with glass doors. Airtight wood-burners require little compensatory air, as long as the doors remain shut, and they seldom cause backdrafting problems.

Wood Stoves

A freestanding stove can change a drafty, wood-guzzling fireplace into an energy-efficient heat source. If the house you're remodeling has an inefficient heating system, whether it be furnace or fireplace, you'll want to consider adding an energy-efficient stove. Some of these stoves are designed to give off convective heat, others primarily produce radiant heat. Some will heat an entire house, others will provide auxiliary heat to supplement an undersized furnace. Check with dealers for additional information and costs; prices usually range from $300 to over $1,000.

A wood stove's thermal efficiency is based on the percentage of Btus it's able to deliver to a house from a given quantity of wood. The stove's increased burning efficiency is due to a controlled combustion process, which burns as much of the volatile material in the wood as possible. In addition, internal baffles, plus the increased surface area of the stove, transfer more radiant heat into the surrounding space. Usually the efficiency between even the most airtight freestanding fireplace and such a stove is from 50 to 75 percent.

If you use an existing chimney and hearth you'll save a bundle of money. The stove can be placed as close as you want to a masonry fireplace face, if it doesn't have a wood mantel. (By code, wood-burning stoves must be placed 36 inches from combustible materials, walls, and ceilings; a stove pipe must be at a distance of 18 inches from combustible materials.) The floor beneath, however, must provide a safe base for the stove. A masonry hearth or a stove pad are usual choices.

Clearances are clearly specified by the National Fire Protection Association (NFPA): If the stove's legs are 18 inches or longer, all that's required is a piece of 24-gauge sheet metal; if stoves legs are between 6 and 18 inches, you'll need 2 inches of masonry on top of, or covered by, 24-gauge sheet metal. If the legs are shorter than 6 inches, codes require that stoves must be placed on a noncombustible, hollow-masonry base at least 4 inches thick. The base should also extend at least 18 inches on all sides of the stove and butt to the front of the fireplace face.

There are several ways to convert a freestanding stove to an existing fireplace. On a top-vented stove, run the stovepipe straight up the fireplace front and through the masonry above the mantel position. If the masonry doesn't go all the way up, you must install some sort of a heat shield on the wall or keep the pipe 18 inches from the wall. Wood mantels should be removed or protected by heat shields applied to their leading edge. While this particular installation is more time-consuming, it does have its advantages. Because there's more exposed pipe in the room, more heat is radiated. Also, you shouldn't have draft problems because the pipe rises vertically. Other advantages: the damper is accessible, and the flue is easy to clean.

If the chimney has an unlined flue, you simply chip a hole in the masonry above and fit the flue through. If your chimney has a tile liner, your job will take a little more time and patience. Be careful not to crack the tile liner when removing brick or rock facing. When the tile is bared, draw a circle on it slightly larger than the collar (thimble) that surrounds the pipe where it passes through the masonry. Use a masonry drill to make holes around the circumference line. Then gently tap it with a hammer and remove the circular piece. Spread refactory cement (fireproof adhesive used inside boilers and fireplaces) in the opening, then insert the thimble sleeve. Twist it back and forth as you insert it so that gaps will fill up in masonry and liner. After the cement is dry, run the stovepipe from stove to thimble and insert the end of the pipe in the thimble.

If you go through a framed wall instead of through masonry, you'll need to provide an 8-inch clearance all around the thimble. This may mean removing wood framing materials. Refill the hole with noncombustible material: masonry, asbestos millboard or other fire-resistant boards. Stuff all gaps with ceramic wool or seal with refractory cement. The original damper must always be kept closed on this installation.

If you prefer not to chop through your fireplace masonry, you can consider two other ways to install a free standing stove in front of an existing fireplace. Both installations call for rear-venting stoves.

First, run a stovepipe through the fireplace's throat after you remove the fireplace damper and replace it with a flue shield. A flue shield can be bought, or made by a welder. It has a hole in it to accept the stovepipe.

If you can't remove the damper plate and don't want to go through the trouble of buying, making, or installing a flue shield, you can do the following.

Remove the fireplace damper plate and install a sheet of ⅛- or 3/16-inch-thick sheet steel as a hearth shield, covering the entire mouth of the fireplace. The shield must be bolted through the masonry face, and all gaps between must be filled with ceramic wool or fiberglass gasketing. Next, cut a hole in the shield to accept a short length of stovepipe, which should extend a few inches into the hole. On this installation, smoke sometimes gets vented into the fireplace opening and cools before it goes up the chimney. This causes a creosote buildup, in which case you'll have to remove the stove and clean the fireplace interior more often.

Inserts

If a freestanding wood stove will take up too much space in the room, you can buy a special kind of wood stove that nestles inside the fireplace. It's called a fireplace insert. While not as efficient as a freestanding stove because its radiant surfaces are enclosed in the fireplace, it does deliver a goodly amount of convection heat. Almost all inserts come equipped with an electric blower to circulate the convective air into the room.

RESTORING A BRICK FIREPLACE

Under layers of paint, fireplace brick offers all of the original beauty of natural building materials. If you want to salvage the existing brick, you could use a sandblaster to get the old paint off, but it's messy. Try, first, to strip it off with one of the solvent-type paint strippers and refer to instructions on p. 98.

If the old hearth, the surface on which you build the fire, is made of anything but brick, it must be removed. Most likely your tools will include a heavy hammer and a cold chisel. If you're going to redesign the fireplace and extend the hearth farther into the room, plan so it projects at least 16 to 20 inches into the room and 10 inches on each side of the firebox. Frame this new area with 2 by 4s.

Lay down wire lath, trimmed to fit inside the framing of the new hearth. (If the old hearth did not project into the room, you can apply the lath and mortar directly to the existing floor in front of the firebox without taking it up.) Use as much mortar as it requires to build the hearth up to the level of the old firebox.

A good mixture for mortar is one part portland cement to three parts clean sand. Or, if you wish, use a ready-mixed compound, which requires only the addition of water. Pour the mortar over the lath so the lath is completely covered; trowel the mortar. Then go over the surface with a length of 2 by 4 to make sure it's level, paying particular attention to keeping the corners neat and even.

After the foundation is fully cured, start with a row of bricks along the front edge of the hearth and work back, row by row, until you reach the rear of the firebox. Lay the bricks on top of a ½-inch-thick bed of mortar, and keep all mortar joints ½ inch thick. Using the same amount of mortar in all joints will keep your courses properly aligned. Do the pointing with the handle of the trowel or other round-edged tool; or keep the joints flush with the bricks by scraping the excess mortar off with the side edge of the trowel. If you reach the front edge of the fireplace or the back edge of the firebox, and you find that there's not enough room for a full-sized brick, cut the bricks to the size using a hammer and cold chisel.

If you're refacing the old fireplace with new brick, be sure to do it *after* the hearth is completed. Plan how many bricks high and how many bricks wide you want the face of the fireplace to be. Begin by building up a column of bricks immediately to the right and left of the firebox. Use full-sized and half-sized bricks to form whatever design you'd like. When you reach the top of the firebox opening, you may need to replace or install a new lintel.

The *lintel bar* is a heavy brace placed across the full width of the fireplace opening to support the brickwork on the upper part of the fireplace. Lintel bars come in lengths that range from 24 inches to 78 inches. Mortar the lintel in place, apply a smooth layer of mortar over it, then continue laying the next row of bricks across the entire width of the face of the fireplace. Build up the fireplace face, row by row, until you reach the desired height of the mantel.

At this point, provision must be made for anchoring the mantel in place. The mantel of the fireplace could be a wood beam, or you could use marble, slate, or even a variation of the brick used for the face. To secure a wood mantel, lead plugs are imbedded between bricks at the desired height. Mark the location of the plugs on the back edge of the mantel and drill corresponding holes at a diagonal down through the bottom of the mantelpiece. When the mortar has set, screw through the mantel and into the plugs. An alternate method would be to use decorative brackets at either end of the mantel. The brackets are screwed or bolted into the top of the mantel and then toggle-bolted to the fireplace wall. Any irregularities between the back edge of the mantel and the fireplace face should be scribed and fitted.

FACING A PREFAB FIREPLACE WITH STONE

Prefabricated fireplace units are designed for top efficiency and easy installation. They can be placed right next to an existing wall and installed directly over a wood floor without danger of heat or fire damage. Massive masonry foundations are not required. Fireplace faces can be finished off with a variety of materials, imitation or authentic. But for a very custom-crafted, rustic look, check out a product called Featherock (*Featherock, Inc.*, 2890 Empire Avenue, Burbank, CA 91510). Featherock is a volcanic rock mined in Mexico or California. It's extremely lightweight and comes in shades from gray to black. Featherock can be cut or shaped with a small hand axe used as a chisel, instead of with a chopping action. It's applied with mastic or mortar over a clean, sound substrate.

Form the hearth first with 4-by-5-inch beams. Be careful not to cover any vents on the front of the unit. Use patio blocks for fillers, add wire lath, then fill the framed hearth with cement. Finish the top of the hearth by setting in pieces of slate. Strike the joints with a dowel.

If you choose to make an entire wall of stone, install a ¾-inch plywood base to the area to be covered. Then apply wire lath over the base of plywood. Secure the self-furring metal lath to the plywood with 1½-inch, randomly spaced, galvanized roofing nails. When installing the furring lath, you'll find that it has a "grain" direction to the twist in the lath. Apply this so the projections point upward to hold the cement.

You can use a good grade of ceramic tile mastic or mortar. The mortar mix can be Featherock Adhesive Mortar, preformulated for a proper bond with Featherock, or you can mix your own, using a mix of 5 shovels sand, one shovel portland cement, and one shovel masonry cement. Use a 3-cubic foot wheelbarrow for a mortar box and a garden hoe for a mixing device. Use a plasterer's hawk to trowel a supply of the mortar onto the wall; hold the bottom edge of the hawk against the wall, and trowl the mortar upward from the hawk onto the metal lath.

Most stone suppliers suggest you wait until the basecoat has set, a period of 24 hours, before applying the stone. When the basecoat of mortar has become firm (but not dry), "butter" the stones and apply them immediately by pressing them against the wall with a twisting motion to get a good bond with the substrate. Apply the large rocks or stones to the entire wall first, then fill in with the smaller stones, or rubble. The voids between the rocks can be painted with black mastic of the type used to apply artificial brick in lieu of grouting; then rock dust can be pressed into the black mastic, making the wall appear to be solid stone rather than grouted.

Featherock applied with mastic can be supported by nails until the mastic dries.

If you get mortar on the stone while installing it, wash it off immediately with water and a sponge. If this doesn't work, use a 5-percent solution of muriatic acid as soon as the mortar has set, so as not to disturb the joints, but before the mortar has cured. Muriatic acid is extremely caustic. Wear rubber gloves, and goggles to keep spashes out of the eyes.

[12]

Attics

Increasing habitable space in a house 50 to 100 years old is usually no problem. Cavernous basements with sanctums and inner sanctums formerly used for housing boilers, furnaces, wine, laundry, and coal, afford excellent potential for new living quarters down under. Furthermore, basic utility lines are already in place and there's usually direct access to the outdoors. Upstairs, attics that resemble unfinished third floors are usually so large that they have enough headroom for full-sized windows. Large front and back porches on the main floor also beg for reincarnation into usable living space.

In pre-1940 houses there's often enough space in the attic to carve out two small rooms and a bath, and still have enough left over for a hobby or sewing area. Even in today's modern houses, you can find convertible space in car ports, garages, and unfinished patios. So look down, up, and out. There may be a gold mine under the eaves of your house of which you're not aware—space that would make a good candidate for rental income, or additional square footage that would up the market value of the house if you plan to offer it for sale.

RENOVATION TIPS

For a few hundred dollars worth of building materials, your own labor, and a large dash of imagination, you can convert a dark, and back-bending attic into a comfortable living space; be it a cozy bedroom and second bath, home office, guest suite, hobby and sewing center, or study.

Finishing an attic is one of the most rewarding and economical remodeling jobs that you can undertake to maximize a house's space. Attics are easily convertible. Your house might have an expandable attic that is reached by a finished stair, a subfloor already over its joists, and supply and drain pipes that have been brought up from the floor below and capped off for future use. It might even be blessed with finished dormer windows.

Most likely, though, the home that you're remodeling has a "storage" attic with partial floors over joists that are insufficiently sized for "live" loads (people and activities). You will have to add more support. Take measurements of joist depth, joist span, and the distance between joists to your local building department for an opinion. Your local lumber dealer also has a safe-span chart for wood of various sizes that you might want to check. A weak floor can generally be remedied with little trouble or expense. Usually there should be 2-by-8 joists on 16-inch centers, and they should not extend unsupported more than 14 feet. If 2 by 8s span over this length, beef them up with 2 by 8s on 12-inch centers, or nail a new 2 by 8 joist to every other joist.

The best subflooring is ¾-inch, tongue-and-groove, underlayment-grade plywood nailed at right angles to the joists.

Forget about remodeling an attic with trussed rafters, or attics that have headroom under 7 feet. The two major considerations before an attic can qualify for remodeling for living space are ceiling height and access. The ceiling height must satisfy the building codes in your community (a height of 7 to 7½ feet is the usual minimum). That generally means that the peak has to be at least 10 feet high before you squeeze out any reasonable living space from the attic according to code. Kneewall heights are not regulated.

The attic must be accessible by stairs. If the existing access is a drop-down folding stair, check to see that there is adequate room somewhere to add a new conventional stairway. If space is limited, you can always use a circular stairs.

The ideal location for the stair is dead center, allowing easy access to all upstairs rooms from a landing at the top of the stairs. Stairs entering the attic from one end or the other will mean waste space from halls, or having to go through one room to get to another. Also, fire codes often required that you have an alternate access out—even if it's as simple as an escape ladder kept within easy reach.

With the common problems being too little headroom and too little light, you may want to consider dormers and skylights. You can enlarge space by adding a dormer, or dormers, at additional expense. This will also give you the option of including a partially enclosed patio between the dormer windows, which can substitute as a fire access. Perhaps a pretty view from a small deck will be a very worthwhile investment.

Installing a skylight is a lot cheaper than adding a dormer window; but be sure that you buy one that won't overheat the attic and that can be used for venting heat, also.

In many cases, major architectural changes in attics are not required at all. Left unaltered, an angular, under-the-eaves ceiling can be very appealing, especially when emphasized with an all-over pattern. But you might want to make the space more convenient by adding kneewalls to aid in furniture arranging and for additional storage. *Kneewalls* are short walls built under the room on the long side of the house. If you keep them at a height of 4 feet, you can use common 4-by-8 sheets of drywall or paneling with minimum waste.

INSULATING THE ATTIC

Attics usually become quite hot in the summer and very cold in the winter. For comfort and energy efficiency, thoroughly insulate your new attic space. Insulation doesn't cost much and the job is not difficult when you have open stud cavities. If you live in a warm climate, you might want to staple a radiant barrier to the bottom of the roof trusses or rafters. This is one of the most inexpensive improvements you can make to reduce energy bills and increase comfort. In summer, as the roof gets hot it radiates heat downward. This heat is absorbed by the insulation and ultimately transfers through the ceiling into the rooms below. A radiant barrier, such as plain aluminum foil or builders' (unperforated) foil, will reflect about 80 percent of the heat outward from the roof before it gets into the attic insulation.

If you plan to use the original attic floor insulation, or add to it, check to see if there's a vapor barrier in it. Remove this vapor barrier, or slash it, so that you don't trap moisture in the floor. If the existing attic is un-floored, by all means, put down a thick blanket of insulation between the joists. This will not only keep the room warm and cozy in winter and cool in summer, it'll cut down on sound transmission to the floor below. If an attic floor is already in place, drill small holes into the boards and have insulation blown in.

The energy expert at your local utility can give you additional information on where to install insulation, how much to use, and what kind of a vapor barrier you should use with it.

PLUMBING, HEATING, AND ELECTRICAL WORK

Plumbing will be one of your major expenses. If you plan a bathroom, locate it above a bathroom on the floor below so that it can be connected into existing plumbing and sewage lines; likewise for kitchen hookups.

A heating and air conditioning contractor may be able to tie in the attic rooms to your existing heating/cooling system. If not, consider electric baseboard heat or radiant ceiling heat—these are easy add-ons. A room-sized air conditioner in a window or installed through the wall can handle attic cooling.

Almost surely new wiring will be required and this is best left to a professional.

FINISHING INTERIORS

Make your final decisions about finishing interior walls, floors, and ceilings, after dormers and other structural additions have been built. This way, you can accurately assess what and how much material you will need to cover the numerous jogs and slanted angles.

If you panel, you may find existing wall studs on 16-inch centers, while roof rafters are on 24-inch centers. Mark nailing positions before you begin. Panel the ceiling first, starting at the joint where the roof meets side wall, and work up to the peak. Then go back and panel side walls, making sure the grooves line up. Cover the joints with moldings.

Whether you use paneling or put up drywall overhead on slanted rafters, buy construction adhesive to spread on rafters or joists before you nail each sheet. The adhesive will help hold the sheets in place during and after nailing.

[13]

Basements

Like attics, basements can provide convenient space for new living quarters. The walls are already there. The ceiling and floors are there, too. So are the basic utility lines; and access is usually no problem. Certainly, square footage is ample. Yet, space down under is usually occupied by only the furnace and laundry equipment, and completely ignored by the homeowner as usable living space.

This is a mistake. Not only is it a waste of space—an unimproved, dark, cold, and damp basement is a definite turnoff to a potential buyer. If there are visible signs of water problems, it almost certainly will mean a "no sale." Wet or damp basements are common problems in homes and can generally be overcome, once you determine the source of the water that's causing the problem.

WATER PROBLEMS

Basement water problems can arise from: 1. condensation of moisture-laden air when it contacts cool masonry walls or concrete floors; 2. improper grading of the earth around the house so surface water runs or seeps toward the basement walls (an inadequate guttering system can greatly aggravate problems caused by improper grading); and 3. a high water table, which exerts a constant hydrostatic pressure upward through floors or walls.

Condensation or Seepage?

To tell whether your problems are caused by condensation or seepage, tape a piece of aluminum foil onto the basement wall, making sure all four sides are airtight. Leave it up for several days, then examine it. If the foil is wet on the surface facing the room, the problem is condensation. If the moisture is on the side facing the wall, the problem is seepage. Condensation means simply that you have to dry the basement out. To begin with, your basement needs heat in winter and cross-ventilation in summer. Cold water pipes should be wrapped with insulation made for this purpose, and clothes dryers, and other sources of moist air, must be vented to the outside. You might also consider using a dehumidifier and exhaust fans, especially in summer.

Minor seepage caused by cracks and holes from settling can be patched with silicone caulk or by hydraulic cement. Large cracks must be patched from both sides. Silicone caulk remains flexible after it dries, allowing it to move with your house as it settles. Hydraulic cement will expand as it sets, tightly filling the breaks. The area must be cleaned thoroughly and wet down before patching.

When all cracks are sealed, paint the walls with a specially formulated masonry waterproofing product, which consists of a cement base and sealing material. These come in powder form and must be mixed, but they're more effective than premixed waterproofing paints. Efflorescence (water soluble salt deposits on cement and concrete), if present, must be removed first. Wash walls down with a 20-percent solution of muriatic acid and water, then seal it with a masonry sealer prior to painting.

Fortunately, most seepage problems are caused by faulty drainage systems that can be corrected inexpensively and easily. Approximately 95 percent of all wet basements are caused by surface groundwater seepage through walls or floors. So if the leakage problems persist, take the following steps before you go to the expense and labor of installing a new drainage system around the footing of the house.

1. Leaky gutters or downspouts on a house can pour hundreds of gallons of water around basement walls. Repair or replace gutters and downspouts, or install new ones to direct the water away from the foundation. Splash blocks placed beneath downspouts, or a tile-lined trench leading away from the downspout, will also move the water away from the foundation quickly.

2. Surface underground water can also drain towards the house and force its way inside. Check the grade around the house to see that it slopes away from the house on all sides. The grade should slope at least an inch per running foot for a distance of at least 10 feet, so the water will be less likely to soak back into the basement.

3. Even though a proper grade may have been established when the house was built, it may since have been altered. The earth fill around the house can sink away, leaving low spots where water can collect, or it may have been altered by flower beds, gravel, or bark placed around the foundation, or by trenches dug for utility pipes. Once the soil has been disturbed, it no longer will shed water. Haul in some black dirt and build up the grade at the foundation.

4. Concrete slabs, such as sidewalks or driveways, can trap water next to the house. It is especially important that downspouts do not direct roof water into areas that are dammed by concrete slabs. Slope all concrete slabs that adjoin basement walls away from the house.

5. The drainage condition of the earth around your home has a lot to do with how much water pressure your basement must withstand. When drainage is good, rain water percolates into the ground and dissipates rapidly; therefore, in-ground pressure has little chance to build up. But if your area has a high water table and the ground remains sodden after a rain, water in the earth will exert pressure on the foundation of your home and may force its way in.

Also, even if the soil has good drainage, a problem can present itself if the terrain slopes toward your house. As rainwater sinks into the soil, it gravitates downhill. When it reaches a concrete wall, it's momentarily stopped. As the water builds up, hydrostatic pressure increases and water may be pushed through a basement wall; the wall may even be pushed out of shape by the pressure. To prevent water from streaming downhill toward your house in the first place, dig a trench across the slope and fill it with layers of gravel and a perforated plastic pipe surrounded by crushed rock. The pipe can then channel water into a dry well away from the house.

If the earth around your house does not allow water to percolate into it, and the pressure built up around it allows water to find its way into the basement, you'll have to take the most extensive—and expensive—route: excavating around the basement.

To relieve pressure:

1. Excavate down to the level of the footing, so the entire foundation wall is revealed. Clean off loose debris from around existing cracks and fill with a mixture of cement, sand, and lime. It's best to coat the wall with hot tar and tar paper if the water level is high, then dump crushed rocks in and put down drain tile.
2. Lay the tiles 4 inches from the footing in a trench dug along the exterior of the foundation. If plastic perforated pipe is used, the holes should face down.
3. Cover the tile with 6 to 8 inches of crushed rock (1½ inches in diameter) before you return the topsoil. This remedy will assure that the water, as it reaches the crushed stone, will follow the least path of resistance—away from the house.

INSULATING THE BASEMENT

Once you've cured your water problems, you're ready to insulate to make the room warmer in winter; but first you need a framework. Foundation walls are seldom straight or plumb. Because of this, it's usually better to frame a whole new wall than to try to install furring. If you can't afford the extra space framing would take, you can install furring strips using masonry nails (1½ inch for ¾ furring) and use rigid foamboard sheathing between (not over) furring strips on 16-inch centers (see p. 131 in Chapter 6, "Walls"). Foam board must be covered by gypsum, according to fire code, before you apply any finishing materials. Be sure you also include a polyethylene vapor barrier over the insulation. Be mindful of some complications when furring; extensive nailing may cause the concrete to crack, and nails could loosen. Then you'd be right back where you started—filling and patching.

You can frame the outside walls with 2 by 3s or 2 by 4s. (Interior partitions should be of 2 by 4s.) It's easier to lay out each wall section on the basement floor and nail the studs and plates together before raising the framework (see p. 117 in Chapter 6).

If your concrete floor is excessively wavy, you may have to build the framework as you go—nailing the top plates to the joists overhead, and shoe to the floor, then cutting and fitting studs individually before nailing them in between.

Before you frame outside walls, strike a chalk line on the floor, indicating the distance from the concrete wall where the inside of the studding will fall. Nail the shoe to the floor with 2½-inch masonry nails. Don't expect to get the shoe to hold tightly. When the studs and top plate are nailed in place, they'll keep it from sliding around. Plumb up each end of the shoe to get the location of the plate. Where the plate runs at right angles to the joist, strike a chalk line across them, then nail the plate on with 10d common nails. If the plate is parallel to the joists, the construction is the same as in attic between ceiling beams.

After the shoe and plate are in place, mark off 16-inch centers for studs on both shoe and plate. Make the space between the first and second stud 15¼ inches, center-to-center; this will assure that the edge of 48-inch-wide paneling will fall on stud centers.

To fit studs: Take a stud slightly longer than needed and stand it up on the shoe with the other end next to the plate. Make sure that the ends are aligned with their marks. Then stand on the shoe to force it tightly to the floor, before you mark the top of the stud for cutting. Cut the stud without obliterating the line. Then toenail it in place.

Before the wall is fully erected, lay a stringer on the floor behind it. (After you have the wall up you won't be able to get it in.) When all the studs are in place, hold the stringer tight to the back of the studs about halfway up and toenail it in place, making sure that each stud is vertically plumb. This will keep the middle of the wall straight. (See FIG. 13-1.)

You must provide access panels to all valves, fuse boxes, circuit breakers, junction boxes, telephone connectors, and cleanout plugs in the plumbing. Make sure you frame in removable panels or door openings.

Now you're ready for the insulation. Staple batt-type insulation between the framing studs. Kraft paper or foil facing serves as a vapor barrier and should face the room side. If you use unfaced insulation, install a polyethylene vapor barrier over the insulation and studs before installing drywall or paneling to finish the walls.

From here on you must rely on two words for basement remodeling; "below grade." Before you buy any decorating finishing materials, floor tiles, paint, carpeting, or paneling, make sure it can be used in a below-grade area.

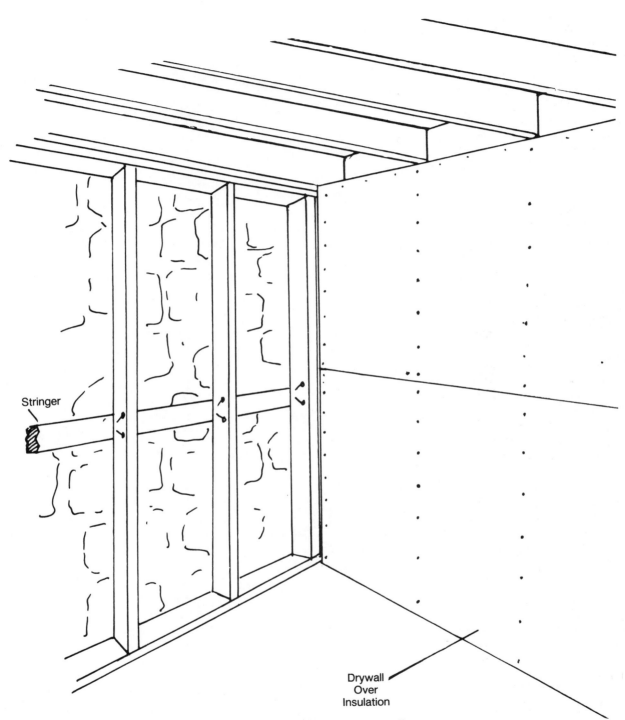

Fig. 13-1. *Finishing Basement Walls.*

Stringer

Drywall Over Insulation

Index

I

insulation
   attics, 279
   basements, 283
interior walls (see also walls),
   inspection, 25
Italianate homes, 18

J

jack posts, 126
joists, 115
junction box, electrical system, 45,
   46

K

kitchens, 11

L

lacquer, 81, 85, 166, 189
latex paint, 80, 81, 168
leaks
   basements, 281
   faucets, 70
   plumbing, 58-60
leather tile, 215
lien sale contract, 27
lineoleum floors, 212-223
linseed oil, 167
lintel bar, 274
lintels, 123
load-bearing walls, 121
long-term renovations, 4
lumber, 33
   grading, 35

M

mantels, 274
marble floors, 204
marquetry floors, 236-237
masonry paint, 85, 98
materials, 32-35
measuring, 30
mechanics lien, 27
metal, painting, 101, 103, 104
metal tile, painting, 103
mildew, 76
mitering, 151-153, 159
moldings, 138, 249
   base, 147, 156-158
   baseboards and base shoes, 158
   ceiling, 147, 156-158
   chair rail, 145-147
   columnar, 144
   coping, 153-154
   cutting, 150
   doors and windows, 147, 156
   gouges, filling, 164
   installation, 150
   locations for, 145

measuring and purchasing, 150
mitering, 151-153
nailing, 154
painting, 151
parquet tile floors, 198
plaster, 169-172
plate rail, 149
plinth blocks, 143, 144, 145
polymer, 140, 142
prefinished paneling, 139
refinishing, 164
removal of, 162
salvaging and cleaning, 160
specialty, 143
splicing with scarf joints, 154
stripping, 162
styles of, 139
vinyl floors, 220
wood, 139, 140
mortar, painting, 100
mosaic tile floors, 203

N

nailing blocks, 116
nails, 32-33
   dating, 7
   drywall, 132
   moldings, 154
newel posts, 249, 262
nosing, 249

O

oil finishes, 167
oil-based paint, 82, 168
outlets, 39, 42, 43
   connecting new wire to old, 43

P

paint mitts, 92
paint pads, painting, 91
painting, 75-105, 168
   applicators, 90
   blistering, 77
   boxing, 94
   cabinets, 98
   ceilings, 95-97, 239-240
   chalking, 77
   checking and alligatoring, 77
   color selection, 79
   doors, 97
   enamel, 80, 82
   estimating quantities, 87-88
   finish selection, 79-81
   flaking, 77
   flat, 80
   glossy, 77
   glue stains, 76
   high-gloss, 80, 81
   lacquer, 81

latex, 80, 81
mildew, 76
moldings, 151
oil-based and alkyd, 82
over calcimine, 79
over wallpaper, 78
paint mitts, 92
paint-failure, correcting
   problems in, 76
peeling, 77
primers, undercoats, sealers, 83
removal, 162
rooms, sequence for, 94
rust, 76
semigloss, 80
smoke, grease, water stains, 76
special jobs, 98
special-purpose, 84-86
spray guns, 92
stairs, 98
tools and equipment, 88-94
walls, 75, 98
windows, 97
wood floors, 189
woodwork, 97
wrinkled or wavy, 77
paneling
   ceilings, 242
   moldings for, 139, 143
parquet tile floors, 191-198
   adhesives for, 194
   borders, 193
   butt-edged tiles, 192
   center guideline method, 192, 196
   corners, 195
   moldings for, 198
   self-adhesive tongue-and-groove,
      192
   side guideline method, 191, 193
   trimming out, 198
   undercutitng, 194
partition walls, 114, 134-137
paver floors, 202
peeling paint, 77
pilaster moldings, 143
pillars, 13
planing, 30
plank and strip (see also wood
   floors), 199-201
plaster, 107
   moldings, 169-172
   repairing, 108-111
plastic plumbing pipe, 60-64
   burying, 64
   couplings, 62
   joining, 64
   metal joined to, 63
   mounting, 64
plastic sponge brushes, painting, 89
plate rails, 149

plinth blocks, 143, 144, 145
plumbing, 51-74
    air chambers, 57
    attics and, 279
    burying plastic sewer pipes, 64
    cleanouts, 54
    drain/waste/vent system, 52-57
    inspection, 24
    leaks, 58-60
    leaky faucets, 70
    mounting plastic pipes, 64
    plastic pipe, 60-64
    plastic to metal joints, 63
    removing walls and, 122
    repairs, 58-60
    traps, 54-56
    unstopping clogged drains,
        toilets, sewers, 65
    vents, 56
    water heaters, 71-74
    water supply system, 51-52
polymer moldings, 140, 142
polyurethane, 167, 189
polyurethane enamel, 85
primers, 83, 169

Q

quarry tile floors, 202
Queen Anne homes, 19, 21
quick turnaround houses, 2-4

R

radiators, painting, 103
railings, 249, 262
ranch homes, 21
receptacles, 39
refinishing woodwork, 164
refurbishing, 6
remodeling, 6, 26-28
    professionals for, 27-28, 27
    restoration vs., 4
removing walls, 120-127
    checking for electrical conduit
        and pipes, 122
    demolition, 127
    load-bearing, 121
    repairing floor after, 177
    support beams, 123
    temporary support system, 125
restoration, 6
    remodeling vs., 4
rise and run, stairs, 257
risers, 249
rollers, painting, 91
roof
    gambrel, 11, 12, 13
    inspection, 22
rotovinyl, 214
rubber tile, 215
rubber-base paint, 86

rust, 76

S

saber sawing, 31
sagging floors, 175
sagging stairs, 254
saltbox homes, 9, 10
San Francisco stick, 20
sanding, 32
    wood floors, 185-187
sawing, 29, 31
scarf joints, splicing moldings, 154
sealers, 83, 169
    masonry, 205
    wood floors, 188
Second Empire homes, 19, 20
semigloss paint, 80
service panel, 36
sewers, unstopping, 65
sheet vinyl, 214
shellac, 166, 189
sinks
    painting, 104
    unstopping, 65
slate
    floors, 203
    painting, 101
smoke stains, 76
spandrels, 140
spiral stairs, 263
spray guns, painting, 92
squeaking floors, 175
squeaking stairs, 252-254
staining, 165
    wood floors, 188
stairs, 247-266
    balustrade for, 261
    carpeting, 263-265
    clearances, 256
    framing, 260
    interior framing, 256
    opening floor for, 258
    painting, 98
    parts of, 249
    prefabricated, 261
    replacement of, 255-262
    rise and run, 257
    sagging, 254
    spiral, 263
    squeaking, 252-254
    stair width, 255
    styles, 249
    under-stair niche, 266
    vertical clearance, 255
    worn treads, 254
stone
    floors, 203, 212
    painting, 101
stoves (see fireplaces; wood stoves)
stringers, 249, 251

stucco, painting, 101
subfloors, 181
suspended ceilings, 243-245
swimming pool tile floors, 203
switches, 39, 42, 43, 44
synthetic marble floors, 204

T

techniques, basic, 28-32
telephone jacks, 39
terrazo floors, 205
textured paint, 86
thermostats, 39
tile floors, 201-211
    adhesive, 206
    cutting, 207-210
    finishing, 211
    grouting, 210
    preparation, 206
    resilient (see vinyl floors)
    spacers, 206
tin, painting, 103
toilets
    dismantling, 68
    installation, 68
    parts of, 69
    running, 69
    unstopping, 65, 66
tools, 28-29
    painting, 88-94
    wall-to-wall carpeting, 228
top plate, 124
traps, plumbing, 54-56
treads, 249
trim (see also moldings;
    woodwork), 138, 160
tung oil, 167

U

unconditional lien release, 27
under-stair niche, 266
undercoats, 83
urethane enamel, 85

V

varnish, 85, 166, 189
    removal, 163
vents, plumbing, 56
Victorian homes, 16, 17
vinyl floors, 212-223
    adhesives for, 216
    cutting, 218, 219
    laying tile, 215
    moldings for, 220
    obstructions, pipes, doors, 218
    rolling smooth, 218
    self-stick, 217
    sheet-type, 220-223

W

waiver of mechanics lien rights, 27
wall-to-wall carpeting, 227-238
  binder bars, 230
  compressed edge starting
    technique, 231
  knee-kicker for, 233
  power stretcher for, 232
  seaming, 235
  stretching and hooking, 230, 231
  tackless strips for, 229
  tools for, 228
  trimming, 234
wallpaper, painting over, 78
walls, 106-137
  bearing, 113
  budget and design possibilities,
    107
  building new, 113-120
  cleaning, 76
  corner construction, 119
  curtain, 113
  door and window openings, 118
  drywall (see drywall)
  fishing electrical cable through,
    40, 41
  inspection, 22, 25

joist location, 115
measure and layout, 116-118
nailing blocks, 116
nonbearing partition walls, 114
painting, 75, 98
partitions, 134-137
planning new location, 114
plaster (see plaster)
raising, 120
removal of (see removing walls)
repairing, 108-113
stained, 76
water heater, 71-74
  inspection, 23
water stains, 76
water supply system (see also
    plumbing), 51-52
waxes, 168
  masonry, 205
  wood floors, 184, 190
windows, 5
  casing, 156
  dating, 8
  framing, 118
  inspection, 24
  moldings for, 147
  painting, 97

wood floors (see also plank and
    strip), 181-190
  blemish and stain removal, 183
  buffing, 189
  finishing, 187-190
  parquet, 182
  plank flooring, 182
  protective finishes, 189
  restoring, 182
  sanding, 185-187
  sealing, 188
  staining, 188
  strip flooring, 182
  stripping, 184
  waxing, 184, 190
wood moldings (see moldings;
    woodwork)
wood stoves, 271
woodwork (see also moldings), 138
  cleaning, 160
  painting, 97
  salvaging, 160
  staining, 165
wrinkled or wavy paint, 77
wiring (see cable; electrical system)
wrought iron, painting, 103